ON
GLORY
ROADS

ELEANOR MUNRO

ON GLORY ROADS

A Pilgrim's Book about Pilgrimage

THAMES AND HUDSON

First published in the United States in 1987 by
Thames and Hudson Inc.,
500 Fifth Avenue, New York, New York 10110

Library of Congress Catalog Card Number 86-50231

Printed in the United States of America

CREDITS

Lines from Jorge Luis Borges: *Labyrinths*. Copyright © 1962, 1964 by New
Directions Publishing Corp. Reprinted by permission.

Line from Hortense Calisher: *Mysteries of Motion*. Copyright © 1983 by
Hortense Calisher. Reprinted by permission, Doubleday & Co.

Lines from Wallace Stevens: *The Palm at the End of the Mind: Selected Poems*.
Copyright © 1971 by Holly Stevens. Reprinted by permission, Alfred A. Knopf.

Lines from *The Homeric Hymns*, tr. Apostolos Athanassakis. Copyright ©
1976 by The Johns Hopkins University Press. Reprinted by permission.

Passage from Thomas Kuhn: *The Structure of Scientific Revolutions*. Copyright © 1969 by The University of Chicago. Reprinted by permission.

Line from Giorgio de Santillana and Hertha von Dechend: *Hamlet's Mill*.
Copyright © 1969 by Giorgio de Santillana and Hertha von Dechend. Reprinted
by permission, Gambit.

Lines from Louise Bogan: from "Poem in Prose" from *The Blue Estuaries:
Poems 1923–1968*. Copyright © 1968 by Louise Bogan. Reprinted by permission, Farrar, Straus & Giroux. Reprinted in *Journey Around My Room: The
Autobiography of Louise Bogan. A Mosaic* by Ruth Limmer. Copyright © 1980
by Ruth Limmer.

Lines from Claude Lévi-Strauss in *Myth: A Symposium*. ed. Thomas A. Sebeok.
Copyright ©. Reprinted by permission, American Folklore Society.

Lines from Marina Warner: *Alone of All Her Sex*. Copyright © 1976 by
Marina Warner. Reprinted by permission.

For Jack:
good companion

The steps [a person] takes from the day of birth until that of death trace in time an inconceivable figure. . . . This figure (perhaps) has its given function in the economy of the universe.
Jorge Luis Borges:
THE MIRROR OF ENIGMAS

Such harmony there is in heaven,
And so many planets . . .
Temistocle Solera:
I LOMBARDI

CONTENTS

PREFACE

Pilgrimage is a global enterprise of deep antiquity and powerful psychological appeal. It draws multitudes to riverbanks, to mountain peaks and lonely desert shrines. Sunrise, moonrise, and star-rise, equinox and solstice, and the arrivals in their stations of the planets are its timekeepers. It could even be argued that going on pilgrimage is, in its widest definition, one of the few universally shared human ritual practices, and that it began in the same surge of evolution that brought about humanity's self-conscious awareness of the world.

As a living practice, it can be witnessed today in the Americas and in Europe; in Asia and in Africa; in Russia and in between. To Lourdes, four million people, many from the educated middle class, go each year. Some two million others, educated and illiterate together, travel annually to Mecca. Ten million pilgrims visit sites on the Ganges in India at specific intervals. And many of the world's 647 million Hindus, 295 million Buddhists, 175 million evangelical Christians, and manifold Jewish mystics would say they are always on pilgrimage.[1] Also, secular travelers may use the word these days to describe trips to sites that move them unaccountably.[2] These self-styled pilgrims may simply feel, as Herman Melville did when he climbed the Acropolis, that in the landscape, the way a monument is set in between the horns of distant hills, is some larger meaning about the structure.[3]

On the other hand, dangerous emotions too can erupt at the cross-points of opposing pilgrimage systems. Today, as we know, Moslems, Sikhs, and Hindus clash on sacred turf from Assam to

Amritsar and Pakistan, and south to Sri Lanka. Jerusalem's centrality to three faiths and arguing sects of those three is an explosive issue. And in the global West-East struggle, pilgrimage to the Black Virgin of Czestochowa in Poland has lately served political ends. In short, political masters have made good use of pilgrimage fever.[4] For in nations with linguistic, social, and ideological cleavages like India, and in religio-political empires that embrace peoples of diverse colors and languages, like Christianity and Islam, the practice fosters devotional unity and, sometimes, subservience to millennialist visions of the masters.

Also, if emotions associated with pilgrimage can arouse masses to violence, what of the practice of individual, self-inflicted pain on the way? One sees pilgrims crawling on bare, aged knees up stone staircases in Mexico, Rome, and Lhasa in Tibet, creeping inchworm style around Benares, piercing their pectoral muscles with wired steel hooks in Sri Lanka and their cheeks in Nepal, immolating themselves, sitting and standing in frozen stasis for periods from days to years, and, in a rite that may seem related, circumcising one another, as well as doing suicidal battle to clear the way of others no less zealous, only less well armed for the moment.[5] By what definition of a good world could such behavior be called for?

A practice with such power to move people calls to be studied broadly in order to find its roots in common—nonparochial—human needs and desires and to understand how these are transmuted into significant forms of behavior and art.

THIS book provides a narrative description of pilgrimage in four of the world's major living religions; the myths on which it is founded in each case; the rites, arts, and monuments it has generated; and the history of their development.

But I go further. This is also a book of speculative vision. I suggest a fundamental myth provides visual setting and internal structures for pilgrimage around the world. I take my lead from historians of art and religion, and from anthropologists, with a bent toward general principles.[6] My own background is in art history and criticism, but my divergent approach to this subject began with my reading *Hamlet's Mill* by historians of science Giorgio de Santillana and Hertha von Dechend, with its persuasive if unconventional argument for the astronomical basis of certain myths and images in art. I moved to the relatively new scientific disciplines of archaeo- and ethno-astronomy that seek to support such argument by tangible evidence, that is, monuments and rituals in which the ancients deliberately embodied astronomical ideas.[7] I put their propositions together with Lévi-Strauss's on mythic thought, Stella Kramrisch's on Indian myth, and Rudolf Arnheim's on mankind's use of perceived information to survive in an unknown environment. Then I proceeded to a general theory about the form and function—and so the meaning—of pilgrimage within the embrace of that Ur-myth.

The theory rests on observations, documentary facts, and ideas that may seem arcane at first. But I hope the reader will share my interest as I gradually moved through these sources toward the powerful imaginative vision that historically shaped the practice of pilgrimage worldwide. For the Asian sages and the Western patriarchs and doctors who conceived the great religions and contrived their pilgrimage structures drew from and then projected back on nature a compelling image, a vastly expanded version of what they saw with their eyes: earth largely unexplored, under the familiar star-fields of the night.

I support the theory, I hope, with sufficient data, most of which, in the interest of readability, is in notes at the text's end. But the interpretation is mine as is my reading of sacred scriptures. Also as a writer and pilgrim of sorts, I am a beneficiary—as are all thinking women and men today—of the surge in women's studies over the last two decades. So encouraged, I accept my personal slant on both history and life-experience, and there is a subjective "pilgrimage" touched on in this book. Another implication of the subjective nature of the text: I could not go to Mecca; I've not been on a Moslem pilgrimage; therefore I say little about Islam. All the same, I hope to have shed some light on the relevance the subject at large has to the world today, in which past myths are painfully and dangerously being reformulated in terms, perhaps, of a life-supporting new one.

PROLOGUE

◆

Where the journey begins . . .
Hortense Calisher:
MYSTERIES OF MOTION

◆

✦ ✦ ✦

One December, when I was living on Cape Cod, I watched for the first time (because I'd lived so long in cities where it never occurred to me to notice) the sunset inch its way along my kitchen windowsill each evening a little farther south. At the implication of that slight notching descent I was struck in my mind like George Fox the Quaker, who was walking one day outside London when, as he wrote, "I lifted up my head and espied three steeple-house spires, and they struck at my life."[1]

A little later, I found myself in the Hebrides with my two sons, exploring circles of old standing stones, those strange geometries of upright rocks found across the British isles, northern Europe, the Americas, and India.

We rambled one circle, then trekked to another about a half-mile off. Cold wind blew off the sea. The sun lay at a low angle over the horizon. The light was pale and lifeless and drained the color out of the heaths.

Reflect on this light, I said to myself. How does it address itself to the brain?

I was used to a sun riding at a higher angle over the world. The angle of the sun I lived under at home gave my brain its psychic center, made the outer world look real and the inner one feel stable. By contrast, this alien sun set the world adrift and me from it.

The boys and I at last reached our destination. I went and stood in the middle of that circle of stones and looked around the horizon, and when I came to a certain point, my own eyes locked into an alignment that struck at my life.

For in the distance were two small gray peaks like horns and, coming up between them, a third peak, smaller and so pale it seemed ghostlike. Between me and that far-off configuration, I could see in the middle distance that other circle where we'd been. And then I saw, right in the center of it, an upright rock I hadn't noticed before, as perfectly placed as a compass pin.

I'd strayed across a connection as live as a high tension wire, and my mind flickered with the shock of it. I was looking down a sight line laid out, I suppose, millennia ago. I felt the pull on my mind of another mind's will to orient itself by this sighting system on the plane of the earth.

I was in the Hebrides then because my Highland-descended father had recently died and with him, except for my brother who had no son, the clan name he took pride in. I wanted to show my sons the country though it was theirs only by the obscured connection of matrilineality.

My father's people had come to the Hebrides from the mainland; they then moved on to America for good. Through the few letters and books that survived those sea voyages and homesteadings, our clan's generations were known as far back as the carnage at Culloden. But at that point there was just a single line in a book about a refugee who had sailed around Cape John O'Groats with his remnant of a brood to settle in Skye by the mouth of a river called Snizort. George the Fair Miller of Strath, he was called. But no one knew for sure whether he had actually lived to take up his trade of a miller after so much had been blasted away of his earlier life.

It was a day or so later that we found ourselves beside that very Snizort, at the place where it met the tides of the Bay of Strath. After rambling the banks, we waded to an islet. There was a hundred-year-old wall there, deep in nettles. There were yew trees and thistles, and buttercups that brushed our knees. Against the wall were two crypts with knights carved on their lids, with their toes pointed to the sky.

Then on the other side of the wall, but out in the shallows, I saw a big jumble of dressed stones. The boys clambered over and walked out into the water. I followed. We were looking around, and there were iron wheels and gears fallen down. One of them looked like a broken mill staff. And then it struck me, and I lifted my head with the certainty of it: we were standing in the very water that washed the bones of the Fair Miller's mill.

That mill, turning in its good days around the upright iron staff, had ground time and our ancestors and scattered the flour of their lives across a hemisphere. But even fallen, the staff had kept on turning in the minds of those who came after, drawing in what it had cast out, so that in our own times my father, later my brother, later my sons and I had been pulled back toward that great helix of a screw.

Now on all sides where I stood ankle-deep in the ancestral river I seemed to see the water flowing both toward me and away. Off by the shore, sheep were grazing half in green grass, half in silver. Suddenly the gray-green moors and far hills turned transparent. Shapes began to shift in the light, mobile and glancing, and in the midst of so much motion, the broken stones and we beside them stood like the gnomon of a sundial, able to mark us a meaning had we only the science to read it.

Wait, these stones now seemed to say: one day the meaning of your coming to stand on this spot will be made clear, will slip as easily into understanding as that peak that yesterday rose like a summoning ghost between two nearer, darker slopes.

SUCH mysteries began to haunt me, and eventually I set out to make what I expected would be a study of the alluring artifacts of pilgrimage. I dug out my art-historical notes on past trips to places like Abu Simbel in Egypt and the Borobodur in Java. I also planned new trips to places and monuments called sacred by generations of pilgrims. I was trying to establish a correlation between traveler, architecture, and world that I couldn't yet define. To this end, I watched many a sunrise bring an ancient ruin back to life, watched many a living shrine dim out at dusk to be soon after illuminated by a firelight procession winding around it. Everywhere, it seemed there was a language the monuments and rites were speaking, simpler than details of doctrine, more relevant to life today than the archaic trappings of the rites made it seem. But its grammar eluded me.

Eventually, I found myself on a course divergent from my usual one, deep in readings in ethno- and archaeo-astronomy, which argue for a common origin—in early astronomical ideas—for many of the world's myths, rites, monuments, and developed theologies.

For a while, as I followed these scholarly arguments, my very life seemed caught up in them. To supplement my art-history library, I acquired maps and star charts, books on cosmology and the myths and scriptures of the great religions. I was possessed by the feeling that I had tremendous research to do. Teilhard de Chardin somewhere remarks that one is not always aware how close a relationship exists between research and a subjective emotional need.

Unconscious of it still, I was being drawn myself into the pilgrim flow.

NOT long before, I had watched my father struggle to prepare his mind for death. A true son of the Enlightenment, an empiricist and humanist, he had preached that scientific method brought to bear on life and death would plumb the one's mysteries and draw the other's sting. In the end, however, fate was cruel to him. He suffered a long decline, and we suffered it with him.

For a while along the way, though, I saw him possessed by a yearning energy that carried his thoughts in a direction opposite to his usual one. He began reflecting in a kind of transport on the image in Lucretius of the gods who live out long, happy lives between the stars, aloof from the earth. Homer of course had said it before and many said it after—what an abyss of space and idea lies between the Olympian highlands and the ways of human beings on the earth's floor. These meditations gave my father solace, but then he would cut short his flight of mind as if honor-bound to do so, for the gods were only wish-fulfilling illusions to be rejected by an honest man. He became more solitary and, at the last, with a resignation that was painful to hear, repeated Longfellow's lines about men dying leaving only footprints in the sand of time.[2]

I was his child in spirit, and it troubled me to hear people decrying the value system he'd lived by—secular humanism is its redundant name—as responsible for all the ills of the modern world. But his atheism had hedged him in, I decided as I looked back. He had not let himself experience the freedom his imagination craved—almost as if it had a life of its own. I decided even a humanist might allow him- or herself to live among, and fear and love, the gods by calling them *natural,* that is, functions of the mind's own reaching out for new representations of its little-understood nature.

It was in that spirit that I prepared to leave on a research trip to India. It would be the first leg of a prolonged journey that would also take me to Indonesia and Jerusalem, then homeward via the Santiago trail through Spain.

ONE evening before I left New York, I talked with a Hindu visitor to the city.

"What shall I look for in India?" I asked.

"Look for Shiva."

"Where should I look?"

"Look in Benares."

"Where in Benares?" I asked.

"Where you look, there you will find him."

I knew Shiva was a Hindu divinity of boundless energy, now only latent in space and matter, now awakening, coming into his own, breaking into visibility in cascades of forms and shapes. In devotional poetry, he is called Lord White as Jasmine. In a turbulent mind, he is Lord of Wrath. He is Lord of Caves and of Mountains. He rises as the sun and rises again as the moon. He has a female self and several selves as animals. He stirs the cosmos into being and back into nothingness, surviving to reappear as King of Space and in it, Lord of the Dance.

But what that plastic extrusion from an alien mentality could mean to me personally, I had no idea. Yet the bid to come and find out was there: "Shiva is in your own face," writes the great Indianist Stella Kramrisch. "Shiva you taste with your tongue. Your senses are sharpened by Shiva the more exquisitely to savor Shiva. He is the parrot with red eyes who cries from the temple beam. He is cloud, lightning, seasons and sea. He has entered all these, and they vibrate with his intensity."[3]

"Shivaratri, the birthday of the Lord, is the most fantastic night of the year," said the prime minister of an Asian nation whom I met in New York. "To establish total union with the divine cosmic force of which you are only a fragment . . . this is the lifelong effort

of every Hindu, illiterate peasant or educated, Westernized, politically aware person. And in this pursuit, Benares is the most, the
most important city."

"It is in the sky and not on earth," writes Diana Eck, Harvard
Indian scholar, quoting the sages. It is "a destination without the
going." It is "the intensification of all space." It is all cities in one.
It inflates, in the mind's eye, to encompass "the whole of the
Cosmos."[4]

DEPARTURES for the unknown can be frightening. I myself dream
of ships sinking, cars running out of control.

The day I was to leave, a friend pressed a good-luck charm into
my palm, a little hand cut out of tin. But that morning, the newspaper ran a photo from El Salvador showing a house whose oc-
cupants were marked for death by a handprint in dripping white
paint.

The plane was already darkened when I boarded. It held Indians
of various decorated appearance, little girls ajangle with gold jew-
elry, women with diamonds in their noses, men in fluttery white
blouses. I took my seat next to a sleek, round-headed man in a
pink shirt, who at once offered me a number of Hindu religious
tracts. "Are you a Swami?" I asked him.

"No," he said gently. "A saint."

I spent the hours rereading V.S. Naipaul's bitter study of Indian
society and Ved Mehta's on the rising tide of political and social
violence in modern India. I leafed through a folder of clippings on
Indian life and customs. When an eclipse of the sun had occurred
earlier that year, the streets of Delhi and Bombay were nearly emptied of people. Parliament closed and nuclear reactors were turned
off. Westerners were warned by Indian colleagues not to look up
into the sky, even with protective glasses.

Imagery of the stars, I read, permeates the rites of common life.
A Hindu bride, in ceremonies of great antiquity, is given twelve
gold bangles—one for each zodiacal constellation and month of
the year—and she brings into her new life twelve bedsheets and
twelve tablecloths. In the wedding ceremony itself, she and her
groom stand side by side before a sacred stone or fire and take

seven steps around it, like the sun, moon, and the visible planets, going around the pole.

We landed in Paris in daylight that had come too soon, disembarked, reboarded, and in a few hours had crossed back into night. We arrived at Delhi in pitch dark. In my hotel, I took a purple tablet from a vial, watched it dissolve in a glass of water, waited, then gingerly drank. There was low rolling thunder in the distance. When the day dawned, muddy-brown, I returned to the airport to fly on to Benares. This time, it was a little old Fokker prop plane I boarded.

We took off and rose, and rose further. We climbed and climbed. We leveled off and climbed anew. For a while I could see the brown and gray-green details of the earth below. Webbed through the dust were footpaths and burrow trails like the lines on the back of my hand.

Then roads disappeared. There was nothing to be seen but the color brown. At one point, however, we flew over a silver-green weaving of rivers and islets, straits and sandbanks. It was the confluence of the two great rivers Ganges and Yamuna, the site of the famous Festival of the Water-pot, the Kumbha-mela. There it is that, when the planet Jupiter enters the house of Aquarius, many millions of pilgrims, more than congregate for any other event on earth, come to dip themselves in the merging rivers. I looked down and wondered how ten million people would look from such a height, whether they'd be visible as separate beings or only as a spiral galaxy turning across the axis where the rivers meet.

I opened a book of Indian scriptures.

"In the beginning," I read, "what stirred the world into becoming?"

The answer, I read, was: desire. Desire caused the void to shudder into created being. A further answer was even stranger: it was the play of the mind of the ancestors.

Their thoughts produced an embryo, globular, gold, floating in the dark. It split. Its upper half became sky. Its lower half held water. Between lay the earth. Earth and sky were veined with rivers that fed the seas.

Sweet water ran in the earth-rivers. Star-rivers ran overhead. The ocean tides rose up to wash the constellations. All forms were conjoined and enclosed, all shaped in the same shudder, all shining gold.

For a thousand years the embryo floated. Then it burst to release the First Man. Thousand-eyed, thousand-headed, thousand-footed, he moved out in all directions. Look west: there he was, ever-extending. Look north, south, and east, the same. The First Man filled all space. The cleft in his skull was the arch of the zenith. His navel fronted the wind. His feet trod the sea bottom.[5]

The First Man, I read on, saw a figure approaching. It was a vagabond with black face, tattered clothes, and a female heart. Its name was Rudra.[6]

Rudra made the gods give him six more names. By these names he located himself in space. Look north, south, east, west. Look up and down. In the center, where the six ways meet, Rudra danced at the crossways.

Rudra, I knew, was the primitive mythological source out of which Shiva would come in historic time.

Again and again as I turned the pages, I read the same message in the metaphors of the myths—mind coming into self-awareness desperate for location in the world, for the "six directions" of identity. Again and again, the voice returned to the source of its amazement: that out of nothingness it, conscious mind, had come, and into nothingness it would return.

Now we were flying into dark again. Black clouds appeared ahead. Shapeless bursts of lightning began to fill the sky. They flashed on one side, then the other. I pulled another book out of my bag and read, "In the lightning, the light of an eye, the light is the Self."[7]

At last we began our descent. We came in on storm winds, slipping sidewise on the drafts, banking in to touch wheels light as raindrops on black tarmac streaked with reflections. And I remembered someone had told me Indian pilots are the most daring in the world, for they grow up accepting that the material world is an illusion, and death has no relevance to the eternal courses of the spirit, whose habitat is space.

PART ONE

POLESTAR SIGHTED

◆

Through such strange illusions have they passed
Who in life's pilgrimage have baffled striven . . .
Herman Melville:
CLAREL

◆

◆ ◆ ◆

Starting my four-legged journey in Asia, I unwittingly gave the whole of it the shape of an Asian pilgrim's tour of a shrine. Generally, he enters the sacred enclave at the east, turns south, and carries on around the field or shrine toward the west. The doctrinaire meaning of the route is that it imitates the sun's daily flight.[1] To me, the cumulative meaning would be this: I dived straight into a world of "strange illusions"; then I traveled south toward a major clarification of mind under the death-star of myth, Canopus. Finally, I came traveling westward toward a reunion with the sources of my own heritage.

What the North means in myths and, also, to me as a pilgrim, I would learn in time.

As I walked out in Benares before sunrise my first day there, I saw the pilgrims coming. Down the feeder alleys leading to the Ganges they hurried, sometimes twenty or thirty to a party, arrowing along like segmented caterpillars, the women in each batch dressed alike, hung with gold noserings, earrings, necklaces, anklebands, portaging bundles of firewood on their heads along with cooking pots, food, and extra rags for feet and loins. They came from villages sometimes hundreds, even thousands of miles away, padding along, often barefoot, over roads and city pavements, past government buildings, in and out of shrines, unstoppable and inseparable, bent only on their destination.

As I stood and watched, four men came trotting out of the dusty haze heading toward the river. Their thin legs moved in tandem. Their loins were wrapped in gray rags tucked up for speed. They trotted along carrying a litter on long poles resting on their shoulders. A shape was on the litter, wrapped in red cloth, tied with a rope, thin and flat as a folded newspaper.

They were chanting a mantra, trotting to its beat. Again and again they voiced it, never breaking their stride—"*Ram . . . Ram*

. . . Satya Ram"—as their feet slapped the stones. They'd come a long way, trotting day and night.

When they sighted the river, they turned as one and ran down the ghat alongside the water toward a gray column of smoke. Now one runner's voice rose over the others, higher and more piercing.

With each step now, that voice peaked and pierced, a young boy's voice, more urgent than grieving, or with grief heightened by urgency.

Ram is the fire-mantra. Saying it as they ran, the runners were fire. Their feet on the stones were fire in dry grass as they carried their burden to the river to put out its pain.

THE ghats, or paved banks of the Ganges, were strewn with sacred stones. Here and there stood spindly trees. The stones were streaked with yesterday's saffron powder. The trees were hung with yesterday's tinsel. The walls along the ghats were plastered with posters of gods and saints—old saints, bald saints, saints with white beards; naked saints sitting on dry cow dung, on elephants, and on piles of bones.

Underfoot and in all the corners, swept back but spilling out again, were shards of clay cups used yesterday for offerings in the temples, thousands of cups melting back into the mud out of which they had been molded.

Down the feeder lanes came bullocks and cows, roused from their beds in the ditches where the pilgrims had slept. Back where the lanes disappeared between buildings, the lights of breakfast fires flickered in tin cans casting pale gleams onto the figures bending over them.

The light widened and citron-pink filled the east. The sun rose across the river like a vagabond in rags of clouds. Lifting clear of the mist, the egg of light split into two, one flow spilling toward us on the ghats, the other rising, an ever-lengthening column of gold in the sky. The paling sky lifted away from the world. The river ran on, streaked with froth.

"Welcome to the auspicious river," said a soft Indian voice in my ear. "Since the beginning of time it has flowed, never diminishing. As long as it flows, it will protect the people. There is also

Mount Kailas in the north, shining like crystal, indestructible. As long as it stands, the people will live."

Men were swimming out into the orange water singing. "O Ganga!" "O Bhagiratri!" "O Govinda!"

How many gods, I wondered, were listening? "O Ganesh!" "O Surya!" "O Ganga."

The Brahmins were saying the Gayatri, the mantra owned by males of their caste alone. Let no female or lower-caste male listen! "Let us meditate on the most excellent light of the Sun-god," it goes. "May he guide our minds . . ."

"To Shiva, robed in space, I bow down," others were praying. "Rising sun, Lord of the Blue Throat . . ."[2]

Bare-breasted, the Brahmins drew in big, chest-inflating breaths. They cupped up the water, turned precisely to the four quarters, and tossed water each way.

FARTHER down the shore, the women were clustered in fenced-off areas, washing the dirt of the roads out of their saris. They too stepped in and out of the water, shaking wet hair, then sitting down to press red paste into the center partings in their hair.

Behind them, market stalls were being opened. Heaps of powders, fuchsia, silver, citron, and red, were being laid out in neat baskets, to be sprinkled on the stones and rubbed into hair parts, foreheads, palms of hands, and soles of feet.

> Colors, orange, yellow, blue, red, these are in the sun and also in the blood vessels of the body . . .
> The sun's rays flow down, entering the body, flowing through the veins and arteries, flowing out and returning to the sun. (The Upanishads)

Sidewalks and steps were being decorated with patterns of powders, shells, scrolls, mythical beasts, dots and darts, flowers, and stars. By nightfall, the colorful designs would be streaked with mud and excrement, ready to be washed away to be redrawn tomorrow. People were bending over the waterside to launch little boats of green leaves filled with marigolds, rice, butter. "The color is the Shakti," said the Indian who had elected to enlighten me that morning.

Shakti is the energy that caused the void to quicken into creation. Shakti is the quickening in the blood when a human being feels sexual desire, or creative inspiration. Shakti is female. In Benares, she flows openly between the riverbanks. Bathing here washes away your past crimes though you have committed 84 million of them. The gods drink nectar, but people drink Shakti, the milk of the Goddess, who feeds the pilgrims even while she feeds upon them, for never does she assuage her hunger for ashes and bones, for flowers and the slimes of Benares.

From the ghats, from pipes and down gutters, raw sewage poured from the waking city. An iron spout belched and a geyser of urine flushed into the river. Down where the water lapped, scum thickened and drew flowers into its clots. "Beauty of Benares is best from the boat," said the voice in my ear. Its owner pointed to a line of long, curved passenger boats filled with tourists, gravely poling by, well out beyond the shore.[3]

Nearby under an umbrella sat a Sadhu or Holy Man. Pots of colored pastes and powders, rice and seeds were arranged at his feet. "What do you think about?" I asked him through my interpreter.

"God. Worship. Worship the Guru. The Guru's footsteps."

Next to his seat was a plank on which were a number of worn sandals, huge, ungainly, inhuman-looking footgear. "Guru's sandals are full of glory," said the Sadhu, fingering a shoe and smiling.

Pilgrims came toward him pressing their palms together to signify that their double-selves—material and spiritual—are meshed together in this world, then touching their heads at the place from where the soul exits at death. In the same posture, they stopped at other places along the ghats. An old woman pattered by, head down, shooting for the river, till she saw me, a Western woman in traveling garb with camera. She turned to face me, stood stock-still raising folded hands, bowed, and moved her lips. "She's worshiping *you*," whispered my interpreter. By a blacksmith shop stood a flower-decked table and on it a broken hunk of metal wrapped in a rag. "We worship the iron," explained the blacksmith, "as the farmer his seed and the cowherd his cow."

To join this worshipful flow, the Hindu abandons his work, his home, and his web of natural social relationships. Yet once launched on his pilgrimage, he finds himself in a social modality with its own rigid forms. For the duration, he will eat only certain foods. He or she—for both sexes are bound by the rules of the road— may offer a head of hair as a gift to the gods. All pilgrims must remain continent or at least avoid copulating by crossroads, burning grounds, gardens, or water, under tall trees, or in temples. If the male is a Brahmin who has survived the three passages of a normal lifespan—student, householder, retiree—he may himself go as a Holy Man. In that case he will have undergone symbolic death and cremation. As a dead-man-in-life, he will wear special dress, white of the wind or red of fire. If he is a Buddhist, he will wear ochre, once reserved for criminal outcasts. If he is a Jain of a certain sect, he goes dressed only in empty space.

On the ghats now, the lepers and cripples, the blind and dwarfed had come to work their separate begging grounds. They raised their begging bowls, small suns of polished copper. Among them, barbers had set up operation. Their clients squatted before them, peering into little tin mirrors hung on strings from poles. Light glinted off the mirrors, flew through the air and glanced on all sides.

Drums and chimes sounded. *"Hare Krishna!"* sang a line of Western hippies. From all sides came a drone of sound—of engines and wheels, of conch- and air-horns, of loudspeakers and, under these, a never-ceasing, heart-shaking vibration, deep as if it came off the strings of some universal instrument, of voices, shouting, crying, praying, groaning their mantras, all to the ear-splitting accompaniment of electronic recordings of the same.[4]

The sound was the Shakti!

Now the sun was falling on the scene with an eye-splitting brilliance. It traced the edges of the umber, carmine, and ivory palaces along the ghats, the thin throats of their Islamic-style windows, the long streaks of decay down their sides. Orange light washed over red-brown skin. Gold flickered across the oil-stained pavement. Silver dazzled off the hems of vermilion, saffron, green, and turquoise cloth. Reflections met and melted into reflections of buildings, towers, boats—a daylit aurora borealis over a city sinking daily into the rank darkness of its foundations. For when the snows melt in the north and the monsoon rains come, the Ganges overflows, and the riverbank buildings sink a little into earth too soft to bear their weight. Then the walls crack while banyan and pipal trees draw their nets ever tighter, so that in the end Ganga will carry them all away.

THE most desirable pilgrimage for each male Hindu is to carry the ashes of his dead father to the Ganges. In the big riverside shrine cities, Brahmin priests keep palm-leaf ledgers of the deposition of ashes, family by family, some going back centuries. Census of the living is relatively new in India. For centuries in that land, one came into being officially only when one died.[5]

Theoretically, the ashes may be thrown into any capillary of the Ganges, that is, by inference, any river, brook, or pond in the world. The theory is that all the world's waterways feed into that great central artery, therefore that all lesser streams feed eventually into the sea. For this reason, Hindus abroad have been known to deposit their ashes in such alien waters as the Thames.

The ash-eating Ganges itself, says the Hindu, thunders down out of the sky in the far north, plunging onto the head of Lord Shiva where he stands on Mount Kailas. The flood then dives underground only to burst forth some distance south, within the border of India, from a fissure in the ice called Mouth of the Cow.

From there, the Ganges shudders and leaps, slows and nearly dies, revives and flows on for nearly two thousand miles till it reaches the colossal delta that empties into the Bay of Bengal. Thereafter, *Ganga* loses her name and her identity, though she is immanent still in the salt seas that diffuse southward till they meet the horizon where they fuse with the sky, wherein she rises back into identity as the River of Stars.

And, as she coils through the sky-dome, running from south to north, then flows back across the earth southwards, so there are pilgrims who make the trek in the same directions, clambering north through gullies and glacial moraines to the ice-rivers by the Cow's Mouth, there to fill bottles with holy water to carry back down to the Bay of Bengal, there to empty them into the tides. Meanwhile, along the road, other pilgrims are making their way northward carrying bags of sand from the Bengal beach to sprinkle on the headwaters that flush it south again. So the great vascular system of sky-and-earth is kept flushing and filling, thanks to the millionfold labor of the pilgrims.

In this ecosystem, the earth is a living member that the Hindu devotee calls Mother India.[6] She can be seen on a map, lying on her back, her head in the Himalayas, her feet amid the triple seas—the Arabian Sea, the Indian Ocean, the Bay of Bengal. Her children have only to dip up a palmful of water out of any free-flowing brook or spring-fed tank to drink of her life-supporting fluid. Scattered through fields and cities, at the foot of trees and skyscrapers, buried in last year's fallen leaves and at the intersections of highways, are sure to be little cult shrines—a clay snake or horse, a couple of flowers, a pinch of rice—where the Hindu may pay homage to her.

She lives and breathes around him in his imagination, yet it is separation from his real mother that, according to some scholars, helps provide the psychic ground in which Hinduism thrives. At the age of eight, the Brahmin boy enacts a ritual "Going on pilgrimage to Benares," in the course of which, for the last time in his life, he shares food with his mother. Thereafter, he is bathed and given an adult's white loincloth, and a degree of willed alienation becomes his lifelong lot. "If a hairsbreadth separate you from the Universal, you suffer anxiety," says a respected Hindu psychoanalyst.[7] Then the cure for anxiety, as for all other woes attendant on material life, is to sink one's flesh back into the flesh of the Universal Mother, that is, into the flood of what the Hindu calls the River of Illusions.

HOWEVER, as wild plants are picked out of fields to be dissected in botanical gardens in the interest of science, so the terrain of India, flesh of the untamed Mother Goddess, has been subdivided by the Brahmanic priesthood in the interest of bureaucratic control over her pilgrim devotees. Therefore, a Hindu seeking intercourse with the maternal divinity today is likely to buy a bus or train ticket for an official, government-promoted "All-India Pilgrimage" to one or more of her discrete body parts.

An ancient myth, surviving in modern Hindu temple art and popular books, provides rationale for the widespread distribution of separate shrines to the Goddess. She was born out of immanence-in-nature into the shape of a young woman, Sati, who fell in love with Shiva. When her father refused to bless their love-match, Sati set herself on fire. In fury, Shiva took up her corpse and danced with it through the sky. As he whirled, scattering fire-tears to all sides, Sati's body flew apart and fell across the land.

The place of her suicide is a rich and revered riverbank temple in North India. In Calcutta, where her skull fell out of the sky, stands another rich temple today. Her tongue is worshiped in the Punjab; her elbow, in the central Indian town of Ujjain; her navel, in the fabled pilgrimage town of Puri, halfway down India's east coast. Even the poor woman's eyes, or rather three qualities of them, are worshiped by pilgrims: "huge eyes" in Benares, "fish-eyes" in Madurai, and "libidinous eyes" in the South Indian temple city of Kanchipuram. But her holiest shrine is in Kamakhya, in Assam, where devotees of the Tantric sect make pilgrimage to a particular cleft in the rocks where a male goat is beheaded each eventide and where, in the monsoon season when the Goddess menstruates, the ground is drenched in blood from the opened veins of thousands of animals.

Kali is the Goddess's name in these temples. She represents the resurgence into modern cult-life of a prehistoric demoness, Durga, who personified the decay of organic matter.[8] Priests of the Hindu middle ages tried to banish Durga from their pantheon of male sky- and sun-gods, for she kept reminding them of death. But they failed. Like decomposed matter, Kali-Durga is black, and like death, she returns.

As a pilgrim, I came upon Kali-Durga in such a place as this. Down on the floor of a pitch dark, bat-hung shrine, in a scatter of garbage and dung, lay a humped black stone with silver eyes pasted on and a protruding tongue, bright red from lapping up blood.

Someone had come into the place and laid flowers and rice before the stone.

"What of this?" I asked my friendly guide. "What do you make of this?"

"Peaceful," he said in a reverent voice. "Quiet. As in a cemetery. You can rest. Lie as if dead."

Until I understand Kali as "peace," I considered, I would not be able to say I understand India.

Later I would go to the temple in Calcutta where Sati's skull fell out of the sky.

We approached through sunless alleyways. Somewhere a dog howled. Dark-faced people spilled from doorways of blackened bamboo huts. Atop a stone wall, a waif perched on her skinny knees to shake dice with a crippled boy in red rags.

We turned a corner and were in an open square. On a high platform stood the temple, thronged by pilgrims. Gongs were clanging. We clambered up and joined the crowd that pushed toward the altar. I saw red banners flying. Suddenly I was thrust to the front. I stumbled to the edge of a stone trough and looked down. Dancing in the pits were flames of oil lamps amid scarlet flowers. "Hail, Mother of the World of Illusions!" pilgrims were crying behind and around me. There, down in the fire and the flowers, lay Kali again, again a blackened stone, this time with three piercing red eyes, a gold tongue thrust out, and red hands like the stumps of a thalidomide child, raised in supplication.

Had I expected to see the Virgin Mary down there with pink cheeks and a nimbus? I turned to my friend and guide again in confusion. He looked at me with softened eyes and said it again: "Peace."

✦ ✦ ✦

To travel India as the Hindu pilgrim does is to experience geography enlarged and glorified. The most audacious and hardy, for example, ascend the full length of the Ganges to its headwaters, then circumambulate the foothills of Mount Kailas, whose sheer peaks can't actually be climbed, then descend the opposite bank of the river to its end.[9] These two conjoined trails, in the terms of myth to which the Hindu subscribes, circle and scale and so define the cosmos itself. The Mountain is the axis that touches the top of a golden egg that floats in nothingness, and the River curves inside the egg, mixing ashes into slurry to sink to the riverbed, delivering some organisms back to shore in new forms and some rarefied spirits, stripped of their material pods, off to the stars or beyond them into the void.[10]

Other pilgrimage routes, however, crisscross the land, north to south, east to west. On a map, Mother India's body is laid-over by another huge figure, outlined by trails sacred to Brahma, Vishnu, and Shiva—the famous triad of male sky-gods introduced into India by migrants from the north in the dawn of history.

The head of the figure lies in the mountains of Kashmir, beyond snowfields passable only in summer. In a cave there, a massive stalagmite of ice, accreted from glacial melt-off, represents the brain and as well the phallus of Lord Shiva, for anatomy must give way to concept in Hindu iconography, and this form represents the generative power in the cosmos. Pilgrims who have made the trek affirm that it radiates an unearthly light and swells as if alive when the moon is full.[11]

The arms of the imaginary figure span the oceans. Its right wrist beats on Benares. Its left fingers touch the Arabian Sea. Its heart beats over a four-lobed cluster of towns where the love myths of Lord Krishna are enacted by pilgrims each year, after the monsoon rains have greened the earth. Its legs and feet lie along the great South Indian temples, where Lords Shiva and Vishnu are worshiped as wind or fire, energy, empty space, or light.

But that figure is only the start of the male-oriented pilgrim trails Mother India bears, perhaps as her tattoos. There are four All-India Abodes of the Gods at the cardinal points of the nation, and seven All-India cities and numberless other shrines between, mostly participating in more than one god system, so they will be bound to be visited by multitudes.

But of all the sacred cities in India, Benares is the most important.

I walked on the ghats with an Indian scholar adept in brisk introductions to Hindu philosophy.

"What is the nature of spirit?" he inquired conversationally as we walked, fast, by the cremation ground. On a litter lay a body with gauze tightly tied over its face. Smoke curled over a pyre nearby. Red feet protruded from the stack of logs. The toes were puffed.

"The spirit is captured, bound into flesh, sorrowing and in pain," he continued, laying out principles in everyday tones of voice, high and positive, as if he were talking politics. "The spirit's pilgrimage is away from the material world. Its longing is never to be captured in flesh again."

Smoke from the pyres went on staining the sky. A dead dog floated by in the river. "The riverbanks are the lungs of the city!" my host cried. "In the city, one suffocates!" He rushed on ahead, pressing his handkerchief to his nose.

This city with lungs is one of the oldest human settlements, old as Babylon. Its significance is worldly and cosmological. It lies in an ancient east-west trade route linking the furthermost Orient with the Mediterranean. As cultural nexus, it was renowned when the man Buddha walked by in the sixth century before Christ. It was a center for Hindu philosophical discourse in the Western Dark Ages. It was besieged by the Moslems in the eleventh century, again in the twelfth, again in the fourteenth, and again. Each time, new palaces, temples, and mosques were built out of the ruins. But no siege can bring down mystical Benares.

A horseshoe-shaped road, joined to the riverbank at both ends, bends around and encloses the city. To walk it takes five days. It leads by little stalls where buffalo milk boils in copper cauldrons to refresh the pilgrim. It leads through fields where the wind rocks marigolds by the million, ripening for pilgrim devotions in the temples. Once the road has been walked, the pilgrim has in theory encompassed the cosmos and made it his home.

Inside the large circle are four smaller ones, five in all, for five is

Lord Shiva's sacred number, the number of syllables in his mantra—OM NAMAH SHIVA—that the pilgrim will be mouthing with each step he takes. The second-to-last road can be walked in one hour. But the final circle has only to be entered. It is the sanctum sanctorum of Benares's most sacred shrine, the Temple of Shiva in his manifestation as Lord of the Cosmos. A single step by a pilgrim pierces it as a sperm pierces an egg. The metaphor serves, for the sanctum of a Hindu temple is known as its "womb chamber." The stone icon on its altar is the cosmic Lord's phallus rising straight from its stone base that represents his wife's vulva. And both are embraced in the mystical confines of Benares itself, for the city entire is the phallus of the Lord made manifest as pure light.

Benares, then, is the bridal city where Shiva as stone and light copulates with the Mother as stone and riverwater. To die in the churn of their passion is the pilgrim's desire.

In the evening, the professor led me into the suffocating core of Benares, to the very Temple of the Lord of the Cosmos.

"Stand up high!" he cried, for as a non-Hindu I was not allowed to go in. Through the door I could see clouds of glowing smoke and the backs of priests sitting on the floor. I heard bells and cymbals. I saw oil lamps lifted and lowered. Ashes covered the priests' bald heads, and yellow powder spilled over their shoulders. By their knees I could make out a silver-railed stone tub in which stood the upright stone that is the symbolic representation of the mysteries of creation-out-of-nothingness: the sacred phallus or linga. A bronze snake encircled it. Holy water was being poured over it, vented off through a stone pipe to a catch-basin out of the way, for anything that has touched a linga may be infused with lethal energy.

"The god has come! He is in this very place!" said my guide. He was leaning back against the wall of a facing building not four feet away, appreciating my interest in the brilliant display, the noise and confusion and even the continual pressure against our flesh of various animals that stood around. A cow with gaping anus and blue horns swung her flank sidewise, knocking me against the wall. A Holy Man with feather baton and coat of rags was stationed at the temple door, stamping his feet and shouting but never entering. He was, I was told, a member of a brotherhood of perpetual pilgrims called Ramanandi, who neither cross thresholds nor stop in their lifelong marches save to sleep, or in the monsoon.

Indeed, like that Holy Man, the stone linga is considered to be in perpetual motion. Its function is to extract out of the cosmic air a stream of energy that, at every moment, is embodying itself as material reality—landscape, city, temple, and ourselves. At the same time, the stone rises like a sundial's gnomon and so, by extension, serves as a support for the sky. Furthermore, under that sky, the upright object that it is stands for the First Man of creation, the Hindu Adam: Purusha.

The linga's theoretical extent and power, then, is macro- and microcosmic. It stands at the center of a whirlpool of light and energy that engenders the material world. The four elements, fire, earth, water, and wind, are engendered by it. Therefore, these elements themselves are worshiped in some places as separate aspects of Lord Shiva's cosmic being. In the city of Arunchala in South India on the winter solstice, a Linga of Firelight rises from a bonfire on a mountaintop. In Kanchipuram is a Linga of Earth, and in Jambukeshvara, a Linga of Water. In Kalahasti a draft blows through the temple, and that is a Linga of Wind. In Chidambaram the sanctum is empty save for the altar-stone with a small depression in it, and such is the Linga of Space. In addition, there are twelve more Lingas of Light in a wheel of cities, from the Himalayas down to the Indian Ocean, that replicates the wheel of the constellations.

For the literal-minded Hindu pilgrim, however, like his brother and sister in the West, arcane theory must come packaged in humanized images. That evening in Benares I stood on tiptoe to regard the marvel of the linga heaped in carnations, roses, jasmine, and green leaves. All day long it had been attended by pairs of priests—one married and so mired in matter, the other celibate—who together signify the bond between world and sky, ensuring that rites performed down here have their repercussions above.

Long since had they wakened the linga in the morning with kettledrums and bells. Long since had they bathed it and fed it the five nectars as well as cloves and betel leaves, sugar and nuts. Then they dressed it in garlands and held up a mirror before its silver eyes. They fanned it with fly whisks and entertained it with music. If this were a festival day, they would have offered it a turban and jewels, and eyes of gold.

Eventually the pilgrims had come with their gifts of flowers and food, to say rosaries and throw holy water or oil onto the stone. A gift of great worth would be a cup of clarified butter so clear the donor could see his face in it: that would be a "shadow gift," for with it, the pilgrim offers his visible self. In less-frequented temples, these shadow gifts pile up, coagulating over years, a rotting crust of reflections of faces that have, no doubt, passed out of being altogether.[12]

In these ways, worship of the cosmic energy-source goes on all day until the evening star comes out, signaling a change in the day's pace. One of these shifts in the cosmic rhythm comes just before dawn, a quickening through all nature. The other is at dusk, when the light shifts toward the red, turning the sky violet-umber. Then all material beings slow down and draw into themselves preparing to rest. Trees and stones, river and pilgrims share in this inward quieting. Then in the far North, the ice-peak of Kailas flares red-gold. In the myth, Shiva's consort, the Mother of the Three Worlds, takes her seat on a throne that glows in the snow as the sun goes down. Then Shiva himself stands up before her and, as the moon climbs the sky, begins to dance. All night he dances in his glory, which is the wheel of stars.[13]

Now I could see the pilgrims crowding the linga that, to their eyes, was dancing. They seemed to scoop up the air that twinkled around it, cupping it onto their foreheads, breasts, and arms.

After a while they would depart. The priests would wash the stone down and perform the sunset fire ritual over it, feeding the five little flames of the fire lamp, raising and lowering it and ringing bells and chimes while drums rumble a low good night. Out on the riverbank, other priests would be standing with fire lamps drawing other fire diagrams over dark Ganga.

Then for a while in the streets of Benares there would rise a howling cacophony of sociability, with motorcycles, cars, rick-shaws, water buffalo, pigs, and beggars all contributing, while pil-grims too poor to buy beds would drift toward the parks and into the protective shadows of big buildings, squatting in circles to light their little cook fires in the exhaust of the city's traffic.

Then there would be silence, with only those little flames glint-ing in the dark where people and animals bed down together.

But all night long the cremation pyres would smolder, separat-ing the atoms formed in the cores of stars, which then flew into this enclosure of space and time. And strange it is to consider how, once here, those atoms fell into alignments that let them turn and look back up as if at lighted windows seen at a far distance—over snowfields impassable under any circumstances, at any season of the year.

✦ ✦ ✦

After some days in Benares, I took off with my Indian friend for the South, going the way of the ashes but the way of the River too, held to its bosom, if I could only remember that—that though Ganga might carry me to depths too deep for me, she would bring me back up in the end.

We boarded a night train to Calcutta and climbed into a sleeper car so coated with diesel fuel we couldn't see out. We were ordered to bolt the compartment door against bandits. The train started rolling. Four soot-blackened fans stirred the air. The train gath-ered speed, its whistles screaming.

We were sharing the compartment with a family on pilgrimage from Assam, where the Goddess's vulva is guarded, to Rames-waram, site of one of Shiva's twelve phalluses of Light. Man, wife, and grown son, wrapped in white pilgrims' clothes, slept all night leaning on one another's shoulders without strain.

In the morning the woman from Assam set a box on the window ledge and took out a mirror. Slowly she combed her long and glossy black hair, never speaking. She took a pot of red paste and touched a finger to the spot between her brows where the material world melts into the intangible one. That red spot marked her as a living crossways between the two worlds. It also marked her as a married woman. Female and male, coupled, represent earth and sky. After death, the male may rise out of nature. But she will be reborn into it. If her husband should die before her, the red mark would be wiped off, for her metaphysical function would cease to exist.

With her right hand, the woman drew a long, deep-scarlet, moist sweep of paste along the part in her hair. Then she leaned back in her white wings of a sari. She said not a word nor focused her eyes on anything in particular but fell into a dream, resting her head on her hand. Her arm was bent; one knee was bent flat, the other raised. She had composed herself into a posture of triangles so stable no lurch of the train could unsettle her. For hours, she moved not a muscle but drifted as the train drew her, while I in my topside bunk at first twisted and turned, brushing off biting insects that fell from the ceiling, then gradually also fell into thought, drifting through my maps and books as the train rolled on through what Indians call the Rose-Apple Land.

I reflected that the pilgrim's trail unwinds through both landscape and the seasons, that is, through space and time. Since space and time are fundamental modes of coming to grips with the physical world, pilgrimage must be a response to fundamental human needs.

I was attempting an interpretation general enough to account for the tangible structures of the pilgrim's world—sacred sites, monuments, and roads—and also the round of calendar time that brings on rituals in these places. Carl Jung used the word "constellate" to describe the appearance in a researcher's mind of a long-sought idea or image: it "constellates" out of thought. In this case, the astronomical term itself is a clue to the way my thinking ran.

Wondering about the origin of pilgrimage, I found my thoughts drawn back to the beginning of conscious self-questioning on the part of the human race and of each new individual in his and her lifetime. According to one theory of knowledge, people learn about the world through experience in it. By an opposite theory, the human mind imposes self-generated categories of understanding—like space and time—upon a world unknown and unknowable. According to this view, only thoughts are real. "The world" is an illusion. This is the Hindu view, echoed variously by Western idealist philosophies and certain linguistic schools. The issue is relevant, for the question arises: does the pilgrim travel the natural world or only the inner world of thought? If he attains his goal, will he have achieved deepened understanding of the natural order or only solace for his longings?[14]

Rather than either of these extreme explanations, some psychologists and philosophers propose the true process is a dialectical one. People receive information about the world through their senses—sight, hearing, and so on—then give it meaningful form according to the mind's bent. By these tandem means, they achieve stability and orientation in their surroundings. "Man's orientation in his environment," psychologist Rudolf Arnheim writes, "essential for survival, takes place first at the perceptual level . . ."

Then, in order "to possess a cluster of percepts, the mind gathers them into coherent structure." That is, the mind then selects, out of the perceived field, a "regular, symmetrical, stable form . . . the simpler . . . the easier the understanding."[15]

What is not always taken into account by those who write of such things is that for early humankind, as for many a rural child today, the field of vision from which those basic clusters of percepts were gathered extended not only horizontally across the earth but also vertically toward the sky.

In antiquity, the sun, moon, planets, and stars served as sources of information about the nature of the world before the earth was traveled. Long before recorded history, people had devised techniques to record such data, for example tabulating the recurrent motions of sun and moon as scratches on bones. Much later but still before recorded history, people in many parts of the northern hemisphere built sighting devices—circles of standing stones, upright posts, sky-sighting pipelines across hills and up the faces of cliffs. Thus well before written proof of it can be shown, a body of astronomical information was possessed by the human family.

However, a leap of mind beyond the gathering of data had to take place before the world could be "possessed." That move would not be a trivial one. It was impelled by the instinct for survival.

THE "coherent structure ... regular, symmetrical, stable" that thought derived from this body of astronomical data was, it seems, a visual image, magnificent and enormous: an earth-enclosing pod of space, bounded by the stars, which the anthropologist Mircea Eliade has called the "Cosmogonic Egg."[16] An inspiration for the image may have been the cave, where human beings first came together in firelight to question the nature of the world beyond its confines. A later model may have been a hut or tent, held upright on a center pole and staked around its circumference. But however it was inspired, the image was so efficient in affording a sense of stability and self-definition that it became a, perhaps *the,* fundamental archetype by which externality was brought under the domination of consciousness. It could be called the Ur-myth: the Myth of Cosmos.

Cosmological myths worldwide describe the Egg in much the same way. Adrift in chaos or an infinite void it hangs, hollow and upright, turning on its axis. Across its center lies the flat earth.[17] Above the earth curve the fire-paths of sun, moon, planets, and stars. Below the earth lies the abyss, where dead organisms sink to undergo sea change. Fire, earth, and water: the famous "Three Worlds" of world myth.[18]

In terms of the myth, the earth itself is generally square; its four corners are the points on the horizon where the sun is perceived to rise on solstice and equinoctial mornings.

Here a word of explanation is needed for city dwellers like myself who lack the art—and have forgotten the relevance—of marking sunrise points on bits of bone. Because of the tilt in the earth's axis vis-à-vis the sun's, that body of fire appears to be in constant motion traveling not only east to west but also north or south in the course of a year. At midsummer and midwinter, it reaches its north and south extremities. On my windowsill I have marked the points of solstice sunrise as I see them on the horizon. When the sun reaches these two points, it appears to halt in its flight, then reverse its course. So, common sense suggests, it must do year after year if the Cosmos is to survive. Therefore, the solstices were experienced in antiquity as times of danger, actually reflected on earth by extremes of weather.

Halfway between solstices, the sun's track crosses the points of spring and autumn equinoxes, where the great circles of the earth's and the sun's equators cut across one another out in space. The equinoctial sunrise points are marked, curiously enough at first thought, by one and the same notch midway between the other two. But since the celestial dome continually appears to revolve, it brings around an opposite background of stars to the point of opposite equinoxes. And these stations too, as if to prove their mystical import, are experienced on earth in terms of unsettled weather, rain, and reverses of seasonal winds. Thus, in logically visualized theory, the Cosmos is held upright on four sun-pillars, which stand in space and mark earth time.

Initiated into this pseudoscience of Cosmos by rituals and spoken communication, early people acquired a sense of stable, centered location in it. The mind itself acquired an outer limit to its flights and, as we shall see, internal structures by which to orient both thought and travel.

Later in time came myth to explain the origin of the Cosmos in humanized sexual terms. While the primordial parents lay embraced, there was no time or space, nor separation between the sexes. Then the father sky lifted off the mother earth. As they drew apart, three-dimensional space opened between them, a field of force centered on the shadow of the organ that had joined them—the cosmic axis, Axis Mundi or World Tree of world myth.

With the creation of space, it was considered that time too had begun. From that moment time ticked on in the enclosure. The next event would be the descent of the life-plasm from sky to earth.

THE star-bounded, internally articulated Cosmos has had a long life in human thought. In historic time, it gave rise or shelter to the ideas of Pythagoras, Plato, and Aristotle. It shaped Christian imagination up to and including Copernicus and Kepler.[19] For it was inconceivable unboundedness from which both these late-Renaissance empiricists recoiled, as Pascal did and, later, Einstein.

But its great gift to humanity through the ages has been a metaphysics of light in which believers have found answer to deep existential concern. "I know you want to keep on living," wrote St. Augustine. "You do not want to die. . . . This is what you desire. This is the deepest human feeling . . . the soul itself wishes and instinctively desires it." On the earth, many forms of natural regeneration after death were and are witnessed save the single one for which people most ardently yearn. The lights in the skies, however, neither failed nor faltered. Year after year they returned in sequence. Out of an instinct for more life, then, came the idea that the dead live on among the stars.

Theoretical access to the star-fields, it was believed, could be had at certain sites, such as mountaintops, tall trees, or stone markers where, sometimes, a star seemed to stand. Or the sun might raise the dead out of their graves as it drew its fire-columns up to the zenith.[20] Also, by common perception, the sea plainly flows into the sky at the horizon, and rivers flow down from sky-scraping headlands into the sea thence back to the stars. So the Ganges has been called the "flowing ladder to heaven," and the Nile "the earthly continuation of the Milky Way."[21] Across such trails that lead from the earth to the sky via rivers and seas, many pilgrim-heroes of cosmic myth made their way in search of restored life: Gilgamesh, Ulysses, Aeneas; Abraham and Joshua; the mythical Buddha; later Christ, Peter, Paul, James, and others.

WHERE and when cosmological speculation began is unknown.[22] A few fanciful writers have proposed it was in the northern latitudes where the standing stones are today. In that doubtful case, the teaching would have been carried south through the Pillars of Hercules to the Mediterranean to inspire myths recorded on the tablets of literate antiquity. A more likely source was the region around the Caspian Sea, from where the great nomad migrations out of landlock began, it is now thought, around the fourth millennium BCE.[23] Some of these tribes, blessed by fate, moved westward into the fertile river valleys of Mesopotamia. Their brothers, cursed by fate some say, settled in the Gangetic plains. But they came from the same language pool, and their scriptures are alike permeated with astronomical images and poetic meditations on them. "Undying, shining, swift-horsed" was a hymn of the Persians to the sun, to which the Hindus of Benares still daily say yea. Surya, the sun in Sanskrit, is Ahura in Persian.

Eventually, from the Euphrates eastward toward the Indus, there arose culture centers where cosmological science flowered rapidly and from where it radiated into Asia, Africa, and Europe.[24] In all these regions, surveillance of the skies was a perpetual communal activity to pinpoint the rising and setting sun, the new moon, and certain star and planet risings. People took up their stations on the flat roofs of mud-brick houses, as those in hot climes do today.

How accumulating astronomical lore was spread is easy to suppose. One trader on a horse or camel can sow information correct or false a long way. And the coalescing science would be added to by those who had to plot journeys "toward morning" or "toward sunset." For on earth you can see at most a few miles off, but you can walk toward a star for months. Or, stand by a river and you see neither headwaters nor mouth. But stand under the sprawling constellation Eridanus and you see that star-river in its entire flow.[25] "First the celestial fields were known, then they were identified in terrestrial geography," writes Eliade. "The skeleton map of the earth was derived from the sky," reads *Hamlet's Mill*.[26]

The tribes who moved eastward toward India, for example, took their lead from the sun as they entered their future home, and their epics reveal their imaginative efforts at orientation in the wilderness. Myth, for example, says that the first God-king of the Indo-Aryan tribes commanded a "Thousand-horse Sacrifice" to see how far his kingdom would run. That is, he set loose a thousand white "horses of the sun" to range where they would for a full year's time, while his warriors, no doubt, followed with swords. At the year's end, the horses were slain and laid in the thousand beds of the king's wives. When that coupling was done, the king ate the marrow out of the horses' bones, laying claim to the land they had traversed and the people as well. And it ran from shining sea to sea.

Scattered through the Hindu epic of the settlement period—the Mahabharata—are tales of heroes going on pilgrimage following the sun's course. They travel south, then west, circumambulating much of the subcontinent. Along the way, they make sorties up the big rivers, penetrating forested land corridors populated, in that era, by aboriginal tribes. By later generations' reenactment of these epic adventures, the holdings of the Aryan empire were enlarged and consolidated.[27]

So cosmic myth, pilgrimage, and political formation came into being as a continuity and still, in modern India, reinforce one another. Modern Hindus still travel to a sacred tract of land, some hundred miles north of Delhi, which scholars think was an actual staging area for the migrants. It is still mythologized as the center of the Cosmos. Here, the Mahabharata records, the transcendent Sun-god, "Krishna-Govinda of the Intolerable Beams," came out of the sky to teach a reluctant warrior-chief, Arjuna, the facts of cosmic law and, in the light of it, human duty. No one comes new into the enclosure of being nor dies irrevocably out of it. Slayer is bound to slain like the rising sun to the setting sun. When blood falls on the ground, spirit flies up toward the light. Therefore the moral is: *"Arjuna, fight!"*

In this way, out of cosmological myth sustained by pilgrimage, ethical propositions that still shape Indian life were derived and are passed on.

STILL one may ask what use is all this myth and theory to understanding pilgrimage in the rest of the world today?

My answer is that the religious pilgrim worldwide moves in the light of it still. He projects the old cosmic geometry onto the natural world, or in nature he discovers the old geometry for the old reason: to find his bearings in a world in which, from the moment he comes into self-awareness, he does so with a will not ever to be without being again.

Then pilgrimage can be said to be a traveling, in body or thought, toward a point on earth that affords access to the outer curves of the Cosmos, whose geometry still signals to the mind relief from disorientation, suffering, and the need to die.

The religious pilgrim aspires to the modality of the stars, which is eternity.

THEN what does the heritage of cosmological myth hold for the modern (or even postmodern) secular pilgrim? Such travelers probably agree that an earth-centered pod of space doesn't curve protectively around them. For them—for us—the globe turns at a slant and wobbles in space. For us, the fundamental notions of space and time have lost their finality. We even wait for science to tell us whether the universe will collapse, rendering the concept of space meaningless, or enlarge "forever," which would render time meaningless. Our commonest possessions reflect the relativity of our sense of location nowadays. For example, the digital watch on my wrist annihilates the old image of circularity that once defined the day, the year, the horizon, and so the All. And so I steal a glance at the kitchen clock that sets me back into earth time like an astronaut cocooned in artificial gravity.

All the same—all the more—the notion of a single abstract, archetypal form embracing and so giving unity to the many-sectioned world survives. To bring that form onto the mind's screen in meditation is to transcend the discontinuities of ordinary life. One way to spiritual peace is still, as Plato said, to contemplate the "revolutions of the universe," or, with Meister Eckehart, to meditate on such a notion as "symmetry with lucidity." If Spinoza determined to "analyze the actions and appetites of men as if it were a question of lines, of planes and of solids," and Cézanne to "deal with nature by means of the cylinder, the sphere and the cone . . . ," so, as an Indian art historian writes, "images are to the Hindu worshipper what diagrams are to the geometrician."[28] Within such a geometry as the Cosmos of myth and imagination, not only all roads and lines of thought but also time past and time to come have their reunion, as many a writer has said.

As for myself, as I reflected on the image of the light-shot Cosmos, I fell under its spell. With awe, I read how its components— the pole of it, the zodiacal wheel, the sun, planets, and certain stars—gave birth to myths in coherent linkages, whole families of structures born and reborn the world around, for all people see the stars, and "the gods are really stars, there are no others."[29] Under the figurative turmoil of diverse systems of religious iconography, east and west, and running through diverse rituals associated with pilgrimage, I saw the world-enclosing, death-refusing geometry that holds their meaning and promise.

Then eventually as I traveled and wrote, there came an intuition of what such a form as "cosmos" might hold for me personally and what the quest for connection with the stars might convey me to in the end—thoughts that would prove as clarifying to my ongoing research as the axis around which the mythic Cosmos turns.

For to return to the old question about thought and its relationship to the objective world, I asked myself in what realm does the secular pilgrim seek orientation—in the inner world or the dimensional one bounded by the visible stars? and if in both, in alternating or simultaneous measure, then what are the subjective correlatives to the stars if not stabilizing, guiding figures remembered from an earlier time, retained in the mind though long passed out of visibility?

✦ ✦ ✦

We were greeted in Calcutta's Howra Station by a pulsing scream of engines and wheels, a continual blast from conch- and air-horns, a howl of loudspeakers, and, under it all, that increasing vibration, deep and continual, of the voices of India.

My friend led me down into a subterranean passageway that piped pedestrians under a choked highway. Ahead I saw a waterfall! Light was falling at a slant through overhead grills. Dust was being kicked up from underfoot. The waterfall was a staircase with a dozen risers. People in gray rags were climbing up it and down, thousands of them. The waterfall carried along a slow transport, bobbing and eddying, of bales and baskets and water pots, all being borne toward us or slowly finding their way up and out of sight.

What is it that, when known, makes us know everything in the world? . . . Light first, then water.

It was light that produced the illusion that human beings were water. *Worship light.* I had read that too, on the train, in the Upanishads.

WE entered the churn of Calcutta.

We visited Mother Teresa's Home for Dying Destitutes. It was a tiny Moslem-style building with domes over its four corners. "Dear Lord the Great Healer," said a sign over the door. And "I have loved you with an everlasting love."

Inside, novices in white saris edged in blue walked among the cots ranged in rows, two on a platform for "walkers," two at floor level for "non-walkers." A youth from West Germany bent blue eyes and a headful of blond hair to swabbing the rectum of a man with cancer. The invalid, ravaged and gray, lay on his stomach watching us with a stare unmoving as stone. "The Poor are the Body of Christ," said a sign on the wall. "Touch one of them and you touch His Body."

"Two died today," said a sister, showing us the Keeping Room. There they rested in glacial chill, wrapped in muslin, already stretched on bamboo litters.

In an alcove was the kitchen. Nuns stirred huge cauldrons of soup. The walls were marked with the Stations of the Cross. From over the door, Pope John Paul looked down in full color. A sign-board said "I am on my Way to Heaven."

OUTSIDE, we turned in the churn to the nearby cremation ground. It was a paved courtyard with a number of bathtub-sized brick-lined pits. There were also some unlined dirt pits and a brick plat-form on which stood a rosewood bed complete with bedding and in it, a dead man. His hands were folded on the blanket. Flowers were around his neck. His gray beard was neatly trimmed.

Suddenly a young women standing by the bed shrieked and fell to the ground. She was carried away weeping.

"It is the most pathetic thing for a Hindu," said my friend. "Other women will take off her bangle bracelets and break them. They will wipe the red auspicious mark off her forehead. I know. My own mother was left a widow at an early age, and it was as if she too had died."

WE turned toward a mirage at the V of a dusty intersection: white columns supporting a Grecian pediment. It was a Presbyterian church, hung inside with memorial tablets: Broughton, "lost in the Punjab" . . . Bowman, "lost in Burmah" . . . Ogilvie, "in Penang." Their wives were named as well, dead "in Rawalpindi" . . . "Sialkot" . . . "at sea."

An elderly Britisher with bulldog jowls came out, leaning on his cane. "Things have sadly changed," he said. "The people have all gone away."

WE turned on, to the Temple of Kalighat where I saw Kali-Durga in the pit of flames. Then we made our way back to our hotel through industrial suburbs, ironmongers' shops, scrap-metal piles, electricians' dens. Everything, tools, machines, people, was coated with black soot. Trucks ground by, blowing dust over rickshaws jouncing in the gutters. Pigs shuffled between the wheels. People were picking through garbage. It was twilight, shopping time. On wooden tables by the highway, lit by lanterns, were oranges, eggplants, lemons.

The sky was turning gray-blue. Rain was coming. There was lightning.

At the hotel, I stepped onto the balcony and looked down on what could have been a corner of Rome. I saw amber and gold scrolls holding up domes, Doric pediments, and balustrades.

Lower down I saw lesser domes, cracking walls. I saw the Victorian city under the Neoclassic one. I saw under those the ghost of an Islamic city. Under all that was the Hindu city. Down in pockets of darkness at the root of my building I saw little pit fires and smoke. It was suppertime for those who live in the dust.

That evening a Communist journalist came for a drink. I told him how I had seen many graffiti that day for the Party, but among them another that announced, "Only Brahman is real. This world is just a jiggery of words."

"Take away poverty," he said, "and you still do not remove chaos and violence. Caste is still there. Agrarian violence: peasants against landlords. Sexual violence: men against women. Of late, I hang my head in shame." He sighed. "China and the Soviet had a philosophical tradition. We on the other hand are trying to modernize a country while permitting democratic chaos."

I thought of Mohandas Gandhi's pilgrimage to the sea back in 1930 to break the British salt law in a democratic way. The poor through whose villages his path led strewed it with green leaves. Seventeen years later he walked again on pilgrimage for friendship between Hindus and Moslems, and people strewed his way with broken glass.

I asked the journalist what he foresaw for India. He took a swallow of Scotch and quoted Mao Tse-tung:

The situation is excellent. There is great disturbance under the sun.

✦ ✦ ✦

Disturbances under the sun, painful events that randomly afflict all people, impelled the sages to meditate on the bounded light-shot Cosmos, in which such events seemed irrelevant to the order of the eternal star-fields. Following that proposition, it was conceived that the Cosmos might be replicated in miniature on the earth to provide pilgrims with a foretaste of eternality. Various architectural structures conform to that principle: the Hindu fire-altar and temple, the Buddhist stupa, the Jewish ark and temple, the Christian church and cathedral are only the best-known of humanity's uncountable models of the Cosmogonic Egg on earth.[30]

The technique of replicating the Cosmos was to measure its parts accurately, then build the model on the same lines. The structural components must duplicate both space and time as they exist in the Cosmos. Cosmic space was visualized as a round enclosing a square: the sky above the earth. Cosmic time was visualized as a series of rounds: of a day, a year, a cycle of years. To replicate either space or time was simply a matter of counting. Are there numbers to be found associated with pilgrimage shrines and the seasons on which they are visited? Undoubtedly those formulae derive from antiquity, when the Cosmos was being searched by priests, sages, and architects for its "sacred measures." Most Westerners today, at least, consider numerology as fantastic as astrology or palmistry. But in the past, the pseudoscience of sacred numbers was taken seriously. The efficient working of shrines and rituals depended on it.

The sun, moon, earth, and other planets visible to the naked eye, that ride on the zodiacal wheel or the circumference of the Cosmos, are seven. Always and everywhere in religious rite and doctrine, that number would signify a natural whole.

Seven and then twelve, another whole: to the count of twelve, Jupiter completes its orbit and the year turns, the moon and women following. "The twelve-spoked wheel revolves around the heavens. . . . The wheel is One," says the Indian text, the Rg Veda.

Combine the numbers as one will, the meaning is there. 84 is 12 times 7. Hindus say that 84,000 Sadhus live in the Himalayas, and there are 840,000 postures in yoga.

Then there are roughly 360 days in the year. "There are 360 lesser spokes in the wheel," continues the text. The fire-altar used for worship by the Indo-Aryan migrants as they entered north India was built of 360 bricks. When he was ready to put together a new one in newly claimed land, a priest first laid down a ring of stones representing the great circle of the horizon. Inside, he laid bricks in a square homologous with the earth, brick by brick to the correct number, five layers deep to represent the five elements in space: sun and moon, rain, wind, and fire. Thus the fire-altar was homologous with the Cosmos. It represented the sky, the year, and the earth, with fire at its center, as its axis. This sacred fire that burned in the sky and again on the altar was not to be considered a natural flame. It was older by far than its embodiments as this flame or that. In the scripture, it is "universal Agni, whom age never touches . . . who wanders on forever, unresting in his fiery splendor."

The fire-altar clock, as it might be called, was figuratively wound and set each spring. As the equinoctial dawn approached, the priest stationed himself before it, standing in for the Father-creator of the Cosmos. As the stars directly above the rising sun began to pale, the priest lit the flame and began to burn a sacrificial animal, collecting the melting fat in a dipper, pouring the fat back to feed the flames. The rite continued till the sun reached the point in the sky where the leading star had stood when it disappeared. By this intricate procedure, the day-measuring sun was locked into place with the year-measuring and eternal stars.

According to some historians, the altar was constructed with reference also to the human lifespan, for each was kept in use for three generations: in other words, the time of possible transmission of the science to one man from his father and on to his son. Thus migration and settlement were held to a slow but steady pace, and the accumulated lore of the tribes preserved. In this sense, the fire-altar also embodied memory.

When the migrants settled into communities, the altar was walled in and roofed and so became the sanctum sanctorum of the free-standing temple. Huge elaborations of the ground plan were developed during the Hindu Middle Ages. Those buildings of the later style, with cavernous darks and densities, flickering lights, and earthy smells all enclosed in a "soaring, battle-scarred mass," still project the old meaning. The temple is the Cosmos with the fire-mountain, Kailas, as its axis.[31]

STRUCTURALLY powerful the aesthetic of the Hindu temple may be, but a Westerner trained to other aesthetic values may fail to find the monument itself pleasing to his eye. Standing before a specific temple, he may look in vain for qualities that to him suggest nobility, such as logic among the parts and harmony between them and the landscape. By contrast, the Indian shrine may seem to sprawl like a monstrous sea creature in the low reefs of its city setting.

A Hindu cosmogonic myth helps account for this contradiction between theory and appearance. The temple, in theory, is a relic of an oedipal drama played out in the sky before humanity was born, when the Father-creator awoke one dawn to the sight of his star-daughter glimmering in the clouds just out of his reach. In a spasm of lust, he leapt toward her but was stopped by an arrow from a hunter's bow. The Father was stunned. He ejaculated in the air. His seed fell to earth, "dark, hideous . . . wrapt in the darkness of his nature." What fell from the sky, writes Stella Kramrisch, was "some of the precious substance of the plenum, the Uncreate." It burst into flame. From that fire came our sun and also the divine energy that invests gods, priests, and temple builders—and demons.

The origin of the world is recounted in the myth, and also the origin of consciousness. For at some time in the past, without a doubt, humanity woke to the natural facts of generation and death and leapt hopelessly, ludicrously, after what is taboo: more life than the natural life span. All the works of man, the myth implies, are rooted in that primal wrong, corrupted by that primal disorder.

A later myth focuses on the temple itself. A chaos-demon, formless and nameless, leapt out of a thunderclap and began eating the world. The gods rushed toward him. On each of his legs sat a god, pinning him down. Belly down under the stones of every temple lies that demon still.

Laboring to contain such a charge of frustration and rage, how could an architect make a work with grace? At every step, the burden must weigh him down and make his going heavy. Every work of thought or art must be wrested from chaos, redeemed from entropy. "Every building activity means a renewed conquest of disintegration."[32]

Another myth gave the formula for success in this metaphysical struggle. Here Shiva led the way. Of unbounded chaos, Shiva made an enclosure of space: the term in Sanskrit is "vastu." Of the wild demon, Shiva made a coherent being, a man-in-space: the term in Sanskrit is "vastupurusha." Now when a temple is required, the architect draws on the ground a "vastupurusha mandala," a "man-in-space map." When the temple is built, though it be in wilderness, it itself will be oriented to the four directions and stand upright, shapely and firm like the First Man, Purusha.

When the mandala-blueprint is drawn, the temple already exists in theory. Only the hauling-forth of raw materials remains to be done, and the piling of it into a form already existing.

Under the spot where the sanctum will stand, a jarful of gems and grasses is buried. A stone slab is laid over the pot. Then bricks are laid down enclosing the sacred area: "Lay ye down 360 enclosing stones and world-filling bricks . . . ye will be laying down all my forms and will become immortal."

In years to come, in theory, the pot's cervix will dilate, the sprouting seed force the slab, and its expansive energy fill the sanctum. That energy, demonic in its raw state but generative when controlled, is what the Hindu pilgrim walks thousands of miles to receive.

DURING the Hindu Middle Ages, the temple plan acquired open courtyards, corridors, and side-shrines for attendant gods, often represented in over-life-size sculptural reliefs, fighting, dancing, or making love, actions also engaged in by humans in imitation of the immortals. The exterior walls of the temple—Purusha's flesh—were worked in cellular modules set at various slants to glitter and gloom, forming a "visibly breathing epidermis" that protects him from the rain of entropy outside. For Purusha is not yet immortal, though some element in his brain is on the way to becoming so.

The door to the finished structure would likely be at the east, not south or west, for those are the ways of ghosts. But in fact the temple needs no significant entry at all, for, like fire, mountain, and tree, it exists in the round, centered, from where its energy radiates up, down, and out to all sides. However, the door of the innermost sanctum is often flanked by carvings of the river-goddesses, Ganga and Yamuna, so that pilgrims entering may consider they are dipping their bodies into those streams.

Once the walls have been piled up, the temple's icon must be put in place. If the shrine is sacred to the beneficent god Vishnu, the image is friendly and can be carried in the door. But a Shiva-linga is explosive and has to be swung down on a hammock through a hole in the roof. The moment it is nudged into place, its juice flows and the temple is charged. If the icon should be damaged one day, it cannot be simply thrown out. It has to be rendered impotent. An uncastrated bull will be hired to haul it over the threshold into the open air. Perhaps then it might be consigned to a pilgrim on his way to the seashore, who would hire a boat, sail out, and drop it safely in the deep.

The sea bottom is the only place to dispose of a dead linga.

As the last step in the temple's construction, a little gold statue of a man should be thrust into the tower and bricked in. There he is to hang till the temple falls, primordial man, mixture of matter and light, trapped halfway between mortality and illusion.

Then at the four corners of the temple's sanctum stand guardians of space, each staring fixedly to the horizon, locking the structure in the Cosmos and the Cosmos itself in nothingness. Such bindings are required, for the whole complex, in theory, is revolving. Like the smoke from the old fire-altar, the tower over the sanctum marks its axis. Around it the sun wheels, the stars, moon, and planets turn. Under it lies the Father's sperm and the demon's bones and perhaps a bit of Sati's flesh, all turning around the axis.

Indeed, the forms of the Hindu temple are to be experienced shifting back and forth between reality and illusion, and within them, Purusha, the Golden Man, sports in the stones like the old Greek demigod Proteus in the waves. For example, when Purusha stands up in the sanctum, his spine is the temple's tower and his head is a little stone lotus bud at its terminal. Or if Purusha lies down, his mouth is the temple gate. Or he may turn end for end so his feet are the gates, and a flagpole down the way his phallus, a table set with food for demons his navel, and a platform for the temple's dancing girls his beating heart.

Or call the whole temple Purusha's brain and the walls its "rugged cortex," as Stella Kramrisch does. Or call it a leafless tree in April, with branches fraying at the ends into filaments that seek to draw life, more life, out of thin air.

In the great pilgrimage center of Bhubaneshwar, halfway down the coast of the Bay of Bengal, between the seventh and thirteenth centuries, some seven thousand shrines were built around a sacred lake. Some five hundred remain today, more or less in ruins but recapitulating the course of Hindu temple architecture. Among them the great Temple of the Lord of Three Worlds is said to be the finest in all India.

But I would never see him, that Lord, a nine-foot-high block of granite that daily endures twenty-two ministrations by priests who wash his teeth, assuage his hunger, enliven his days with musical treats. Nor would I see the Lord's procession by chariot to the nearby Ocean Drop Tank, filled by water from all the streams in India. For not being a Hindu, I was excluded from the precinct. As I stood by its fabled entrance, an aged toothless fellow in rags shrieked at me. "Will you enter?" he shouted. And when I said probably not, he lifted his fist and shook it in the air.

"No! You cannot go in! No one who is not born so can become a *Hindu!*"

I therefore sat myself under a banyan tree in the center of a dirt crossroads to wait while my friend paid his respects. I reflected that even Stella Kramrisch did not enter here. Now I, and a number of beggars, sat together outside, only I was fuming and they were not. I meditated on a souvenir-stall signboard across the ditch: USELESS WANI—ARTS AND CRAFTS.

Further south, sometimes, I had better luck. In the central plains where the red-gold Seshachalam mountains rise out of sun-baked flatlands, a great cluster of pilgrimage shrines exists, sacred to the Sun-god. In the most renowned of these, Tirumala, he is present in the shape of a large black stone. Sometime during the Middle Ages he was roofed and walled in. Along the way, he garnered four golden arms, a serpent girdle, and a wardrobe of jeweled collars and crowns. Some ten thousand people come to worship him daily, and four times as many on festival days. "I am a rationalist, but after observing this god, I return to him with folded hands," said the president of a regional Rotary Club as we lined up together, before sunrise, to greet that Lord.

We entered with the orderly throng through massive gates bristling with carved animals. The line took disorienting turns through pockets of dark, then light. We crossed bare stony courtyards, then entered corridors increasingly narrow. We shuffled forward, pushing and craning, standing on tiptoes, and a long sigh went up from the line ahead, passed over us, and was sent on back.

Then I was before the image in its radiance of lights, lights from oil lamps, hanging and in the hands of priests. What I was looking at was a seven-foot-high humanoid shape with silver rays on its brow like a Martian helmet, a form blackened by smoke and ancient drippings of butter and musk, draped in crusts of costume and gems. And the pilgrims were crying its popular name, "Oh, Govinda!" and reaching out to scoop some of its immortalizing energy into their hands.

In South India certain temples are so oriented that a shaft of sunlight pierces the womb-chamber at the spring equinox.[33] East of Bhubaneshwar stands the so-called Black Temple of Konarak, which is wholly shot through with fire each day when the sun comes up.

Originally, it had the shape of a twelve-wheeled chariot pulled by seven horses. It was built in the thirteenth century by a king who had stemmed the Moslem tide as it spilled south. To celebrate, he plundered all the surrounding shrines for stones for the Sun-god, who had trampled down Allah. Of it all, only a great pile of broken stones survives—a truncated shaft covered with fragments of superb carving, and the chariot wheels, each one nine feet tall.

To reach the site, we traveled through jungle toward the Bay of Bengal. We drove through shafts of light and shadow. We crossed the Happiness River, silver between dark mango groves. A bright blue bird dipped across the river and was gone. When the bus came to the shore, we ran into the waves and stood knee-deep until our trousers were heavy with salt water. It was dark before we made our way back a quarter-mile through the woods to the temple. We must wait, said my friend, for the cow of dawn, the red cow, to come.

We went to sit in the wattle hut of the temple watchman. The black cow of night was standing over the hut. Inside, the watchman's family was cooking on a clay stove. The grandfather stirred a cauldron of buffalo milk. He lowered his bamboo dipper, drew up the milk, and let it fall in long, thick strands. The mother was preparing beans. A son chopped something. A daughter kneaded something.

The family spoke little, but my friend spoke to me. They did not understand him when he did so, but they made room in the dark for me, and for his voice. My friend is a Westernized man with a doctoral degree, and he was saying to me, "The cow is everything. From her udders, you get milk. From her horns, combs. From her skin, leather. From her hooves, gelatin. From her dung, fire. And from her body, more cows.

"All these parts of herself she gives us. She is holy, our mother. Go-mata, Cow mother." The old man went on stirring the buffalo milk, drawing it up and letting it fall in long threads from his dipper.

I was thinking how in Benares I had been pained to see people living on the level of their animals. But in that hut dark as a cow's belly, what held my curiosity was not that these people lived among their animals, but that their animals seemed to live *in them,* alongside their other selves, each looking at the other with peaceful eyes, shuffling, each making room for the other.

By first-light the next morning, we were seated on an embankment facing the temple, waiting to see it by sunrise.

At 5:30 the sun was still low in the trees behind us. By 6:10 it topped the rise. Birds sang in rising cascades. The trees made shivering motions. The light cleared the trees. The first rays striking the temple set its ramparts into action.

On the top ledge, large figures of musicians stepped forward, holding cymbals, drums, and stringed instruments. We saw their arms move and we heard their cacophonous welcome to the Fire.

Step by step the sun mounted the sky and the edge of light notched down the temple's face. The musicians' flourish ended, and courses of animals began to move. Elephants and horses rode eastward and westward. The great wheels turned. Flames rose from the niches.

By 9:30 the sun was high. The upper registers began to burn. The stone filled with light. The surfaces simmered, and the sundance began. Snakes and dancers writhed. Amorous pairs moved into intricate embraces, sexual and acrobatic, voluptuous and stylized. They were the coupling sons and daughters of the sun, with power to protect the temple from thunder and lightning.

One of them, broken, seemed to press her body to her lover's, lifting her cheek to his lips. Tenderly he leaned what was left of his broken form to hers. Their jewels sparkled like fireworks. From a pocket of shadow in the ruins came the sobbing of pigeons thrashing their wings for leverage over one another, while among the pilgrims clambering over the stones passed thin brown urchins, their arms strung from wrist to elbow with coral necklaces to sell and their hands full of postcards, who softly inquired as one passed, "Sex photo, sir or madam?"

By ten o'clock, the sun stood to the south. There in full glare the god himself appeared, a life-size figure of green chlorite holding two long-stemmed lotuses. The planes of his eyes are bowed slightly so he seems to look off as if in a dream. His curved breast swells. His chest is full of green light. In all art there is no expression of calm amidst turmoil equal to his unless it is that of Shiva, Lord of the Dance, in his cosmic ring of fire, and in the iconography of myth they are "the same."

✦ ✦ ✦

The world's most dramatic pilgrimage events owe their drawing power to a single astronomical principle. The best way to approach it is, again, through myth.

"From the beginning," as the story teller says, sages and priests who watched the sky knew which constellation rose in the east just ahead of the sun on equinoctial and solstice mornings. By that visible lock between the sun and specific background stars, the architectural lock between earth and sky was made manifest and reinforced each season.

Back in the age when the sky-myths were first generated, some scholars now believe, the spring sun rose into the house we call Gemini for its twin stars, Castor and Pollux. Hindu myth calls them the Asvins. In Greek they were the Dioscuri.[34]

World myth gave them many titles, sometimes Sons of the Sun or the Sky, or Sons of Thunder. But as the ancient heralds of the spring sun, they were everywhere said to have power to grant new life to old men. A Hindu myth describes them: two youths in white hats flanking a bent elder, dipping with him into a pond, then surfacing, all of them in golden ear-hoops, the old man restored to beauty.

Such was the triangular geometry that rose in the eastern sky in the springs of prehistory: two stars, raising the sun. World myth still reverberates to that imagined celestial configuration that signified—or would when it had "fallen"—a lost Golden Age.

For over an immense span of time, with a sense of disquiet one can only imagine, those original sky-watchers would have observed that the lock between the equinox and Gemini, which had been thought eternal, was coming undone. On a time scale of awesome slowness and a spatial measure of magnificent immensity, the outer shell of the Cosmos that had been thought eternally attached to the earth was shifting.[35]

There is no other way to appreciate the power of the observation than to put one's modern eye to the primitive sighting device. Such gradual motion could not have been detected save by sighting instruments used to keep track of the more obvious motions of sun, moon, and planets.[36] The phenomenon would have been noted over very long periods of concerted attention, becoming more obvious as the stars behind the place of sunrise continued to drift on. Then the looked-for constellation gradually would have seemed to "fall" or perhaps "drown" in the abyssal sea under the horizon's edge.

The circumstance went on unfolding. In massive time slippages known now to measure some two thousand years each, constellation after constellation came to stand in the place where the spring sun rose. Thus Gemini, the place of sunrise around 6000 BCE, gave way to Orion around 4000 BCE, then to Taurus and the Pleiades in the neighborhood of 2000 BCE. And still the celestial dome moved on, toward Aries, then Pisces around the year One. And still it moves, grinding toward Aquarius.

The phenomenon, known as the precession of the equinoxes, is the result of an added wobble in the globe's tilt, which sends its axis around the axis of the ecliptic in some 26,000 years. As a result, the actual north pole of the earth has been visibly marked through the millennia by a changing series of "North Stars." Meanwhile, the dominating axis of the whole solar system, that of the sun, is not marked by a star visible from earth and so may be said to exist, so far as we are concerned, only in theory.

To this ill-understood circumstance, the mythic mind responded by generating, among other structures, a cyclical narrative beginning with the Golden Age of the Sun-twins, proceeding through successive cosmic Ages, each coming into being, thriving, then decaying.[37] When a cosmic Age reaches its end, the fire-pillars that support the sky threaten to collapse. The axis of the world wobbles in its socket and the Cosmos itself must fall and drown, or sicken and die, or, as the Hindu conceives it, go up in universal flames. Secular history has experienced the myth in terms of collective foreboding as millennial turns approach, and fundamentalist rhetoric from many religious quarters heralds such a turning point these days.[38]

If they are so old, the springs of apocalyptic thinking lie very deep, and their power to move human groups to action is understandable.

All around the world, therefore, even in these days of nuclear weapons, pilgrims gather to enact events whose function is to stabilize the Cosmos and save it from destruction. Astrologers time the gatherings that must take place if the Cosmos is to survive. For example, in December the sun lies in the pit of the south and needs an infusion of energy to return. So bonfires are lit all over India, and indeed ancient fire-ceremonies are performed, overtly or in disguise, around the whole wintry world. The six months that ensue are auspicious, leading to spring when, in India, equinox is celebrated in a madcap event called Holi, when pilgrims fling powder dyes, flowers, and holy water at one another. But under the apparent chaos of Holi, in each handful of powder a Hindu throws into the face of a passerby, staining him magenta, scarlet, or yellow, he contributes his particle of energy to the saving of the world by the equinoctial sun.

When these and other ceremonies are performed correctly—holy water is dipped up and poured back, a sacred stone is circumambulated, star-imitating rites and dances are performed—then the Three Worlds of water, earth, and sky are realigned and joined. Then the great axis of the Cosmos—around which these Worlds with their load of life (fish, foliage, animals, and birds) are conceived to turn—is lifted up, re-set, crowned, and bolted at the top by the polar star, "as it was in the beginning," and so the communal prayer goes up in many languages, "as it shall be, world without end."

ON the Field of Kurukshetra north of Delhi in India where the Sun-god lectured Arjuna on the inevitability of war, such a Cosmos-saving pilgrimage takes place during a solar eclipse.

As the eclipse approaches, all the rivers of India are said to turn in their beds and flow uphill into the holding tank at Kurukshetra. Then pilgrims by the thousands follow to make thunder on their kettledrums and conch- and cow-horns and to sink their bodies into the sacred waters, to turn the rivers back into their courses, the sun onto its way, and the faltering worlds to order again.

But the pilgrimage event of supreme importance in India is the Kumbha-mela. Its function is to restore sun and planets, rivers and people to their places at the end of an astronomical cycle. The festival itself cycles slowly through time—twelve years—and places—four cities.

Again myth sets the scene. "Long ago" the Cosmos sickened and began to die. The Sun-god woke in his bed in the sea and came to help. On the sea floor, he explained, was a pot or "kumbha" full of the fluid of immortality. The trick was to bring it to the surface.

Now, many good things can be drawn from their matrix by a churn, a grinding mill, or twirling-stick. Butter is extracted from milk that way, and flour, and fire from tinder. During the centuries of migration and settlement, horses churned empire out of the wilderness by the beat of their hoofs. So the male churns new life out of a woman. And all these essences—butter, fire, empire, and life—

bear primary correspondence to sunlight, and sunlight to immortality. "Immortality is gold," say the sages.[39]

Then to deliver the jar of immortality out of the sea there must be a churn or mill of the ancient rope-pulled type. Mount Kailas would be its axis. A sea serpent would be its cord. Demons would pull one way, gods the other. And so they did till the pot was drawn up.[40]

With that event, the Cosmos was saved. But now the demons claimed the prize for themselves. A tug-of-war began and went on for twelve days. At the end of that cycle, four drops of juice fell to earth. The demons faded away, and peace returned to the Three Worlds.

The four stations of the Kumbha-mela are, as one might expect, the places where the immortality-bearing drops landed. Two of them, the cities of Prayag and Hardwar, receive the event in turn three or four years apart after the winter solstice; two others, Ujjain and Nasik, receive it during the period of solar descent. But the event enacted in Prayag is the culminating cosmogonic ritual of Hinduism today.

That city, otherwise called Allahabad since the time of its Moslem overlords, lies at the confluence of the Ganges and Yamuna Rivers. The event there coincides with the return of Jupiter to the House of Aquarius, in Sanskrit the House of the Water-pot, after its twelve-year cycle of the heavens. The event also harks back to millennia past, when that conjunction occurred at the winter solstice, and pilgrims flocked to Prayag to dip pots of seed into the "heavenly rivers" to ready them for planting.[41]

The ritual calls for the pilgrims to dip their bodies into the conjoined streams at the moment of astrological conjunction. Correctly timed, the rite ensures the preservation of the Cosmos and life in it, and renders it immortal.

Indeed, for a pilgrim to die at a Prayag Kumbha-mela is to attain the stars without delay. Scriptures spelled out the best means of dying there—drowning, scorching while hanging head down over coals, being sliced into pieces to feed the birds. A Chinese pilgrim who attended the festival back in the seventh century wrote of ascetics clutching log posts in the river and staring at the sun till they were blinded, then jumping. Others fell headlong from banyan trees. Philosophers and kings, some with trains of wives, were drowned. There was death by combat too, for cult-proud Sadhus regularly slaughtered one another until the British put a stop to it. But with Indian independence, the gatherings began again. At the first one thereafter, in 1954, hermit-Sadhus came out of their Himalayan caves and far-off swamp huts and gathered at the site. At the right moment, they marched toward the water, militants among them armed with iron spears, tridents, and tongs, and encountered a traffic jam of other pilgrims, elephants, jeeps, and tourists. Hundreds were crushed, speared, and drowned, but there was a certain opinion voiced, even by officials, that those who died had got what they came for. And, to be sure, the world went on.

That year, over three million people bathed at Prayag. In 1966, five million entered the river on a single day. In 1977, ten and a half million gathered there.

But the strangest enactment of the Churning of the Ocean takes place perpetually in the now ruined Cambodian city of Angkor Wat, amid stone carvings of demons and gods pulling away on ropes, churning peace into the world, though the god-kings who ruled there have long gone and even the Khmer Rouge, who a few years ago tried to wreck what archaeologists had earlier restored, have like demons filtered back into the forests from which they came.

If some pilgrims travel in flocks, others travel alone in solitary consecration to the task of upholding the cosmic order. For example, that Holy Man whom I saw stamping his feet by the temple in Benares was on such a mission. He was a member of a sect of moon and sun worshipers, who walk a perpetual ring through four sacred cities, pacing their movements to the lunar and solar passages.[42]

The sun-moon-man's year begins in the ancient city of Ayodhya, northwest of Benares, when the spring full moon announces the birthday of the god Ram-Chandra, or Sun/Fire-Moon. Thereafter, each full moon in a new part of the sky finds the traveler at a new point on his road. From the winter solstice on, he camps nightly before a little fire-mandala of flaming cow dung. In the full moon of the summer solstice, he bathes one last time before the great rains. For during Ganga's menstrual period, Ram-Chandra hides his face in shame, and so do his followers till the autumn full moon marks the Goddess's return to purity and Ram-Chandra's emergence from his cave.

In their solitary flight between stations and the periodicity of their appearances, these pilgrims, I suggest, reveal the hidden meaning of pilgrimage itself. The sun-moon-men travel in imitation of their patron-gods, for to imitate the motion of the sun, moon, planets, or stars is to share in their eternality.

Perhaps for the ancients the meaning was not concealed, nor is it perhaps an alien concept for us, only buried in language. The Greeks called the planets "wanderers," and we, drawing on the Latin "perigrinus," call our wanderers pilgrims. For the logic is there: heavenly bodies and pilgrims on earth are shadows of one another, alike in orbital motion, cycling, ascending and descending through the slowly turning, everywhere interjoined cosmic system, particles in a tremendous work of the imagination that is indeed a "strange illusion."

And how many illogical-sounding but oft-repeated descriptions of pilgrimage unfold from this explanation! "The way forward is the way back" is a popular paradox impossible in a world of forward-flowing time and perspectival space. But it applies perfectly to the pilgrimage road as an orbit. Steadily on that road, the traveler moves toward its "perihelion" or turning-around-the-sun point. That turning-around point may be, in practice, a stone or temple, or riverbank or mountain. There he turns in the "sun-wise" direction around it, keeping his right shoulder to the source of holy fire. And when his pilgrimage is done, if he is only an occasional wanderer, he returns to the darkness of secular life, only to begin there to prepare for the return journey toward the light that may take place only after his death.

"I learned," writes an Indian scholar-monk, *how to move about within the precincts of the monastery: always in the direction in which the planets move around the sun*"[43] (my italics).

IN the context of myth, then, pilgrimage takes place on the great wheel of the ecliptic, around the sun, alongside the moon and planets, against the background of the precessing stars.

It leads, as poets before and after Dante have described, through a grid of hoops and planes and their bejeweled intersections.

The authentic language of pilgrimage, stripped of anthropomorphisms and slippery nonwords—the linguistic sludge of popular tracts of *all* the religions—involves instead curves, crossings, and triangulations, and the golden arches drawn by the sun year around: "Such harmony in heaven . . . and so many planets" indeed!

To move through these catwalks and uprights that open in the mind like a golden Piranesi is to go without fear of the emptiness that lies beyond. To the pilgrim, the universe is not infinite, alien, corrupted by human suffering. And understandably, he appears single-minded, even blind to what he stubs his toe against, sights that might offend his eye or conscience, because his head is full of the light that shines around and through him.

And there is also this: since he carries the image in his brain cells, the pilgrim can be said to turn around the axis of his own thought. He is, in a sense that logic cannot explain, traveling around his own center. Therefore the pilgrim is to be considered, as he often proclaims, "always in Benares," or as well, "forever in Eretz Israel."

"Sadhu, where is the Temple?" you may ask.

"I am the Temple," comes the reply.

THE sun-moon-man carries with him a small object of vast significance. It is black and round. For one man it may be a stone, for another, his iron cook pot. But it is always with him, and when he ends his day's march, he sets it on the ground before him. It is the black core of his Cosmos of Illusions, but it is comparable, too, to the jar that Western poet Wallace Stevens set on a Tennessee hilltop, to watch it change the surrounding wilderness to form.[44]

✦ ✦ ✦

When the elements of a project have been assembled and a core insight—what one book calls the "controlling destination" of a pilgrimage—is required to give them focus, it is sought in the mind as the North Star is sought in the sky by travelers.[45] But that quest for an orienting insight is better not pursued in the head alone, *pace* the Hindu and the Western mystic. For many a self-absorbed pilgrim has the illusion *a* North Star stands over his own head, and what has been gained for human society by so many conflicting illusions is continual collision among the planets.

Instead, to find the actual polar star and so place oneself under the guidance of natural reality, one has to go outdoors on a clear night and watch the great wheel coming up out of the east then driving down toward the west. In all that tilted turning spectacle, there is only one steady point toward which all humanity looks as if with a single eye.

All people are after the same thing, that star affirms: more life, always rising out of the past.

And on the heels of that affirmation, a directive: Seek the forms of that life not in illusions but in nature, as it opens itself slowly to the questing mind.

From existential need and astronomical understanding, then, arose the myths of Polestar, who focuses the mind in its quest for a form of enlarged life. Single, solitary, unmoving in its station, it appears in some myths as a creature with one eye and a peg leg. When highest divinity was attributed to the star, it was called Creator of the Cosmos, promulgator of its fundamental Laws, Judge of the living, not one of whom can evade its beams. Its agent on earth is the mountain goat, perched on a peak, dead-center of the ranges that surround him.[46]

In human psychology, Polestar is the beloved teacher and guide, ascended into death, sought and discovered in another form. He is *father, risen into myth.*

From early times, certain pilgrims of mystical bent have sought immortality by imitating the imagined postures and states of mind of that transcendent and personified star.

We learn of this strange intent from artifacts in the ruins of

Mohenjo-Daro, the Indus River valley city that antedated the Indo-Aryan migrations and gave up the ghost to the newcomers.[47] Among these artifacts are stone seals carved with miniature pictures of star / animal / human creatures. One of these is called a "horned deity," another the "high one," and the "black buffalo." But among these images, one strikes the mind with the power of a living icon. It is a male seated with crossed legs and arms outstretched and resting on the knees. The outline is an equilateral triangle rising on the axis of the figure's spine. The face is a dehumanized horned mask topped with a star. To this figure, animals come to bow. Some scholars refer to it as Lord of the Animals.

The figure is ithyphallic, that is to say in a state of static sexual erection. It is a solitary icon of power. There is no suggestion of consummation to follow; the sexual drive is inhibited for religious reasons.

"Inhibition is a mark of evolutionary advance," suggests an anthropologist.[48] Then that little figure comes down the millennia asking a momentous question. Was it just there in Mohenjo-Daro, in some unknowable discourse among sages, that a portentous turn in cultural evolution took place? It was the invention of what must have seemed an utterly simple strategy of defeating death.

In the world of seasons and sexuality, grain ripens and falls, animals rut, and humans die, but for Polestar who sits atop the axis, since there is no time-that-moves, there is no end of time either. The sexually inhibited image of the Lord of the Animals says that, though time may wheel in its cycles, he stands on, Polestar's stand-in. Indian scripture would spell out the conditions:

> The stars and planets shall turn around you. You, however, shall be immobile as the axle around which the oxen turn. People will come and go. You . . . motionless, will be forever visible. . . .[49]

In Asia, the cross-legged, straight-backed male in meditation would forever signify rejection of natural sexual life in exchange for lordship over death. The image would reappear some 2,500 years later as the signature of the Buddha and later be the sign also of the Hindu Yogi, who "attempts to realize absolute concentration in order to attain entasis."[50] Some scholars suggest the notion was carried by Buddhist missionaries to inspire celibacy-preaching Jewish sects like the Essenes and, later still, the Christian Desert Fathers. So it may not be outlandish to propose that on the model of the old Lord of the Animals, Christian chastity, virginity, and the full range of mortifications of the flesh would become Western technics also of ascent to the sky.

Once conceived, the image would never lose its power—nor the gift its price. To join Polestar in his remote eminence is to renounce natural life.

On the peak of Mount Kailas, says myth, the Father lies down on his back looking up. Polestar beams down over his head, and their locked eyes lock earth and sky together. A male Hindu of ascetic temperament may model himself on Father and Polestar, one and both. "We have reached the heavens, reached the gods. We have become immortals . . . ," says scripture, to which the Holy Man says, I too.[51]

He stands on one leg under a tree. He looks up through its branches as the sun moves toward the meridian. When it reaches that point, it stands atop the fire-axis that, in the Cosmos of myth, is crowned by the sun and, beyond it in theory, Polestar.[52] Then the Holy Man is "the same as" the axis. And the pilgrim squatting in the dust before him, gazing at him in an open-eyed trance, is also "the same"—one who is dead in life, alive only in death, immobilized in his imagination as the star of the North.[53]

POLESTAR then—the progenitor gone and rediscovered—is the summoning principle in the sky and the mind. But His loneliness at the top of the sky is absolute. He neither rises nor sets and therefore does not approach the earthly horizon. Even in the protean richness of Hindu myth, there is no attaining His lap directly. He never comes nearer earth than is His eternal station, save in the Occidental myth that requires perpetual vigil on His arrival here.

Access to Polestar can be gained, however, through intermediary structures in myth and art. Primary among these are gods, angels, saints, and spirits who have intercourse with humans and so are partly "of the sky," partly "of the earth." Then there are tangible works of art and architecture that also connect what is otherwise held apart.

Writers have employed various terms for such a device. Kramrisch calls the Hindu temple "the hinge by which a changeable panorama is linked with the structure of the universe."[54] Lévi-Strauss talks about a "mediator . . . halfway between two polar terms." Eliade takes up the Latin *coincidentia oppositorum*.

I like the term "hinge structure" for its clarity and visual impact. The hinge is an instrument doubled, that joins. In a pilgrimage system, the hinge structure may be an actual object or monument, an expanded geographical structure, or an intangible essence or symbol that joins sky and earth. Rivers, flowing between highlands and lands' ends, function as vast hinge structures, as do paths leading to highways leading to the gates, ramps, corridors, and ever-nearer approaches to shrines. If natural objects like mountains, stones, and trees, and man-made ones like temples and cathedrals serve that end, so do intangibles like prayers and mantras that rise from a worshiper's lips to heaven, and the mantic voices of oracles.[55]

Myth itself, as Lévi-Strauss says, serves the same end, and so does religious rite.

A particularly revealing class of hinges includes the paired guardian-priests of the Shiva-linga—one of whom is destined to heaven, the other to rebirth on earth—and the Hindu wedded pair. Also in this class are pairs of mythic siblings, often twins, who have different fathers or mothers, one parented by the sky, the other by the earth; or one of whom addresses the sky, the other, earth; or one of whom dies, the other lives. Many of these are to be met in the West—Moses and Aaron, Elijah and Elisha, Pollux and Castor, Romulus and Remus, and James and John, called Sons of Thunder. In this class too belong those who in mid-myth change their name, like Abram / Abraham and Saul / Paul.

Then there is a flood of inventions, hybrid forms of imploded contradiction, like the animal-headed gods of India, Assyria, and Egypt, and also verbal tropes like "a sword whirling and flashing with no hand to hold it." And finally there are creatures that tremble in the gap between clear-cut identity and transformative transcendence, like Shiva, Dionysius, and Christ.

The hinge structure, actual or metaphoric, forces opposites into illogical fusion. It joins the unjoinable: the mortal to immortal life. Paradox itself, it represents the resolution of paradox. Works of the imagination considered in this way, swollen by their cosmic instrumentality, fuse fundamental contradictions of thought and image. They force one into the teeth of their wheels.

In their power goes the Hindu pilgrim, laboring south from the Mouth of the Cow to spill his bottle of Ganges water into the sea. So of him it is both false and true to say his sandals are full of glory and his head of clouds.

✦ ✦ ✦

Rameswaram is the southernmost All-India shrine to Lord Shiva, the goal to which pilgrims bring their little flasks of water.

The temple there may be the biggest in India. So cavernous are its chambers that peasant women winnow grain in them, tossing it in golden clouds from huge wicker baskets. Nearby, I saw a sacred elephant dutifully swing his head to tap the pates of pilgrims, still wet from their ocean dips, shorn of their hair in honor of Lord Shiva.

There came then the elephant keeper with a pike to prod the animal off to some interior stall. I saw the beast's sad rear end drooping, shamed and wrinkled, knock-kneed for all its hugeness. And soon there broke out a noise of horns and rattles from deep inside the walls, setting the whole temple into raucous vibration to call the pilgrims to worship the linga.

And suddenly it seemed that everything I had sought to understand in India was there, in that moment of the elephant's going and the music's explosion: the huge body of immemorial custom that Hinduism is, derived from nature but now temple-bound. And wasn't the elephant tired of tapping heads, mouthing sweetmeats, tired of playing god to these wet creatures, tired at last of the affront of the pike? I watched him lumber off down the gloomy corridor, alongside the threshers and their clouds of grain-dust, ready to go, even longing to go, yawing like an old ship going to harbor.

But the priests had come to summon the pilgrims to their worship with trumpet blasts and drumming, shrill, martial, pompous, and exhorting.

I wound up my Indian trip in Cape Comorin at the southernmost tip of the subcontinent. If you stand on the rocks there, you can watch the sun rise out of the Bay of Bengal on your left, swing overhead, and set at your right in the Arabian Sea. Just offshore is a rock pool where pilgrims wash off the dust of the road. For some of them, it has been a journey of over two thousand miles, on feet with soles tough as animal-hide.

There is a red and white striped temple there, with a pinched entry into one of those firelit, oil-drenched, windowless sanctums. A black stone there represents Shiva's bride. She turns her back on her husband and faces south toward oceans she cannot see.

Her epithet here is Virgin, a feature probably borrowed from Christianity, for female chastity is not an honored condition in Hinduism. That is to say, it serves no immortalizing end. For the woman, says scripture, is sunk in her fleshly nature and will not find liberation from her attachments even in death. On the other hand, there is in the town a community faithful to Mary, who have erected a church with stained-glass windows and a statue of the Star of the Sea outdoors on the rocks, keeping an eye on the curved black sails of fishing boats tacking back and forth like cutlasses being drawn through the waves.

From there at night one sees the star Canopus hanging in the south. It is Polestar's deep and nether double, marking, in myth and old navigational tradition, the southern pole. It lies in the constellation Argo, Argha in Sanskrit, which so plainly sails the heavens that ancient starwatchers called it a ship. Then Canopus, which seems steady as Polaris, is that ship's anchor or rudder, the "yoke star of the sea."[56]

Legendary pilgrims set their courses toward it. Gilgamesh would have sailed south in its rays. Abraham might have sought it in the Sinai, where it is also known to Orthodox Christian pilgrims as the star of Saint Catherine. Ulysses, in Tennyson's poem, may have set his course by Canopus when he sailed through the Pillars of Hercules, which open on the 36th parallel where it first comes into view, hoping "to see the great Achilles, whom we knew."[57]

The two polar lights, north and south, yoke the mind into a vast inhuman geometry.[58] They call the cosmic wanderer and drown him in "immortal longings."[59] In Indian myth, the star Canopus was a traveler who came down from the Himalayas going always south till he reached the sea, where he dived in and was never seen again. A "Canopus-journey" is one from which you never come home.

Halfway between the poles, however, like Purusha in his tower, hangs the great star Sirius, in the constellation we call the Great Dog. It is the brightest star in the skies, marked by a dazzling scintillation from green to steel-blue but most dramatically, till it paled down during our Middle Ages, an extraordinary red. Babylonian texts called it "like copper." "Red or coppery," even like rubies held to light, was the way Ptolemy included it in his lists.[60]

Its worship in Egypt dated from at least the fourth millennium BCE when it rose ahead of the sun around the summer solstice and so seemed to instigate the flooding of the Nile. So it shone beneficently on ships at sea in the summer, as it did over the Fertile Crescent and northern India. And around the first millennium BCE, Sirius had another time of glory in autumn, when through the Middle and Near East, the New Year was observed. In the month called Tishri in Hebrew, the star called Tishya in Sanskrit rose around midnight and gloriously sailed the skies until dawn. For Homer, it was the very Star of Autumn, when rain so vital to harvest either came, or did not.

Therefore it is necessary to know that, where it rose over dry regions in dry seasons, Sirius was also regarded as a star of erratic powers and seasonal ill omen. When it withheld the rain, it was the sign-star of death. In May, when the sun approached the star in its rising, the Romans sacrificed to it, three times, a red-haired dog. And in the West, the dead-hot weeks between mid-July and mid-August are still called the "dog days."

However, of many traditions attached to Sirius, the following may seem most peculiar, particularly considering its apparent reflection in Western myth and folklore. Because of interventions made in the Roman Julian calendar to correct its inaccuracy, that star, sighted roughly along the latitude of the Mediterranean Sea, continued in the Early Christian era to be perceived rising directly ahead of the sun on the day denoted as July 20th, as it already had for over two thousand years—in other words, to be exempt from the precessional drift.[61]

Because of this seemingly unnatural stability manifested on both sides of the year 1 ("Admirabiliter contigit . . .!" was the statement of a Jesuit astronomer in the eighteenth century), as well as because of its brightness and position at the waistband of the sky, Sirius was sometimes considered a second center in the Cosmos, bound in a family relationship to Polestar, his superior in brilliance but still his subordinate in position, like a gifted son or daughter. A tenth-century Persian astronomer explained that "Only the Almighty can say: it is He Who is the Lord of Sirius." And a geography book my ancestors brought from Skye taught that the Creator himself "appointed Sirius and encompassed it with worlds."

For such reasons, Sirius was sometimes called no star at all but rather an "eighth planet," ruler of an eighth sphere of the Cosmos beyond the seven nature presents the eye. Therefore, the number "eight" would reverberate through world myth to denote events outside the natural order. Brahmin boys receive their sacred thread and learn the hymn to the sun at age eight. The Hindu god Krishna was an eighth-born child, and Christ was descended from the eighth-born David. Buddhist monasteries accept acolytes at eight. Circumcision of Jews takes place on the eighth day of life.[62] And the Christian scholastic John Scotus Erigena would confide that when he reflected on the number eight, all the supernatural teachings—Easter, Resurrection, Pentecost, and Immortality—"vibrated" in his mind.[63]

In Hindu, Jewish, and Christian myth, Sirius would generate a single but elastic structure reflecting its radiant, paradoxical, and inspirational nature and its role as a special mediating agent between Polestar and events on earth.

✦

THE greatest mediating figure in Hinduism, according to some scholars, was inspired by that star, Tishya. For on that linguistic base, it has been argued, the concept of Shiva originated, unfolding through the centuries, enlarging in scope and glory as his myths evolved, like a bloom rising out of a bulb.[64]

As humanity generated forms of thought, art, and society, the attributes of Shiva "unfolded in the Cosmos." As the works of humankind multiplied, so Shiva's forms projected by poets and artists expanded in a "crescendo of form." His transformations could never be contained in the minds that bred them. For Shiva, a creature of purest thought, "flared at the limit of the mind's grasp . . . beyond which no mind could reach." His myths both mirror and define the course of human evolution.

In the conceptual space between Polestar and the human traveler, then, lives Shiva.

Then Shiva was the light I saw flying off the barbers' mirrors in Benares to scatter, ever seeking, across the surfaces and undersides of the material world.[65]

Shiva was the shadow I saw pressed to the body of Mother Earth on maps, as if in frantic desire not to be torn from her.

In his transformations, Shiva ranges the Cosmos and beyond until, according to Hindu philosophy, both go out of being in the same shudder. And even then, this never-satisfied creature leaps on to suggest, he has another, still undefined but longed-for mode of survival as "Shiva-Mahakala," Great Eternity, or "Shiva-Mahadeva," Great Being: some quality contained in and passed forward through the chain of life that will outlast whatever an individual or a society might make of his, her, or its time on earth.

For me, Shiva's name is: the traveler's imagination.[66]

I let it lead me now.

PART TWO

POLESTAR GONE

◆

These are not natural events;
They strengthen from strange to stranger . . .
Shakespeare:
THE TEMPEST

◆

TO THE SOUTH : INDONESIA

◆ ◆ ◆

Driving through the dry-baked South one of my last nights in India, I stopped in an inn in a blacked-out town, bolted the door of my room, peeled an orange, drank a toast to myself from my canteen of water because it was my birthday, and lay down exhausted. Then there came from outside a sound, some sort of animal cry between a cat and an owl, full of rage and lament. I heard it near, then far off, moving fast as a witch on the wing.

Later I'd learn it was the wild peacock. But that night it was an unknown call that could have come from my own mouth. It opened tunnels into a place in my memory that seemed the deepest place, indescribable in words save as a place of anxiety and woe.

Like many a Westerner in India for the first time, I was experiencing an emotional overload, a rising of the body temperature, a frazzling of the nerves by so much dirt and din. In the West, even in our big cities, we're used to a plainer visual field. Here, when you closed your eyes you still saw shapes writhing and mandalas showering. *Color is the suffering of light,* is a poet-philosopher's reflection; to no place on earth can it seem more applicable.[1]

That night, I relived my first days in India, when my feeling had been one of desolation unlike anything I could recall. Men in the streets seemed to be walking in dreams, their faces irrationally calm in the midst of chaos. Staring or with eyes unfocused, their faces smeared with dyes, their bodies streaked with ashes, they drifted through my mind on bone-thin legs. Already, before death, their flesh looked charred, as if they had passed through fire.

And what dreams were the women walking through, in their acres of diaphanous sky-blue or peacock-green silks trailed through soot and dung? "The philosophies did not make our life what it is; it was the life that made the philosophies," wrote the Indian Nirad Chaudhuri in *The Continent of Circe*. It was the "vampire of geography," that "sucks out all creative energy and leaves its victims listless shadows."[2]

On that day of my birthday, a crippled man with thrust-out chest and withered legs laid straight across my path had furiously howled, "I am in bad condition! I have no legs! People should give me money!" Nearby a boy lay sleeping face down in the road with his arms outstretched, both hands chopped off at the wrists. A tiny girl rushed out between the wheels of wagons and rickshaws to scrape hot buffalo dung into a basket with her hands. Between these fellow-beings and their plots of begging ground, the pilgrims wound their self-absorbed ways, oblivious indeed as planets.

In my depression that night, I saw again the temples with their black and phallic stones, the animal gods decked with rotting flowers, crusted with oils of past devotions. I remembered a famous Hindu sage's words to describe women: "the unremitting stream of the world of illusions. They are the black-faced ogresses, incarnate. Their flesh is a witch's cauldron. . . . Woman is the name of this cauldron; woman is the name of the prison of death . . ."[3] As a certain result of such teachings, there are carvings of females to be seen even in such revered places as Ajanta, gouged at with iron tools and burned with torches, while by many a road is a stone carving of Sati, lying on her back as on a pyre, drenched in blood-red powder, providing license for dissatisfied males to commit the fairly common crime of murder-by-fire of their wives.[4]

AT last that night, cool air began to seep into my room. I turned and lay across the bed slantwise, so my head was in the corner where two walls met. And strange it was then—and I later returned to the memory as if it held a promise I had not yet understood— what came to me from beyond the walls, from what I imagined to be a courtyard somewhere in that intolerable town, was a faint, faraway, voluptuous singing.

It was a young man's voice, thin and fervent, singing some midnight raga, but so faint and walled-off that I wondered whether it too, like the strange creature's cry, was not coming from an unknown corner in my own head.

The sound stirred feelings I'd experienced before in Hindu India. By now I called them the *peace of Kali*. It was evoked by conversations in which, gently, persistently, my instructors spoke to me of "souls" and "bliss" and "release." It was evoked by the milky-thick environment, of songs, bells, chimes, prayers, bleats of animals; of clashing colors mingling in shadows; of brushings and pressings of animal and human bodies; of briny, acrid, spicy fragrances; by the incomparable images in stone, bronze, cloth, paint, of the gods. It was a rapture of the Hindu deeps that drowned my anxiety and fear.

Freud calls these two conditions the universal source of religious feeling: narcissistic despair and its solace. The Hindu is, by childhood experience, predisposed to these states of mind, and a Westerner adrift in that land, in circumstances beyond control or understanding, may be overwhelmed by the same feelings, which projected outward give rise to the World of Illusions.[5]

It was exactly to correct this set of mind that the teachings called Buddhist came into being. The Buddha aimed to dispel illusions by distancing the student from both despair and the hope of solace. Alone among the major religions, Buddhism teaches, by exercises and symbolic models including imitative pilgrimage, acceptance of the utter extinction of being at life's end.

PROBABLY there were many teachers in India who challenged Hindu philosophy on psychological and social grounds as early as the first millennium before our time, but tradition merged them into one or two timeless Teachers. Of what he or they may actually have said nothing is known. No texts survive earlier than some 150 years after the Buddha's death. But in the first writings thereafter, a simple pilgrimage exercise is recommended. The aim is to break through the fog of narcissism by orienting the novice in the real world, in it but distinct from it. The larger aim is to cultivate a mind able to deal with existential issues without recourse to ghosts, gods, or wish-fulfilling illusions.

The exercise was a trek around the four "pillars" or sites of the events of the Teacher's life.[6] Once the four-cornered path had been paced, it would of course reveal its center: the awakened mind in the midst of its known environment. For Buddhism is simply, however overlaid it would become in time with fanciful details, the cult of location and self-awareness at the center.[7]

The first of the four pilgrimage shrines of Buddhism lies south of the Himalayan foothills in a place called Lumbini. Here Queen Maya Devi, according to the myth, reached up to touch a tree and her infant sprang from her side. At once, the locative details begin: Four gods caught the child in a net. Four kings lifted him out and laid him on a deerskin on the ground, with its legs stretched to the four quarters.

In time, the famous events of his young life unfolded. The young prince witnessed the four trials of human existence: crippling deformity, self-inflicted pain, old age, and death. Reflecting on these, he went to walk in the forest.

Awakening comes for each person in a different way. For George Fox the Quaker, it was three steeples seen against an English sky. For the future Buddha, the process began as he walked in the woods. "As I tarried, a deer came by. A bird caused a twig to fall. The wind set the leaves whispering. And I thought, Now it is coming, that fear and terror . . ."

Disoriented, not knowing the right road but desperate to find it, the prince became a pilgrim. He rejected the blandishments of the Brahmanic priests and wandered to the Hindu sacred city of Bodh Gaya. There he sat down under a tree, facing the sunrise.[8] Even as he sat, there came a warning earthquake. Six times the ground shook. At the seventh convulsion, the Goddess of Illusion sprang out of the air to seduce him. But he reached to touch the shoulder of Mother Earth, and the false goddess fled.

He concentrated on himself, the thinker, a point of consciousness in infinity. Then he let his mind open outward from that point toward the six directions until it seemed to fill the Cosmos. For seven days more, he sat still while only his mind moved.

This is how his mind moved, as I understand it, staking out a track for Buddhist pilgrimage-of-the-mind to come.

It moved cautiously and logically, step by step.

It said: There is being. There is also nothingness. My senses tell me of one; my reason, the other.

That much was already implied in the Hindu scriptures. Hindu philosophy proceeded then to veil the contradiction by calling the one, illusion.

But the man under the tree was what Western philosophy would call an empiricist and a humanist. He would not say the natural world is an illusion. How then accept that both states exist, both real, both natural? There is a paradox here, the same that underlies one of the historic Christian arguments for the existence of God: a perfect being must possess Being and so cannot not-be. If descriptive language and objective reality coincide, then there must be God, for nonbeing cannot be.

But the empiricist knows that "must" as applied to language alone is a false proposition. One has but to overleap the words and one has overleapt the necessity that being be and nonbeing not be.

The mind of the man under the Bo tree moved that way . . . yet farther. Try it, the Buddhist says! It can be said. It is not impossible, though a contradiction: being and nonbeing exist, simultaneously and everywhere.

The mental pilgrimage proceeds, step by step, toward the crux. "Form is emptiness," says the man under the tree. "Emptiness is form."[9]

Form and emptiness, objective reality and the void coincide and overlay. Matter exists, real enough. The ground exists, and I, seated on it. Yet, or but, there is also emptiness. The one does not disturb the other.

There is a fierce, persistent hammering at this contradiction in Buddhist instruction. There is no way to hold the parts together save as a dialectic forced into fusion. It is that exact step that takes place under the Bo tree in the Buddha's mind.

Life in the world is real. Death too is real and total. One who had died has "gone upstream" and exists in Nonexistence. He is simply "without name and form."[10]

That is a hard nut to crack, and hard to take solace in when a loved one dies. But once the principle has been pointed out, there is really no more to say. The rest is up to the individual.

"We ask and ask," said the Buddha's disciple Ananada. "You only smile and say nothing."

Deep is the Tathagata (signifying Truth), unmeasurable, difficult to understand, even like the ocean.

And the nature of the knot wherein the two strands, Be and Be-not, are tied is "incomprehensible, indescribable, inconceivable, unutterable."

All the same, acceptance of the contradiction at the heart of the knot is, for the Buddhist, "the supreme goal . . . the consummation, the eternal, hidden and incomprehensible Peace."

And when he saw the morning star rising in the east, and saw it as if "for the first time," for the man now designated the Enlightened One, the pilgrimage of thought was over.

WHEN he left Bodh Gaya, the Buddha walked north toward Benares. On the way, he stopped in a deer park in Sarnath. There he preached to his first disciples, four in number. Perhaps they were really four deer, for preaching to the animals was common among the sages. That place is the Third Pillar of the Buddha's life-pilgrimage and still a gathering place today.[11]

The message he delivered included acceptance of the paradox and commitment to lifelong reflection on it. Further, as concerned life in the natural world, it was a call for respect and tolerance among all people and for a humanistic perspective toward the structures of society.[12] Theravada Buddhists, followers of those original teachings, still maintain their commitment to empiricism. There is no spirit world. There is no invisible, immortal "soul." *Anatta:* no soul. There is only the flux and occasional coalescing in one "aggregate" or mind of transitory sensations, perceptions, and so on that give rise to temporary states of what we call consciousness.

Consciousness is only a function of permutating matter, a flame dancing on a bed of coals. But who has seen the flame without the coals?

"What is a chariot? the wheel? the body? the shafts? It is none of these. So for the human personality. It is but name and form, mind and matter. Nothing more.

"Light a candle. From where does the light come? When it goes out, where has it gone? No-where."

Death is a going into no-where, only to be feared in anticipation, as Epicurus and the Stoics would be saying two centuries later and, later, Lucretius and also, sometimes, my father.

"Love is a binding and will only give rise to grief. Then cut it out."

There is only one solace for a person of Buddhistic temperament. It is to accept that with one's death, one vanishes entirely. There is also an eschatological projection: in the long future, all living things will have passed out of existence. Then the Cosmos will have returned to a condition of stasis and formlessness. Entropy will have reached a maximum.

If "religion" implies the existence of a connective bond between earth and heaven, then early Buddhism was not a religion but an order of life.[13] People of a monastic bent may elect to leave the world ahead of time and, by withdrawing their love from it, prepare for annihilation. But for them and also those who keep their interest in the world alive, compassion must be the rule. Therefore, exercise "charity, discipline, patience, energy," and work for peace.

Eventually it came the Buddha's time to die. He accepted his fate and, even in dying, says the story, was faithful to the principle of location in space. He lay down on his side with his head toward the polar star. Then he closed his eyes and gave in to the "utter passing away that leaves nothing whatever to remain behind." That event is supposed to have taken place around 480 BCE in Benares, which became the Fourth Pillar of Buddhist pilgrimage.

AROUND this track the early Buddhist pilgrims went, meditating on the Teacher's words. If he was the first to say "Life is a journey, the universe, an inn," the phrase coursed the world, and in the third century BCE many other phrases were gathered into a canon. But however it changed in different countries, the simple origin of the cult was remembered in two simple forms, one sculptural, one architectural, by which it was impressed on Indian consciousness.

The image that would unify the Buddhist world is the cross-legged male in meditation, descendant of the old Lord of the Animals of Mohenjo-Daro.[14] The iconic Buddha describes an equilateral triangle. So elemental a shape may make further claim to dominance over the mind by absorbing, while reversing, the shape that before had always signified the female sex. From Paleolithic times, the triangle, point down, signified female fertility. Henceforth, point up, the triangle signified the ascetic, seed-withholding male. Posture itself has become an icon and affords the male pilgrim, seated in meditation, a sense of congruence with the cosmic axis while confirming in the pilgrim, female, her exclusion from it.

Centuries before that geometry was adapted for the Teacher's person, however, there existed as simple a form of Buddhist sacred architecture. The stupa—or reliquary-shrine—like the domed church and mosque of the West and also like the modern astronomical observatory, replicates the upper half of the Cosmos of myth: a hemisphere held upright around its axis. Some were even pocked with niches for oil lamps to bring the dome to starry life.[15]

The stupa took its shape and symbolism from two sources: a mound of dirt a peasant heaps around a germinating seed, and burial mounds in rural India. Beyond these, it takes other references from nature and art, like the anthill that holds energy in its roundish crust, and the tent that shelters a family's energies. The Buddhist Temple-stupa of the Borobodur has been called a "huge tent the evil spirits cannot enter."[16]

What is in the stupa is a symbolic seed or "heap of grain," actually a bit of bone, hair, or tooth of the Buddha or one of his followers. It is a womb of energy, like the pot under the sanctum of the Hindu temple. The oldest stupa still standing, dating from the third century before this era, is in Sri Lanka. Cracked and eroded, spilling out its brick stuffing and overgrown with grass, it looks like half an old planet. But some later examples built in the royal age of Buddhism were enclosed in richly carved stone walls with gates marking the four quarters.

"At the four crossroads, they build a cairn to the King of Kings," the Buddha said. The cairn or stupa, then, serves as a compass laid down at the crossroads. Like the Shiva-linga, like Wallace Stevens's jar on a hill in Tennessee, it sheds its ordering power to the six directions and changes wild to formed. Around it the pilgrim went and goes today, following the planetary "path that both comes and goes" and so circling the Cosmos.

Unlike the Hindu temple, however, the stupa both calls the pilgrim into orbit around it and, at the last threshold, excludes him. In Buddhist symbolism, there is no entry into the mystery in this life. That last step into Buddhahood, which is the same as nothingness, takes place only in deep trance, or at the moment of death.

THE age of expanding Buddhist pilgrimage and mission activity began on a field in east-central India where the historic King Ashoka, after a particularly bloody battle, vowed to change his ways and promulgate the Teacher's pacifism. Pilgrims gather there still to stare at a rock-cut inscription that purports to be the very one with which Ashoka renounced war. Eventually, royal proclamations on stone pillars drew pilgrims to the ends of the empire, and it is likely that some reached the Mediterranean.[17] For tradition says the King divided up the eight original stupas in which parts of the Buddha's body were buried and repackaged them into 84,000 portable packets: a mystical number that symbolically would serve to sow the earth with sanctity.

And in time, the historic transmission of Buddhism by pilgrims traveling the silk routes to China and Japan began, and thereafter there also began a reverse flow, backwards across the northern sands from China to Tibet and also back by water from Japan to Indonesia and the Indian mainland.[18]

Even during the King's lifetime, the doctrine had showed signs of dividing into two streams. One school stayed close to the original teachings. The other took on florid new detail. Theravada Buddhism, the Buddha's original "Little Vehicle," still today rides without the oil of mysticism and wish-fulfilling equivocations. "Mystic wonders, I loathe and abhor and am ashamed of," said the Teacher. By contrast, those purists might call the Greater Vehicle—Mahayana Buddhism—a religion for wishful thinkers.[19] Heavily influenced on its transit through Japan, China, and Tibet, it generated supernatural subcults and mystical concepts of immortality through reincarnation. But all these abandon the authentic paradox that the Teacher seems to have propounded and that modern science affirms: that both matter and the void coexist in this universe, real and interpenetrating.

The first teaching took root in southeast Asia, Ceylon, and Burma; the other, in China and Japan, Tibet, and, for a while, the Indonesian island of Java where the Stupa-temple of the Borobodur, once one of the great pilgrimage shrines of the world, stands in ruins today.

✦ ✦ ✦

I went to Indonesia to see a shadow play and to climb the Borobodur. The shadow play is mobile and living, the temple is now dead. But together they illustrate the separate ways of Hindu and Buddhist thought. Seek in the shadow play for a distinction between the real and the illusion, and you will not find it. The Borobodur rises out of the same insubstantial vision but forces thought on toward a starker conclusion.

NEARLY 150 million people live in Indonesia now, seeded across some three thousand islands of rain forest, volcanic cones, and marshland paddies that look, from the air, like green thumbprints of the gods. In the daytime, these fields are flushed with a paradisiacal gold-green light, where peasants in pink, fluorescent green, and lilac headcloths seem to float above their reflections in the brown water.

Yet this has been called one of the most deprived regions of the world. Its people are subject to periodic famine and epidemic and to political, racial, and religious violence. Today, whole islands are said to be gulags, and ancient blood hatred between ethnic and religious groups underlies all other woes.

Where real life is painful, the cosmic image frequently inflates in the mind to provide release. There is no island in Indonesia that has not been mythologized as a Cosmos entire, afloat in the seas of death. Each volcanic island lifts its mouth to the gods where they drift among the clouds. The principal cone on Bali, as on other islands, is called Gunung Agung, Great Mountain. There are only two ways to orient yourself on Bali: "kaja," toward the mountain, or "kelod," away from it. To go toward the mountain is to approach the gods. To go the other way is to go toward the sea with its population of demons. There is one other term that figures in Bali: "paling." If you are disoriented or in a trance, you are "in paling."[20]

FOR at least two thousand years and probably longer, the shadow theater has existed in Asia, a fragile and passing art form of bamboo and paper, leather and lamplight, voice and memory.[21]

The performance begins around midnight at some forested crossroads where villagers gather before a little box of a theater. The puppets, when they appear, are the ghosts of the heroes of the epic tales of Kurukshetra or Ceylon.

As the puppets are lifted to the paper screen, their painted colors are reduced to black and white, three-dimensional space shrinks to two, and symbolisms may inflate in a modern pilgrim's mind. The theater is the brain; the screen is its cortex, and the puppet master, consciousness. Behind the cortical screen sits mind in its box of bone, lifting the withered shapes from their oblivion to endure, once more, their adventures and deaths, while their plaints and howls pour through the puppet master's larynx to mix with the chimes, bells, and gongs of the gamelan orchestra.

The play begins with a leaf shape that flutters behind the screen, stops, flutters again, comes into clear focus, then pulls back to a blur.

The leaf-puppet is called Gunungan. Its shape is also that of a mountain, a flame, a bird, or a tree, for by the logic of myth all are "the same" and represent the Cosmos. The form is split down the center, so it has also the look of wings or doors, each side richly worked in vines and flowers, and sea and tree spirits. Hidden, as well, in the mat of detail may be twin horses, those guardians of the sun in the ancient solar myth.[22]

The play itself unfolds through three passages of action, set to three modes of gamelan music, during three phases of the nine hours until dawn. Like the island Bali, like the greater Cosmos, time itself in the shadow play is tripartite. You watch its full round while the dome of stars turns overhead and Canopus glows in the deep south. And the next morning, you may hear in your mind: "Now come, yourself, into the shadow house."

THE shadow house of stone is the Borobodur, a million and a half blocks of volcanic rock piled into a pyramid on the high plateau of central Java. At the horizon stand volcanic cones, some, like "fire-throwing" Merapi, still alive, others, like little Tidar, the spike that nails the island into the Cosmos, quiescent. Probably it was these whose eruptions snuffed life from the Borobodur, for only a few years after it was built in the ninth century it was abandoned. Its priests, and the monks who had tended and the pilgrims who had orbited it, moved to east Java, and jungle crept out to cover the remains. Gold leaf which some think covered the stones would have washed into the abandoned paddies and then out to sea, and for over nine centuries—until the British Sir Stamford Raffles happened on it in the nineteenth century—no pilgrim is known to have found his way to the place.

The plan of the structure, seen from the air in a green sea of jungle, is a square island rising to an apex. Centered in the square are circles, three large ones and arrayed around their axis, seventy-two little ones. The diagram is a mandala, a blueprint of the Cosmos: the plane of earth under the dome of the sky, oriented to the directions and fixed between zenith and nadir. Between earth and sky, the Borobodur is itself the axis that both separates and joins. It is the World Mountain over which Polestar shines. Since there was in actuality no mountain in the midst of this plain, only a low hill probably sacred since prehistory, the Borobodur stands there for the sacred mountain in far Tibet, Kailas.

THE doctrinal background of the work is worth spending a moment on, for without it the formidable array of sculpture is meaning-less.[23]

For centuries before its construction, Buddhism of the Greater Vehicle had flooded farther Asia. A center of study was a monastery at Nalanda, within the four-square sacred tract of Lumbini, Bodh Gaya, and Sarnath / Benares. There, pilgrims from the international Buddhist world gathered.[24] Their red and yellow robes spoke of their lands of origin, and their fanciful hats, like truncated pillar bases or extended wings, of their various cults and schools. The air was filled with a din of conch horns marking the hours and also with the cries of sky-watching priests atop a star-sighting platform.

It was there, during the seventh and eighth centuries, that a syncretic Buddhist cult emerged which combined Tibetan with Japanese geo-cosmological ideas. Together, these would provide the theoretical foundation and the formal template for the Borobodur.

The cult taught the existence of an actual point in space where the two realms of being and nonbeing collide. The point that cannot in experience or logic exist, yet does, is the Diamond Point. Mastery of its laws is the Diamond Way. At the Diamond Point, matter vanishes. The point as well. By the time the event has taken place, the point itself is nonexistent. The teaching is medieval Tibetan, but the concept is modern particle physics.

Diamond is "vajra," which is also "thunderbolt." The thunderbolt hits the rock and shatters it, releasing steam, fire, light. The rock is hard to split; the diamond, harder. The paradox of the Diamond Point will not accept penetration. Then shatter it!

The symbol of the Diamond Way is a bronze thunderbolt-shaped scepter, the Vajra. Hold it in your hand. Lift it. Turn it, with gingerly attention to its metallic weight, while from your chest you emit a space-filling groan and, from the recesses of your monastery, drums send forth a continual low vibration. Then like the lightning that splits the skies and the stone, the Vajra can crack the adamantine knot and end the fear of death.

Chinese and Japanese Buddhist teachers conceived of the event taking place within landscape overlaid by two geo-cosmological mandalas.[25] Through the trails of the actual, material Womb-mandala, Japanese pilgrims still make their way today, meditating on the flesh and bones of the Buddha-body. "The river to the right is the Buddha of Mercy ... the river to the left flows from the

Buddha of the East . . . the mountains and rivers, trees and plants, are the body of the Buddha; the wind proclaims the Law of the Buddha . . ."[26]

But then there is the Diamond-mandala that cuts across the landscape too, and these two blueprints have their point of intersection at a particular mountain, where the two realms impact and annihilate the one that is of rivers and trees.

Settle these concepts in the head of an architect looking for haven from anti-Buddhist persecutions that ravaged Nalanda in the ninth century, persuade a rich and royal Buddhist clan to underwrite a building project in the safe haven of upland Java, and you may have the Borobodur.[27]

I traveled to the Borobodur from the modern town of Jodgjakarta, a quiet stir at 4:30 in the morning. A guide, holding an inch of candle between two fingers, led me through pitch dark, over buffalo-dung patties, to a bus filling with Nepalese pilgrims.

On the road outside town, bullfrogs croaked in the paddies and peasants were already abroad, bent under heavy loads of produce for market. The fields lightened. At 5:30 by my watch, a saffron beam struck a peak, lighting the fiery crater in which the Cosmos gestated. The sky lightened, and another peak stood up, cleft at the top like a broken tooth. White mist still lay over the fields of manioc, corn, and tobacco.

We drove across a shaking bridge and looked down upon muddy whirlpools. We crossed another, over a brown stream, swift and flat.

By 6:15 we had pulled up before the east wall of the temple, or the low, bristly mass that calls itself a wall. From the door of the bus, I could make no sense of the pile, neither its scale nor its situation on the ground. Two million cubic feet of decaying gray stone seemed to have soaked in the space around it as if they were a sponge.

So I went to sit down under a Bo tree that was still dripping dew, to drink my bitter coffee and wait for dawn to bring the sleeping giant to life.

And indeed, when the sun broke over the trees at my back, letting fly long red spears against the facade, as suddenly as a piper's breath on pipe holes brings out sound, the light brought forth a vision striking in its clarity. In rows of identical arched niches were multiple figures of the Buddha, all reaching down in one ordered gesture to touch the earth, as the man under the tree in Gaya touched earth to dispel the Goddess of Illusion and prepare to accept the truth.

Now I could see that the Gunungan-mountain had a door. Behind it was a short flight of steep steps, then other flights, above, that led toward the topmost summoning shape of its axis. Once I climbed that first short flight and turned to my left, as doctrine requires, I was lost to the world behind me as well as to my destination, that summoning dome at the top. For the passageway turns and is closed in between high walls, a shadow valley with no sight lines out to the landscape.

However, if the natural world was gone, another opened before me with engaging power. On each side of the path, which turns four times on each of three rising levels, unfolded a moving-show of sculptural reliefs. Here cycle after cycle of tales are told, a mix of myth and folklore describing the supernatural Pilgrim born in bygone Ages as an elephant, a bird, a prince, and at last, in this World Age as the Buddha. Other panels tell of a human pilgrim named Sudhana, leaving India, making his way through Ceylon, finally arriving in Java and this very temple, while intermittently flying off to converse with angels.

In time the scenes of animal-thronged glades, palaces, and ships in sail came to an end, replaced by figures of placid saints standing in monotonous rows, lifting hands in communal blessing. Their formal quiet spoke to me, saying, Quiet, now, and take account of where you have been before you enter the stranger world ahead.

The bus that morning had brought me through the villages of the World of Illusion to the confusing pile of stones: the World of Matter. Sunrise showed me the logic in the stones, and step by step I mounted the levels of the World of Sense-experience. Now those experiences too lay at my back. Of their rich variety, nothing remained but the abstracted postures of these blessing-saints, of the World of pure Forms.[28]

At that point, a transitional terrace impels the pilgrim out onto the stupa's open upper courses, where the sight of an immense sweep of landscape, running in all directions off to the horizon under skies of delicate blue, takes the breath away.

FROM such a height at last, the full layout of the pile can be understood.

For example, the Buddha figures seated across each of the four flanks of the structure make a different mudra, or significant hand gesture. If to the east they make the Touching-earth signal to take courage to face the truth, to the south, where the death-star Canopus shines, they make the sign of Blessing. To the west, where dormitories of the monks once lay, they fold their hands in private Meditation, and to the distant north, they lift their hands in the mudra that says, Fear Not.

These Directional Buddhas, as they are called, are representatives in stone of the cosmological system refined and taught in Nalanda.[29] Sitting facing outward to the four directions, they form a spatially oriented, three-dimensional Cosmos of Buddha-spirits. A fifth Buddha-of-the-Sun, representing the power of the mind to conceive this order, rides at the pyramid apex atop them.[30]

Beyond them, in each direction, lies the void that also permeates them. Deep in the material mass at their backs is the metaphysically impossible Diamond Point. By their meditations and the action of their hand gestures, they bring the stabilized Cosmos into existence out of it.

For the pilgrim himself, there is a mode of meditation based on the Directional-Buddha system. Concentrate. Hold the mind steady, without wandering. Avoid thoughts of yourself.

Meditate till thought begins to stream outward as if in an unbroken flow. At the farthest reach, thought is entering the void. Such is the condition called Directional Meditation.

The theoretical end of the process would be to follow thought into nothingness, like a person riding a barrel over Niagara Falls. At the end of this World Age, all beings will have been raised to such a pitch. Then, as if Niagara crashed on sand, all of them, in a flash of time-becoming-timelessness, will pass through the interstices of matter into nothing, drawing the last sparks in their wake.

In fact, something like that was probably the actual fate of Nalanda. When the Moslems invaded India, they razed the monastery's domes and towers, burnt the texts, melted the bronzes and slaughtered at least five thousand monks, many of whom doubtless composed themselves in the posture of Directional Meditation to await the sword.

Seen from the upper course of the monument that was inspired by these doctrines, the Womb-world, brought into existence by the Buddhas seated all around this sacred mountain, is a green and mild place of small farms, paddies, and fruit trees. The Diamond-world is that same landscape out of sight and mind, emptied of itself and removed from being.

THE mind that plays back and forth between the stones of this monument and the emptiness it floats in is represented, itself, on the Borobodur by as strange an assemblage of sculpture as exists on earth. To enter this region of the stupa-mountain is to abandon the particular for the universal—the Worlds of Matter, Experience, and Form for the Realm of Law to which all being is subject.

At first one sees only three cycles of little stupas like perforated beehives or upturned baskets. On the lower two ranks, the openings are diamond-shaped; on the top, square, as if even such minor shapes could be reduced from an active to a balanced state.

You can look in these windows. Inside each hive, splashed with diamond- or square-shaped spots of light, sits a Buddha making the intricate, intertwined finger gesture called Turning the Wheels of the Law.

Then what is this whole ensemble of stone and sculpture, from the base of it to the top, but a massive shadow play tombed in the mountain? The pilgrim audience is held to the hither side of it. Behind the stone screen, behind the passing drama of worldly experience, unfolds the play of plays: the cosmic round that spins being out of nothing, then living being back into inanimate dead. Between the pilgrim, where he stands in nature, and that metaphysical theater is the gap that cannot be crossed save in thought or works of art like this.

When or if the Borobodur was gilded and painted like Buddhist temples in Japan, China, Tibet, and elsewhere today, its platforms would have shone even more brilliantly against the dark jungle. On the upper terraces, by sun-, moon-, and torchlight, hive would have mirrored hive and between them reflected the passing shapes of monks and pilgrims. Then the whole temple may have looked like a stage alive with presences, drawn out of their imprisoning containing hives to travel back and forth along the rays of the Directional Buddhas' thoughts. Then the pilgrim circumambulating the hives may have felt himself afloat as well, circling the axis of the celestial dome like a planet around the sun.

Or take that hypothetical shadow play from the other side: there in his bone hive sits a person at his or her lifework. He is tombed in stone, and the true nature of the world—its entrances and vanishings, its fragrances of tropical flowers, birdcalls and hums of insects—reach him only indirectly. His thoughts are concentrated on the intricate patterns his fingers make, which may or may not have their larger formulations in the world beyond.

Just so, the Borobodur, this complex of stone and idea, burgeoned out of the thought of a simple Teacher under a tree. In Sanskrit, "budbuda" means "bubble" and may be the linguistic root of "Borobodur" and so suggest the process by which the temple—and other human works—emerge into tangible being. It is the creative worker's turning in the hive of his or her own ignorance and longing that sends forth ring after ring of forms transient as bubbles or fire, whose material residue then sets and hardens into artifacts. However, by that time, the original query and lament that impelled the mind and set it turning may have long since been left behind, forgotten.

THERE is still one last level of stone and meaning on the Borobodur. Above and beyond all these sculptural and conceptual forms and contradictions is a yet more ineffable Buddha, more remote than Shiva-Mahadeva, beyond cosmic Law, beyond the pilgrim's power to describe.

That last stone shape rises against the sky and against one's right shoulder. It is vertical, brute, the trunk of the stupa. This shape that pierces the sky and locks the whole into the Cosmos has no entry and no name. It is called the Realm of No-form, the ultimate destination toward which humanity and all its philosophy and art are headed.

Possibly some object was inserted into its core during construction, a charm or relic like the golden man in the tower of a Hindu temple. But what it might have been is unknown.

Or perhaps there was nothing there—need be nothing. The abstract form of the shaft declares its intention. In theory, it would be trained not upon Polestar but the pole of the ecliptic, beyond which there is only what is lightless and unconfined.

That shaft rises on, drawing thought up through that theoretical aperture, on out beyond the shell of stars till thought comes under the steeper law that Ernest Becker called the "suction of the infinite."[31]

Here the Buddhist pilgrimage ends. For the living pilgrim standing on the Borobodur, the Buddhas and all their directional fields of love and authority fade, and the whole vision disappears.

AT this point a whole movement of self-reflective fantasy on the secular traveler's part may end as well. The dead are really gone, says the man under the tree.

When I looked up, the polar star had lost its patriarchal eminence and fallen back into nature, only one among the uncountable fires of the open universe.

To what end and by what principle was I to continue traveling? When I looked to find my way, it lay in shadow.

PART THREE

POLESTAR THE PILGRIM

✦

*Since the purpose of myth is to provide a logical model
capable of overcoming a contradiction (an impossible
achievement if, as it happens, the contradiction is real),
a theoretically infinite number of states will be generated, each one slightly different from the others.*

*Thus myth grows spiral-wise until the intellectual
impulse which has originated it is exhausted. . . .*

Lévi-Strauss:
THE STRUCTURAL STUDY OF MYTH

✦

TOWARD THE CENTER : JERUSALEM

✦ ✦ ✦

The astronomical term for the dark zone of a planetary orbit is *aphelion*—the point farthest from the solar axis. For a secular Westerner, the axis of an experience is likely to be its fidelity and relevance to natural circumstances. By the time I'd reached the top of the Borobodur, I had received the monument's message to pilgrims: the finality of death in nature. *The dead are really gone, says the man under the tree.*

But for the pilgrim who is not a Buddhist, the quest need not stop there. In my case, my trail turned me around until I was facing west. Western tradition generally rejects both Hindu illusionism and Buddhist stoicism and advocates the use of imaginative reason to achieve orientation in—and a mode of ascendance over—existential absolutes.

Once I accepted this possibility, my research into pilgrimage could proceed, though no longer as a quest for ultimate answers ("How many are the fires and suns in number? what is the number of the dawns and waters? Not in jest do I ask, O fathers. Sages, I ask you for this information . . ."[1]) nor supernatural ones (Where is my father now?). Of the end to which my subjective quest was taking me, I was still uncertain. But I was reading Rilke at the time and took his words to heart: "strive for transformation . . ."

I set out to trace the myths, monuments, and metaphors of Western pilgrimage to their sources. My base and focus would be Jerusalem. There, as the world knows, one great theological system delivered itself of two others. There the arc of history can be discerned and traced from the ruins of the foundation myth to the shrines of the new ones. In that city, when I was there, three consecutive dramas of pilgrimage, death, and transformation unfolded in an octagon of days: Latin Good Friday, Jewish Passover, and Orthodox Easter. Then somewhere between the conjoined Jewish and Christian dramas must be what Rilke calls the flame that leads from form to form.

Jerusalem, its very air and stones, seems charged with flame ready to break out. Phantom sights and sounds are common in the hill city, especially at the equinoxes, when a suspenseful wind, the Hamsin, brings an earthy draft up from the Dead Sea. Then the air grows furry tan. Eddies of pulverized limestone scrape the dry earth, and, even indoors, static electricity erupts in lightning flashes imagination takes for omens that common sense puts down.

THE "High Complete City" lies along a low spur of rock bordered on three sides by wind-eroded ravines. Rising over what was once bare desert, that place, like Benares and the Borobodur, represents the axis of the Cosmos. Like the Hindu sanctum or the core of the Borobodur, its sacred spaces are empty of figurative images, for their function in the abstract, symbolic system of cosmic myth is to afford access to the skies. However, in accord also with Western religious principles, these shrines mark places where supernatural events are said to have occurred. They are the site of the Jewish Temple, the Tomb out of which Christ rose, and the Moslem Dome of the Rock.

Of the Temple, nothing remains today but a behemoth's tooth of wall 60 feet high and 158 feet across, shedding its yellow-white glitter across the black-coated shapes of pilgrims who stand bowing and raining tears at its base. Nine courses of the giant blocks rise above ground. Eight more drive down to bedrock. A single one of the visible stones weighs four hundred tons. For two thousand years, this massive fragment has stood as a bond between the Jews and their Lord.

Men and women in separated prayer yards stand before the Wall facing slightly northeast toward the theoretical but unseen site of greatest magnetism beyond it. That site, for non-Jews who may visit it, is marked by an outcrop of bedrock whose root the myths locate in Eden. Tradition also says it was the floor of the inner sanctum of Solomon's Temple. Each day between the Jew and that unseen plot of ground, the Wall imposes itself.

At dusk, the crying of swallows over the courtyard drowns out the pilgrims' lamentations. The moon rises and a Western woman in traveling clothes weeps. Lamentation engulfs the Hasidim and

Ashkenazim, the Sephardim and those young returnees to ancient ways who call themselves Repenters. An American businessman with a briefcase stands and wipes his eyes. A French girl, with tentative steps, approaches the Wall and slips a note between its stones, a note to God. At midnight, the Wall's custodian enters a stone room that runs a little way toward the Holy Mount. He sits on a mat, smears ashes on his head, and laments. Again at daybreak, again to the birds' piercing cries, the mourning rites begin.

> For the palace that lies desolate . . .
> We sit in solitude and mourn . . .
> For the Temple that is destroyed . . .

The Wall is an artifact of suffering-loss. Mourning that loss goes on day in, day out, drawing Jewish pilgrims from all over the world. All come with their individual plaints, but all the domestic, social, or political losses over which this shaft stands vigil are but shadows of the great original loss proposed by Jewish tradition: the disappearance, long ago, of the Lord from his Temple.

The vanishing of the Lord from the Temple preceded its fall, the fall of the Temple preceded the Diaspora, and the Diaspora is template for all later losses. All lesser woes flow from the original one. All pilgrimage by Jews and their offspring, the Christians, takes place in the shadow of an original one of incomparable mystery and majesty: the pilgrimage of the Lord in the Cosmos.

Now the Lord has gone out of natural experience, the Jew may say. But not out of being utterly as the Buddhist says, nor into the illusions of Hinduism, only gone for a while, leaving humanity to sit in vigil on the mystery of the form of His return.

✦ ✦ ✦

The myth of the Pilgrim Lord unfolds in the Old Testament to overcome a contradiction whose terms are implicit in the flow of events. Each passage of the myth differs slightly from the others. But all are conjoined in their cumulative intent to bridge the gap.

The mythic passages describe the coming of the Lord into visibility on His orbital trail through the Cosmos, His arrival and brief station on the earth, and His disappearance from human eyesight.

Scholars suggest that the Lord entered consciousness in the same flare of insight that opened the patriarchs' minds to differences between their culture and that of their neighbors. In effect, the spatial and psychological self-definition the Buddha advocated was experienced here in terms of doctrine and ritualized social life. A growing sense of discrimination brought the end of cultural childhood and the beginning of Jewish historic and ethical life apart from the rest of humanity.

The background against which Judaism arose is known. For millennia, since the subsiding of the floods of the last Ice Age, there had been human presence in the Middle East. There, bread wheat evolved from the wild wheat of the plains. There sickle scythes came into use, made of curved gazelle horn, to till the furrows and inspire myths of field-gods, cut down and sown again. There grape and olive were trained from native wildness to the grid of vineyard and orchard, perhaps inspiring a love of sequential, or narrative, order in mental life. When Abram would come this way there would be wheatfields and vineyards already thousands of years old.

In the Fertile Crescent, the city culture of the fourth millennium appeared. The economy of city-states coalesced. Canals were built to provide for large-scale farming outside the cities. Population grew and class alignments were clarified. Writing came into use for commercial transactions and, little by little, for poetry and history and myth.

There were two Mesopotamian empires: Sumer, settled by Central Asian migrants bringing the Indo-Aryan myth structures, and Akkad, settled by Semites from northern Syria. The main Sumerian city was Ur; the main Akkadian city, Babylon. There and thereabouts stood temples and ziggurats as miniature models of the Cosmos. Their forms reflected cosmic form: square earth supporting the domed sky, over the abyssal waters. Their towers reached, in theory, to the stars.

In that Triple World, a divinity An or Anu or El ruled the sky. He had existed "before the birth of the gods." He was understood to inhabit the far North where he dominated "the stars of El." Let us say he was the polar star, as yet given but vague personification.

Subject to El were Lords Storm and Earth. The Sumerian storm god was named Enlil. He was the personification of atmospheric blast and turmoil. The tall oak drew the storm into its upper branches. The turpentine-rich terebinth tree burst into flames when struck by lightning. Both these were sacred to Enlil. Among living creatures, his representative was the bull. In culture centers of the Nearer East, the Storm lord would be called Ba'al.

Lord Earth-Water was Enki or Ea. This divinity was the clear-thinker, ever achieving insight into natural relationships. He perceived the dimensions of the cosmic architecture and taught people to build temples to replicate it on earth.

The polar star, the storm, and flowing water were of male gender. For the female presence in the Cosmos, the generic Goddess, a planet and a star of near-equal brilliance, Venus and Sirius, provided inspiration.[2] From them equally or variably derived the Sumerian Inanna, the Babylonian Ishtar, and such other Star-queens as "Astarte of the awesome heavens," sighted in the dew or the glint of waves or atop poles or through the branches of trees. In Egypt, the Star-queen Isis was equally or variably identified with Sirius or the polar star, brilliant and steady, focused on through sighting pipes in temples.[3]

The Goddess arrives in Near Eastern history already venerable and full of contradiction, a sky-creature regent over natural fertility and death, androgynous in her dominant power.[4] In Near Eastern and Egyptian myths, she slept with a young field-god, who flourished for a season, then died. For each local form of the Goddess, there was a field-god who must die: for Inanna, there was Dumuzil; for Ishtar, Tammuz; for Cybele, Attis; for Isis, Osiris. Willingly, the field-god went to his death, "the lamb which is made ready with pure wheat to be sacrificed," trusting that the equinox would bring him out again.

Some anthropologists propose that this mythic drama was acted out in sexual rites culminating in ritual murder. Or the ruling chief or king might be put to ritual test. If he failed the priestess sexually, doubtless he soon died. Tokens of the rite survive today—

little terra-cotta sculptures of the sacred marriage bed, a plain wooden frame on four short horn-shaped legs.[5] On it lie the Goddess and her consort of the moment. He is sexually aroused and reaches to embrace her. On the bed, power and life are bargained for with the Star-queen and either won or lost.

Eventually, such rites gave way to the flushing of female sculptures with animal blood or red powders and dyes, as Sati's are in India today. In time, these coatings of blood and blood substitutes would darken to look like lightning-blasted wood or meteorites, reinforcing the belief that "in the beginning" the Goddess was a star fallen out of the sky.

The Jewish Lord would be the implacable enemy of these divinities who lived in nature, appearing and vanishing seasonally under the dominance of the Goddess and a remote, vague El of the North, and whose careers made it clear that death is inescapable save at the price of biological transformation.

SOME historians say the patriarchs of Judaism found their way out of Mesopotamia into Canaan in the Late Bronze Age as semi-nomads. Others hold there never were such migrations, that the Israelites were Canaanites from the start and Ur but a metaphor for a distant past and divergent tradition, left behind.

The scriptural narrative is precise, however. It says that Tereh, over two hundred years old, left the city of Ur with his son Abram and his grandson, and Sarah. They worshiped "other gods" than the One still to come. No reason is given for that leave-taking, any more than for the first appearance of a mind, or God, in the primordial wind and dark. It simply took place, causeless, unmotivated, and unquestioned.

The first leg of Tereh's and Abram's journey lay to the north. The travelers from Ur would have entered Babylon by the south gate, crossed the Euphrates that ran through the city, then traveled north through its broad streets, passing the royal palace and the Temple of Marduk, a god inspired by the planet Jupiter, honored "as far as the earth extends and heaven spreads and the sun shines and water flows and the wind blows."[6]

The travelers would then have passed the ziggurat or House of the Foundations of Heaven and Earth. A walled tower with twelve gate stations, it represented the axis of the zodiacal wheel and would stand proud for a thousand years and in shambles for the next two thousand. It was the last sign of civilization seen by Tereh's band as they departed by the north gate, sacred to the Goddess Ishtar.

From there, the road lay north by northwest, either through or away from the cities of Ashur and Nineveh, depending on whether they took the course of the Tigris, that flowed, it was said, from the star Annuit, or the Euphrates, that flowed out of the star Swallow.

However, after Tereh died at Haran and was buried there, his son abandoned the northerly route. Myth says that at this point Abram turned west and, after a time, south along the Jordan into Canaan, in fact the general route of migration of the west-Semitic tribes of the time.

SUCH is scripture. But a further story, just as strange and possibly as true, comes to light if one takes up, as a tool for research, a star-wheel.

Mysterious flat time-explorer is my star-wheel! In actuality, it is a simple wheel of cardboard in a stable frame: the revolving heavens bounded by horizon and calendar year. Some people call it a toy. But for me it is a helix of fire, a churn, the lightning-stick of the Cosmos spun in the tinder of the void, flinging off ink marks that are constellations, suns, planets, and, somewhere deep in the crosshatch of the cardboard itself, invisible particles: our ancestors, who tried to understand what was beyond their science to reveal and ended by postulating the gods.

Here then is what a star-wheel says to me of the myths on which Western civilization arose.

From long before Abram's exodus, the polar star by which travelers steered had been a pale-yellow light of the third magnitude, Alpha Draconis—or Thuban—in the constellation Dragon. As late as 2500 BCE it was still Alpha Draconis that stood steady in the sky while the Dragon coiled around it in a year's time. Therefore it was called the Crown of Heaven.[7]

But by the time of Abram, as biblical research fixes it, the awesome fact of the precession would have been detected wherever people watched the sky and kept records. Again one has to put a skeptical modern eye to the ancient sighting pipe. Alpha Draconis would have been seen gradually but unmistakably moving out of the field of a rigid viewing apparatus. Then in the corner of night to which the scope was trained, for a while no star stood. Instead there was only a black void, around which the Dragon went on coiling.

In time, after Alpha Draconis "fell," a lesser star in the same constellation, Gamma Draconis, moved near to the pole.[8] That particular star had long been identified as a female emanation. Gamma Draconis in Egypt was Isis. In Babylon itself in that era, Ishtar was the reigning presence over the blue north gate. So a star-wheel and archaeology too suggest it was under the guidance of a Goddess that Abram set off, at a time when it was accepted by all who traveled that there was a momentum to the grind of the heavens that had once displaced a Crown, and might again.

The need was pressing therefore on both travelers and philosophers to determine the true orientation point at the north. To find that true pole haunted the mind, the unknown star that was *tramontane*, beyond the mountains, as later voyagers would say of it. Centuries into the future, mystery would attach to its precise location and identity, "the Sterre Transmontane that is clept the Sterre of the See, that is unmevable and that is toward the Northe, that we clepen the Lode Sterre."[9]

This need, then—as the star-wheel suggests—inspired Abram's departure toward the north: to find the star that would not drift, slip, or fall but always be "upon the mountain."

And, to follow what was earlier said of the Indian Polestar, a quest directed toward that star represents a quest for absolutes of law and fate. Progress there is difficult and slow, and its outcome uncertain. There is no assurance that one will reach the end of it, nor of what one would find there if one did.[10]

To fix the mind on such an end can drain hope. To keep a whole people faithful to it through millennia there must be rigorous, repetitive exercises for mind and body, to introduce new generations to an enterprise begun in the remote past. Further, if a familial bond should turn out to exist between that star and one particular group of people on earth, then it might be expected they would find their way to its—or His—bosom in the end. And so the reservoir of hope fills up again.

In fact, theories about astronomical sources for Judeo-Christian imagery have been alternately proposed and demolished by scholars for years.[11] But scripture itself seems to support such links. For example, when the Temple would be built on Mount Moriah, the people were ordered to perform a curious choreography before it. Ezekiel (46.8–10) says pilgrims once in the Temple yards must make their way straight across, walking either to north or south. If you came in one door, you had to walk across and leave by the opposite one. The sun-door at the east was closed. In other words, this was no shrine for sun-worshipers but for seekers after Polestar.

Already, Leviticus (1.11) had ruled that a sacrificial animal was to be slaughtered on the northernmost side of the altar, in other words, like a compass needle seeking the Lord.

Lastly, whoever wonders whether in the end old Abram found his way to his goal of goals must follow the tale two thousand years forward and read its last chapter in the Book of Luke: 16.23–32.

✦ ✦ ✦

As I read the myth, then, a transcendent male Polestar would rise into the patriarchal mind to replace the sign star of the Goddess, a new "logical model" to orient the people between earth and heaven. The larger terms of the dialectic would be error and righteousness, corruption and purity, the necessity of death and the promise of immortal life.

Reader, will you follow me, now, as I read the scriptures by my own candle?

✦

BEFORE the star was envisioned, the vaulted Cosmos was formed out of nothingness and wind. Sea, earth, and sky lay inside it, and it turned, generating the seasons. Then space and time existed, but not human beings.

Since they, like a mythical star, would be creatures of contradiction, they must be twice invented, first out of pure thought, male and female equally sharing the gift, secondly out of thought and matter, male only enjoying the gift (Genesis 1.27; 2.7, 22).

Inside the Cosmos, the orbit of the polar star had its origin off out of sight, and momentum brought it by degrees toward earth where people stood searching the skies. Little by little, the star emerged from the distance into the epiphanies of Genesis: fire, smoke, and light.

The star was unseen over Eden but it gave signs of its dialectical nature: animals with wings, and the sword "whirling and flashing" with no hand to hold it.

The star was still unseen by Noah, but the shape of the Cosmos was revealed to be curved, like a rainbow or the Milky Way.

The star was still unseen by Abram, but it spoke and ordered him to build a microcosm for a theater in which it would, at last, appear. The blueprint for this structure was in code: airborne creatures were to be laid out on the ground whole; earth creatures, split and the halves laid out in facing rows (Genesis 15.9–11). The form, unmistakably, is a cosmic mandala representing the whole unbroken sky and, under it, the squared earth.

When the structure was ready, the natural world darkened. Abram, like young Buddha in the forest, felt panic fear. He fell into a trance. And the star—now call it, at last, the true and revealed Polestar—made its appearance as "a smoking brazier and a flaming torch passing between the divided pieces . . . fire and a shining radiance" (Genesis 15.17).

Now unfolding in what Lévi-Strauss calls a "theoretically infinite" series, the myth-passages of the Old Testament trace the reduction of a dualistic natural world—in which female and male coexist under her domination—to a monistic supernatural Cosmos dominated by Polestar, male.

"In the beginning," according to some biblical scholars, the chief divinity of the proto-Jewish tribes had a compound name: El Shaddu or Shaddai—old El of the North in linguistic lock with the term for "breast" or "mountain." The Lord's name, it follows, had been Sky-Earth, or even Male-Female.[12] With His transformation "from a fertility god with feminine characteristics to a seeming male god of war," as a historian puts it, Polestar's career as militant Pilgrim might begin (Exodus 3.14–16).

The covenant with Noah had been a curve of light, revealing the Cosmos of the World Age then opening. The covenant with Abram would be a curve of blood, which is, in the correspondences of myth, "the same" as light. Circumcision, that most extraordinary of human ritual acts of mutilation, takes on logic in the light of cosmological myth. The same movement of thought that reduced an androgynous " 'god of breasts' into an almighty god of war" simultaneously reduced Jewish humanity into a male-oriented family bonded by blood to a paternal star.

In old Mohenjo-Daro, a Lord of the Animals had already sub-jected his person to vertical reduction and, by replicating the cosmic axis, gained the illusion of immortality. Now Abram would be reformed to the same end (Genesis 17.3–11). So dreadful was the act that Abram must throw himself on the ground and hide his face. Even Adam had no such terror of the Lord as Abram as he consented to sexual mutilation and a new name—Abraham, "Father of a Multitude," at once bonded son and patriarch—whose flesh would thereafter "bear the brand."[13]

The hidden meaning of the act is revealed by anthropology and reaffirmed by Jewish rite. According to various tribal peoples still today, a child is understood to be born whole, perfect, and androgynous, male/female in psychic and also anatomical union. So in Jewish law the boy is understood to remain for eight days. Ritual circumcision, practiced today, is a coded act signifying the removal of the residual female in the male anatomy, laying bare the intrinsic, uncorrupted male.[14] "Love is a binding," the Buddha would tell his followers, instructing them in a like discipline, "and will give rise to grief. Then cut it out drastically."

The derivation of this Father-god, his sons' only axis and guide, from a hypothetical polar star was a symbolic act of self-rescue on the part of the patriarchs from the necessity of death, and the effect would remain as long as the men remained cut off from the Goddess-oriented nature worshipers by the covenant of blood. In token of that change, Abraham sacrificed an animal to the Lord on an altar of interesting shape: a flat stone with "horns" at the four corners. It symbolized the earth-plane that supports the sky on fire-columns of equinoxes and solstices. But it also echoed the shape of the sacred marriage bed, on which a male must pleasure the Star-queen or die. Turned upside down, it is the table on which a male priest makes sacrifice to Polestar and thereby wins life everlasting.

Henceforth, the Star-goddess's dominance was rejected. No more would Abraham's descendants visit the star-sighting poles and trees of the Star-queens. As Judaic scholar Gershom Scholem affirms, "the long history of Jewish mysticism shows no trace of feminine influence" but rather emphasizes "the demonic nature of women and the feminine element of the cosmos."[15]

When Polestar set Himself against the other stars, He excepted only one, Sirius, but turned it into a male cohort. Thus that star, which in India gave rise to Shiva, in the West inspired a creature of similar energy, paradox, and portent for pilgrims of the future: Elijah.

Elijah's labors (1 Kings 18.31–39) identified him as an actor in the cosmic drama.[16] He came on stage guiding a plow pulled by twelve pair of oxen. He piled twelve stones into an altar and dug a ditch around it. On the altar he laid a quartered bull. Then three times, from four jugs, he poured water into the trench. By that symbolism, the Three Worlds were brought into alignment, and at the third hour of the afternoon, Polestar plunged down His axis to consume the meal.

In future battles against the worshipers of "sun and moon and planets and all the host of heaven," Elijah would be the War-lord's flamboyant right arm. To be eaten by dogs was, for example, the odd fate this warrior from the constellation Great Dog wished on Queen Jezebel (1 Kings 21.23–24).[17] Indeed, he was forever flaring up, going up mountains to meet his Commander. He had but to open his mouth and fire fell out of the sky. At the end of his career, he was pulled up to the sky in "chariots of fire" by "horses of fire."

Elijah also dominated the rains and so the rivers. When he said no rain should fall, there followed three years of drought. When he countermanded the order, "down came the rain" (Ecclesiastes 48.1–3; Luke 4.25).

As the paradoxical regent of both fire and rain, Elijah was a fit figuration for the paradoxical "eighth planet" and therefore, in the genealogy of myth, brother to the banished Goddess. The family traits are clear. Ishtar's sign was the eight-pointed star, and tradition would fix Elijah in place as overseer of circumcision rites performed on the eighth day of a boy's life.[18] Indeed, a chair for him as overseer of that ritual is seen in at least one Jerusalem synagogue literally painted sky-blue and hung up high on the wall.

So here is a question: in appointing the Goddess's sibling to oversee the rite that signified her exorcism, didn't Jewish imagination turn upon itself and in so doing set in motion a momentous dialectic to be resolved only in the course of time?

Indeed, where there is contradiction, there will be movement toward its resolution. So myths generated by Sirius can be expected to contain a dynamic impulse toward future development. Thus, if Elijah supervises the covenanting blood-rite that initiated this World Age, so will he witness the cataclysmic transit to the next. For the event to come, that "great and terrible day" (Malachai 4.5), a chair for him is drawn up empty at every Passover table in the world.

And finally, as Sirius had first been the Goddess's blazon, then the signal-star of her rejection, so in the future, according to my reading of the scriptural mystery, it would herald her reemergence in a radiant new form.

✦ ✦ ✦

Abraham set up horned altars in many sites as he followed a course that fluctuated like a compass needle, hunting the Lord.

North he had come out of Ur, then west, then south. Then he traveled on south to Egypt and north again by the sea route to Hebron, where he died and was finally joined to the sky by the oaken World Tree that grew beside his tomb. To that burial place, Jews and Moslems make pilgrimage together, or did, and may again, religious wars permitting. Pilgrims go down a flight of stairs into the crypt to pray. But no one may descend to the deepest crypt, where Abraham sleeps on the shore of the abyss waiting for the returned Lord to bring him up to life again.

With the building and dissemination of a "theoretically infinite number" of microcosmic altars on it, the earth was readied for the Lord's arrival. Still His arrival must be rehearsed many times, each time as a miracle appearance bringing the promise of rescue from death. His final emergence into full visibility would bring affirmation that the sons of Polestar were both rescued and redeemed.

Approaching materiality but not yet enclosed in form, He hovered in a state of unstable fusion. His arrival was signaled by bizarre flashes of imagery and elusive snatches of language. On the ground, He blazed in the bush (Exodus 3.2). On the mountain, He shook with killing energy. Gradually He was coming closer, penetrating the earth's atmosphere.[19]

ASIAN thought supports a plasmic luxuriance of images—saints and gods, impacted animal and plant forms—held in solution, as it were, in the myths that for ages defined the limits of being. But in the West, the range of the mind's play has often been self-limited by the notion that cognitive truth can be had about a Creator God outside nature. Western thought then can move like closing jaws on the imagination, to give its output the hardness and monist singularity of stone.

Before he was enclosed in material form, the Lord moved invisible and alone. His loneness was total, like that of an Indian Holy Man on the road.

So alone, He longed to be found and loved. He was forever knocking at the clouds from behind, wanting to be let in. He wanted His family around him, and cymbals to welcome Him home. He wanted a house, where He could warm himself at a fire.

When He went away, His whereabouts were unknown. He left no message and was not to be found in the sky or on earth.

When He reappeared, He gloried in His trumpeting arrival. He was given to bursts of outrage if He was not so received. Secretly, He felt shamed by His past, when He had been in subjection to females or sodomic overlords (Joshua 5.9). He tried to wipe these memories from the record. Then His voice might fluctuate between wrath and remorse. For though He was stubborn and punitive, in hindsight He was always reevaluating His nature, even after causing an uproar, trying to use His powers in a way He called "righteous."

He was, in all these ways, a father like many who have lived on earth.

Moses sought the form of the Lord on the mountain and saw a Presence in sapphire-blue air (Exodus 24.10). He captured the Presence in stone and brought it down from the heights. Tradition has the Tablets doubled and arched at the top: bicameral lobes of Mosaic thought. Paradoxical entities, hinges between air and earth like all constructive thought, they were twice offered in the myth (Exodus 24.12; 33.27–29): the Lord wrote on the first set, Moses on the second, just as, back in the beginning, imagination conceived that God must make man twice over.

Now the Lord entered the arc of his pilgrimage that crossed the plane of the earth. On Mount Sinai, he gave Moses the blueprint for a transit vehicle. In historic fact, the details of Tabernacle and Ark came from Canaanite prototypes based, in turn, on Mesopotamian models of shrines and thrones. But what was thunderingly original about the Ark was that it would move.

"Make me a sanctuary," said the Lord. "Make an Ark" (Exodux 25.8–31). It would be an oblong box of never-withering acacia wood overlaid with never-tarnishing gold. In one end would ride His never-perishing mind.

Every piece of furniture for the Tabernacle was specified by the Lord. "Make a table," He said. "Make a lamp-stand of pure gold.

"Weave linen with violet, purple and scarlet yarn, embroider it with cherubim. Make hangings of goats' hair. Make a Veil of linen. Fasten it with hooks of gold . . .''

The curtains were to be five on each side, twenty in all, sewn into two sections so "the Tabernacle will be in a single whole." The "court of the Tabernacle" would be "oriented to the quarters." There would be "pure olive oil beaten for the light, to cause the lamp to burn always."

A structural part of this microcosmos was the priest's costume (Exodus 28.4–43). It too came from earlier Mesopotamian prototypes. It was stiff and of one piece, with a hole at the top for the head. Over all went an apron. Atop that went a breastplate with four rows of gems engraved with the names of the twelve tribes. On Moses' own costume "the whole world was represented; the glories of the fathers were engraved on his four rows of precious stones, and Thy majesty was in the diadem upon his head."

The priestly dress was to be embroidered with scarlet pomegranates. He would be afire with jewels and achime with golden bells, himself the standing axis for the wheel of tribes. Like the Indian Holy Man on the road, this man might well say, "I am the Temple."

And like the Holy Man, the priest must annihilate sexuality to fulfill his structural function. His sexual parts were to be wrapped in linen lest he "incur guilt and die." At the same time, he carried close to his body in a pouch two mysterious stones, the Urim and Thummim, tokens of male gender and perhaps, more remotely, fossil remembrances of old El Shaddai's breasts.

The Ark and its paraphernalia would be a never-failing image in the pilgrimage of thought through what biblical scholars call the typologies of Jewish and Christian myth. The Ark was itself a transparency laid over the original Cosmos, the Garden of Eden, and Noah's ship.[20] It was a metaphor for that which both moves and encloses and thereby saves, "a shadow from the heat . . . and a covert from storm" (Isaiah 4.6). In time, it would be overlaid by transparencies of the sacred city of Jerusalem and its Temple. Eventually it would burgeon with new formulations: the Virgin's womb, Christ's tomb, the church and the synagogue. Eventually it would even deconstruct back into the particles of fire and thought it came out of, so that by the late age of Christian mythos there would be on earth as many "arks" as there were reliquaries with bits of magical bone, wood, blood, or thread.[21]

But back when the myth was new and the descent of Polestar a fresh intuition, the Ark was singular. Each night in the desert the whole theater was unloaded and set up in the sand. The twelve tribes of Israel, as scripture says, camped around it, three on each of its four sides. Then, as candles warmed the air in the Tent, a cloud of glowing mist could be seen so even Moses dared not enter. In the morning, if the weather loomed and the cloud was still there, the people stayed put. If the cloud was gone, they packed the furniture and continued their desert march. By its gathering and vanishing, the cloud led the way for the tribes. But each night, the Tent with the Tablets would be laid out on the ground in the center of the twelve tribes sleeping.

All night, it would glow in their midst.

The tribes had dreamed it up, and it was their dream.

✦ ✦ ✦

The course of the Lord's pilgrimage may be visualized as a tilted orbit that intersects the earth-plane, then bends off and away through the upper dome of the Cosmos. It led Him away from Mount Sinai with Euclidian clarity, cutting through the contradictions, countermovements, errors, and failures that would have characterized actual history.

The process of the twelve tribes' transition from nomadic to agricultural, then urban life, has not yet been fully charted by historians. But it seems agreed that an original cultic tradition, represented by the cosmic trope of twelve tribes around a single shrine, survived these centuries as an axis of social formation.[22] Following in the steps of Moses who followed the Ark, the tribes moved northwards like a twelve-spoked wheel called "Israel," out of the Sinai into Canaan and toward Jerusalem.

Ark and wheel came to the River Jordan. Like the Ganges, Euphrates, and Nile, it is, in myth, one of the world's "heavenly rivers" that descend from mountainous highlands, course the plane of the earth, and empty into the abyss, rightfully named here the Dead Sea. A person who stands midstream of this river dominates the Three Worlds and can make the river stop running, or let it go again.

Into its stream the priests carried the Ark and stood still while the waters "piled up" above it leaving an earth-bridge, and "the nations crossed the Jordan." Thereafter, it fell to Joshua to reaffirm the integrity of the Cosmos. At his command, each tribe took a stone from the riverbed and with them made a circle. Then he himself took twelve more from the river and made a circle, and "they are there to this day." Then the contractual rite was enacted on the men who had not been circumcised during the desert wanderings. And in the same movement of myth, the twelve tribes celebrated their first "pilgrim feast" of Passover in the new land.

"Joshua" was now the name of the trajectory of the Pilgrim Ark. Joshua "captured," Joshua "massacred," Joshua "turned his forces" and "put to death." Joshua "killed" and "wiped them out." Joshua "plundered" and "put every living soul to the sword."

> Joshua took the whole country, the hill-country, all the Negeb, all the land of Goshen, the Shephelah, the Arabah and the Israelite hillcountry with the adjoining lowlands. . . . All were taken by storm . . . annihilated without mercy and utterly destroyed. (Joshua 11.16–20)

THE final approach of the Ark to its culmination was made in lurching stages. At Abu Gosh, it rested during the last skirmishes. Then David ordered it be carried up the rock called Moriah. But on the first try, a bearer struck his foot on a threshing stone there. Trying to save the holy box, the man touched it, and he died. Therefore it was sent back to a holding station for a quarter-year. Finally it was portaged up the mountain in a scene that, in all poetry of jubilation, has no equal: the young David dancing in no priestly pantaloons but only a smock and so brazenly, against all custom, flaunting his maleness in the face of his Father.

David was the eighth-born son of Jesse and so, as the star-wheel reminds us, of the lineage of the eighth planet, therefore the harbinger of other mystery figures outside the natural order, to come. In his historical lifetime, he was ruler of a small tribal community on the southern flank of present Mount Sion, outside the walls of what is now the Old City. But Ezekiel would describe the city as it stood in the minds of the myth-makers, turned square to the four directions, with three gates in each wall, one for each of the tribes. It would be known, said Ezekiel, as "The Lord is There."

WORK on the Temple began in the following reign, of King Solomon, in the month of April/May in the mythic 480th year after Exodus, which is a figure made of twelve generations of forty years each. The actual time is calculated to have been around 957 BCE. The ground plan again was given by the Lord though its ornament was again conventional of the time and region. The rectangular plot lay north-south, with gates on three sides. The eastern entry was framed with double doors: Mercy on the south and Repentance on the north, the two acts, one divine, one human, by which a person comes into correct alignment with the Lord.

The Temple faced that eastern gateway within a courtyard that opened to terraces, arcades, and noble staircases. The sanctuary was adorned with two forty-foot-tall bronze Pillars representing the northern and southern solstice points, and a bronze basin, held on the backs of twelve oxen, facing to the four quarters, and called "the Sea," for it held "all the springs of the great abyss."

Beyond these were:

an altar of gold and the table of gold,
And the lamp-stands of red-gold, five on the right side, five on the left . . .
the flowers, cups, snuffers . . . and the panels for the doors of the house, of gold. (1 Kings 7.48–50)

and the seven-branched candlestick that, as Josephus would say, "signified the seven planets."

When all was ready, the Ark was carried by the priests to the Temple and fixed into the walls of the sanctum so its long carrying-poles projected out the front of the stone structure (1 Kings 8.8). For this odd detail, there is an analogue not in Jewish myth but Hindu, where the fire-axis of the Cosmos is described as "a mountain of gold . . . passing through the middle of the earth and protruding on either side."[23]

Such now was cosmic Jerusalem, which would also be Christianity's heaven-mountain, "*mons coelius,* whereon sits the Pole star."

And so the installation of Polestar in His lock at the top of the cosmic axle-pole was accomplished. And soon in marvelous enlargements of the myth, the whole mountain beneath it was drawn into the iconographical figure: its crest, it would be said, had held the Garden of Eden. Down its flanks the four rivers of Paradise had flowed. Here too, after long wandering, Adam had died. His burial lay deep under its bedrock. Here the floodwater had spun as if out of an emptying tub into the abyss. It was with the stone used in David's time for threshing grain that the drainpipe was stoppered. And to that same stone, Abraham had found his way and offered Isaac to the Lord, who called for circumcision instead.

Abraham's elder but rejected son Ishmael would later on be claimed as progenitor by the followers of Muhammad, and so Islam too is rooted in the myths of Adam, Noah, and the first patriarch. Therefore on the wall of the Moslem Dome of the Rock in Jerusalem today is a line from the Koran affirming that the famous Foundation Stone lay in Eden and from it flow this world's sweet waters, though for devout Moslems that stone must be mystically doubled, since it exists in Mecca too: the even more famous Ka'ba.

THE dedication took place at the full moon of the month of Tishri, or September/October, time of grape and olive harvest-offerings and prayers for rain. Pilgrims thronged the city from as far as the Great Cataracts of Egypt, and as they gathered, a luminous cloud filled the sanctum and "cherubim spread their wings over the place."

Gifts were then made to the Temple, on this day some 20,000

oxen and 120,000 sheep to be sacrificed. It must have been a river of blood that day and the days after while the Temple stood, a dreadful foreshadowing of human blood that would flow in Jerusalem's streets in time to come. But there was water to wash it away, for underfoot lay great chambers from where building stones had been quarried, and these were turned into cisterns for rainwater to the amount of twelve million gallons. But that figure, again, is a holistic one and signifies that under the Foundation Stone were seas of both life and death: "The sacred sea has many sweet rivers flowing into it. Yet . . . its waters are bitter since universal death is attached to it. Yet when these waters flow outward, they are sweet." So would say the mystical text of the Zohar centuries hence.

Myth then would wrap Solomon in what Northrop Frye called the "royal metaphor," for his crown reflected celestial light and, seated on his ivory and gold throne on a platform bearing twelve gold lions, he was indeed Polestar's representative on earth. When he went traveling in his palanquin, his train could be seen from afar "like a column of smoke," which was the same trope used for the Ark in the old days.

This was the high, golden moment of the pilgrimage myth of the Lord, the station of His orbit to which humanity would be waiting for Him to return long into the future.

At that future time, His herald would come from the east, from where now came the pale pink-yellow glimmers of dawn against the walls of the Temple. Silver horns then sounded, and the cries of watchmen and priests set up their antiphon:

Is the sky lit up as far as Hebron?
It is lit up as far as Hebron!
The sun shines already!

Then trumpets took up the cry and the first sacrifice of the morning was bled toward the north of the altar.[24]

The Lord had come out of the darkness of the Teman and the wilderness of Mount Paran to pour His light over Jerusalem, the

One for whom the ways of the eternal skies were "for his swift flight" (Habakkuk 3.3–4).

✦ ✦ ✦

It is the fate of the imagination sometimes to be trapped in the very structures it invents. The patriarchs conceived the myth of a Polestar mobile through the skies, approaching and finally arriving on earth. But the laws of celestial mechanics grind on. Mobility is the law of the sky, of pilgrimage, and of the mind. Stars cannot be stopped, and thought has its own momentum.

The Lord, as a construct of thought, understood this natural condition. He who had been a wayfarer, coming out of the dark like a wind, standing over Sinai like a flame, traveling north in the Ark, in scriptural fact approached His installation in a Temple with a troubled mind. "Down to this day I have never dwelt in a house. . . . I made my journey in a tent and a tabernacle. . . . Did I ever ask any of the judges why they had not built me a house of cedar?" (2 Samuel 7.5–9)

The priests who sealed this Pilgrim into the Temple sealed their own fate. The standing stones would stand on after the Pilgrim would be gone.

In Judeo-Christian history, the courses of fact and myth run together, sometimes intersecting, sometimes running apart. But the authors of scripture forever make it seem that facts were charged with predestined fatality.

After Solomon's death, his realm fell into northern and southern halves. In the end, Israel, in the north, was lost to Assyria. The south, Judea, became an Assyrian vassal. By the time Josiah came to the throne of Judah, in the seventh century BCE, divergent cults had taken root in the city. There were shrines to Canaanite deities outside the city gates and statues of sun-horses by the Temple gate. And the star-worshiping women went about their old customs

We will burn sacrifices to the queen of heaven and pour offerings to her as we used to do . . . for we then had food in plenty and no calamity touched us. But from the time we left off burning sacrifices to the queen of heaven, we have been in great want, and in the end, we have fallen victims to sword and famine. (Jeremiah 44.15–20)

Throughout the century, struggle between superpowers Egypt and Babylonia spread fear throughout the Near East. Eventually Babylon "stood at the gateway to the country." When Jerusalem was softened by starvation, Nebuchadnezzar's soldiers broke its gates. The Temple was burned and the people's homes. The walls of the city were torn stone from stone, though a few that stood on bedrock were hard to topple. The bronze Pillars of the sun and the great Sea were taken to Babylon and never heard of again. By the Euphrates, from where Tereh and Abram had departed more than a thousand years before, the Lord's sons and daughters mourned in song what they had called into poetic being and lost to force of arms.

The destruction had taken place on the ninth day of the lunar month of Av, or July/August. The actual day fell at the end of August, or so myth preserves the date, and considering the logistics of war it may be correct. For Av covers the deep trough of late summer, when survival itself depends on the whims of rain-spirits. In time to come and by the procedures of myth, the date would absorb into itself also the destruction of the Second Temple and later the disastrous defeat of a false messiah in the second century of the present era. By then, Tishah be-Av, the ninth day of Av, would have become as a fault on the wheel of time, swollen by those later events till it would come round each year with a groan, as if the whole mill might break apart on that day.

IT was after the destruction of Solomon's Temple that the circular form of the pilgrimage theme—its inherent geometry and inevitable end—was formulated and back-entered into earlier scripture. Thereafter, accounts of past triumphs were given the resonance of tragedy in the making, as if in the prophetic mind from the beginning had been the theophany of an uncontainable Pilgrim, now impelled on and away, once again the lonely traveler beyond call of those who had conceived Him.

With every new prophetic voice trumpeting the pilgrim Polestar's rage with those on earth who had failed to hold Him in place, the antiphon was rung again between the cosmic vastness into which He was moving and the helplessness of His sons to change His fate, or theirs. The post-Exilic Prophets had even to return to the ancient imagery of Genesis, when the unknown presence was forcing its way into consciousness; now the *mysterium tremendum* was moving off, and Ezekiel foresaw how out of the north would descend the whirlwind, Gog out of Magog:

> The end, the end, it comes, it comes.
> Doom is coming upon you . . . (Ezekiel 7.6–7)

Prophetic language reached its apogee in these meditations on the paradox at the core of Judeo-Christian theology: that humanity is nothing in the scale of the Cosmos and yet is responsible for its fate there. There is neither justice nor compassion in these recriminations and lamentations, which echo through later history reaching new resonance in our time, when masses of people on earth most helpless to change their lives bear the added burden of being blamed for their condition.

Classical Judaism today still addresses itself to this existential rupture and the resulting "vast abyss, conceived of as absolute, between God . . . and Man."[25] Contemplating the Lord today, a modern Jew may confess he "mainly perceives the remoteness . . . the only framework in which, in his aloneness and his search, [he] will find himself."[26]

Even so, through the centuries, the long-range promise of the pilgrimage orbit held like a steel cord stretched around steel poles, and still it holds for the religious believer. For long, long after His departure, the life-saving Lord would come round to this place again, only from the opposite direction, and therefore then say the reverse:

I am against *you*, Gog Prince of Rosh, Meshech and Tubal.
I will turn you about and put hooks in your jaws.
I will fetch you from the far north and bring you to the mountains
of Israel . . . and give you as food to the birds of prey . . . (Ezekiel
38.1–3; 39.1–3).[27]

By the end of the sixth century BCE, refugees were returning from
Babylon in numbers, though many wandered elsewhere and were
lost to the regrouping nation. By various traditions held today, the
Lost Tribes found their ways to the Americas, to Spain, Africa,
India, and even China. Those who returned to Jerusalem lived
thereafter by the Mesopotamian calendar with its autumnal New
Year, in place of the Egyptian and Canaanite spring-oriented one
that had been theirs, perhaps since Joseph went down to the Pha-
raoh's court.

In 515 BCE there took place a reconsecration ceremony in Jerusalem's restored Temple grounds, in which twelve goats were killed
to expiate the sins of the tribes during the dispersion. Though it
would be often said that five things were missing from the Second
Temple—the Ark, the Holy Fire, the Shekinah, and the Urim and
Thummim—the cosmic figure of twelve still held as a sign of hope
in eventual reunion.

ANCIENT astronomical notions may shed light on later Jewish
response to the fall of the Temple and the loss of the Ark.

Say that the polar star was seen drifting away from its expected
location in space: then that site might be said to have lost its
embodiment in light, that is, its very *star-ness*. Then the north pole
would appear to be, as indeed it is in fact, but a theoretical point
in the skies and so in the searching mind.

Then later tradition wound around that natural fact a descant
of holy magnificence. It was proposed that, when such a rupture
of point and light took place in Polestar's case, there was left behind
but a reminiscent gleam shed off no present light source, to which
Kabbalists of the Middle Ages would give a name, and, signifi-
cantly, feminine gender: the Shekinah.

While the Lord stood in His Temple over this plane of earth, these mystic writers proposed, the Shekinah had been His nimbus. Between that Pilgrim and His cape of light there was no separation; nor had there been from the beginning.

> Long ago, before earth,
> When there was yet no ocean . . .
> Before the mountains, before the hills, I was born.
> When he fixed the canopy of clouds overhead . . . I was at his side,
> His darling and delight. (Proverbs 8.22–23).

But as momentum impelled Him out of human experience, the Shekinah was torn from His body and fell into nature. There she lives in hiding still, a gleam without heat, sparks without fuel, a whirr in the ears after wings have gone beating by. The poets have said all these things of her.[28]

Still today, the mystical Jew thinks of Jerusalem as a woman abandoned by a man, specifically a widow.[29] In the Old City, he discovers her aged glittering body, her limestone flesh, her old groined arches, her domes like knees and breasts. She whispers to him as he mourns at the Wall, and he reaches out to touch her with his hands.

But the abandoned woman's forms are cold and drain a body's heat. The city has, indeed, an uncanny mineral glow as of light without fire, fire without tinder. Even Jerusalem's flowers are burning-cool: orange tulips, golden poppies, violet hyacinths. And the sky can be the very lapis-blue that Moses saw on Sinai.

For the devout, Jerusalem is haven for the Shekinah, who is always longing to be found by the Lord, as He is, by her. Reunion, the mystical resolution foreordained back in the Abrahamic Age, is the destination for both Lord and Lady, as it is for all believing Jews.

THE theme of the Lord's return toward that place of reunion also takes on logic in the light of ancient lore. For as Polestar moves on an orbit in the enclosed Cosmos, so He will surely return. Then the Messiah or Prophet—according to Jewish, Moslem, or Christian theology—will come into sight as Polestar's herald, flying ahead of Him on the track that will bring him back from beyond comprehension into human experience.

In living memory and imitation of Polestar's journey toward and then appearance in Jerusalem, the Judeo-Christian pilgrimage gatherings—Passover, Shavuot, Succoth or Tabernacles, and Easter—take place, timed to lunar and solar events. And the Moslem holy month of Ramadan is inaugurated by the appearance of the new moon.[30]

Like all pilgrims on earth, Jews, Moslems, and Christians add the momentum of their feet to the turning of the cosmic sphere. In all pilgrimage systems East and West, responsibility lies with the people to keep the wheels of the Cosmos turning to bring on the great return.

◆ ◆ ◆

Faithful observance of Jewish customary laws that regulate the days, the years, and larger cycles of time was a factor in the survival of Jewish society over millennia.

Myth served social utility in this case by providing theological support for a code of behavior. If the Lord Himself was subject to celestial law, the people must be subject to laws of behavior revealed in the Commandments and enlarged on by men filled with His spirit. The larger principle to be deduced is that human existence is subject to a larger law than individual happiness or salvation, or the extinction of pain. Concentration on a collective end, fidelity to the laws of the course, persistence, and hope: these were some of the bylaws binding equally on the Lord and on the people.

If the Lord's pilgrimage took place on the great precessional wheel that turns once in a World Age, the people must master an intricate system of smaller temporal wheels to bring him back. On the rhythm of these quicker returns, the Jewish sacred year, with its many holy hours and days, is built.

THE annual wheel in Jewish tradition turns to the measure of the Torah, which includes the "whole thought" of the Lord communicated through Moses. Each Sabbath the year around, one passage of Torah is read in synagogues, beginning and ending on the same day. Thus the twelve-spoked wheel still turns around the Lord.

But around that beat, there wind counterpoints based on the lesser figure seven and also its components, four and three. Again, one has to put a modern eye to the past to see how our ancestors saw time in the Cosmos as a dance with the Lord in the center and His children around Him in a circle, taking seven steps this way, seven that and, after each seventh step, holding still for a fraction of time-out-of-time, as a pendulum stops at the terminus of each arc.

Thus seven are the days in the week and the seventh is Sabbath, when time is perfect and has nowhere more to go, and so stands still. Thus seven songs are sung in the synagogue on Sabbath eve and seven candles lit in the menorah. And in the mystical lore of the Kabbalah, there are seven ways of writing the unnameable name of God.

Each seventh year, moreover, brings back a Holy Year, when in the Cosmos, sky and earth melt together to make a single field of sacred time and space, wherefore all earthly fields are to be considered "ownerless and available to all." And the year after seven Holy Years, each fiftieth as it comes around, is Jubilee, when all fields go back to the Lord as their owner, and no Jew on earth is to keep another Jew in captivity, for all belong only to God.

Then on the smaller wheel of the day, three times some seven hours apart, Jews are called to prayers, and the time of prayer is holy and considered not to move.

And thrice a year, in a loose seven-month period overlapping equinoxes and summer solstice, fall Passover, Shavuot, and Succoth.

Such is the immemorial Blakean dance of sevens around twelve-as-One, to which rites around the world still turn. This to me is the meaning of the vision of Ezekiel, of wheels within wheels whose hubs "have the power of sight" and whose rims were "full of eyes," for truly the "spirit of the living creature was in the wheels" (Ezekiel 1.15–21).

THE wheels are of time and also of space. For at the three Pilgrim Feasts, all Jews—all that is save deafmutes, imbeciles, those "of doubtful sex . . . double sex, women and slaves"—must render themselves to Jerusalem or its correlative, an Ark that contains Tablets containing the Torah. For Jerusalem was in the past and still is the hub of the wheels, and the pin at the center of the hub was and is the Foundation Stone in the Temple.

> The land of Israel is in the middle of the earth,
> Jerusalem is in the middle of Israel,
> The Temple is in the middle of Jerusalem,
> The Holy of Holies is in the middle of the Temple,
> And the Stone of Foundation is in front of the Holy of Holies.[31]

During the Second Temple period, the wheels of approach to the city drew pilgrims from the ends of the earth. In the old desert-wandering days, attendance on the Tabernacle had consisted of a simple "reiyah" or presentation of oneself before it. But when the Temple stood on the mountain, attendance on it was called "aliyah," a going-up on foot, a literal pilgrimage. During the periods of Exile and later Diaspora, the scattered people prayed to be gathered again "from the four corners" to the shrine. And now that the Temple's Wall, at least, is accessible to pilgrims again, a Jew making pilgrimage there says he is "making aliyah."[32]

All Jewish ritual still takes place with reference to Jerusalem. Only on the wheel of sacred space that interlocks with the wheel of sacred time are space and time even to be considered real. Life in the "galut," for outsiders who do not turn on the holy wheels, is null and a-human, void of meaning, a mere illusion of life.

THE three Pilgrim Feasts (Exodus 23.16)—rooted in prehistory but given formal structure and liturgy during the five centuries of the Second Temple's life and still celebrated almost universally by secular Jews as well as the devout—function powerfully in two respects. They enforce social and ideological cohesion among separated Jewish communities, and they function vertically to hold these Diaspora groups to their ancient roots. For the symbolism of these events is rooted in pagan agricultural custom though doctrine has evolved to engage changing ethical and psychological matters. Furthermore, for the religious male who presents himself at the Wall or at a synagogue at these seasons, there is a foreshadowing of utopia, when it will be "as if he had received the Shekinah."

Farmers around the eastern Mediterranean have always required light dews in the spring and pelting rains in autumn. Even now, Jewish liturgy at the equinoxes, repeated no matter where on earth, echoes those old local needs for spring dew and autumn rain.

The spring Passover ceremony echoes distant blood-sacrifice of first-born sons, spring lambs and first-cut sheaves of barley. Historically, it commemorates the rescue from blood-sacrifice of the tribes as they fled Egypt. The secular Jew may celebrate by that ritual meal the psycho-historical ancestral journey and so, perhaps, the singularity of Jewish experience.

The summer and autumn Feasts of Shavuot and Succoth, which coincide with pagan midsummer and equinoctial sacrifices to star- and rain-spirits, contain references to old anxieties and enmities. Shavuot comes seven times seven days plus one after Passover, in the hot month of June / July, when Abraham's descendants were forbidden to contract marriages lest they conceive a child by a demoness by mistake. But it is also a feast of thanksgiving, harking back to the wheat harvest in long-ago Egypt and Canaan, and so a foreshadowing of the harvest by Moses of the Torah on Mount Sinai.

After Shavuot, time runs downhill into the baleful month of Av with its nadir day of the ninth, Tishah be-Av, which hides in its name a spark of the unruly rain-star. On that day, in rural communities, Jewish children still bury wooden swords in graveyards and superstitious adults bathe not at all for fear of contamination from water-spirits. But in a larger sense, mourning is then enacted for all the historic catastrophes that have befallen the nation.

Time then flows on toward the lunar month Tishri that enfolds the autumn equinox when, "throughout the ancient world, the days were marked by rites of mortification, purgation and renewal."[33] The new moon of the month marks Rosh Hashanah, the New Year's celebration of joyful hope, when bread is baked in the shape of a ladder so the good can climb it to heaven, or else round like David's crown or the circumference of the Cosmos in which David reigned. Ten days later comes Yom Kippur, when the Jew, mindful of Abraham's acceptance of circumcision, must submit to ritual atonement. Then while the Temple stood, a scapegoat for the desert-demon Azazel was sent off the cliff to its death.

While that fasting and confessing is proceeding, the moon in the sky waxes full and in its fullness is celebrated Succoth, when new-ripe grapes and olives were bestowed on the Temple and today males in a family may sleep outdoors in huts of palm, myrtle, and willow branches, in memory of the days of desert wandering. A mystery rite performed in antiquity on that day, however, revealed its cosmic reference. While the Temple stood, a priest dipped a golden urnful of sweet water out of a spring below the walls, carried it up to the sacred enclosure, and poured it on the ground, while the area was illumined by thousands of candles.

Soon after Succoth comes Simhat Torah, when the year-round reading of the sacred texts is both finished and begun again; and then, at the winter solstice, Hanukkah is celebrated with the lighting of candles; and on the full moon of early spring comes Purim; and finally the full moon of the first month after the spring equinox brings Passover around again.

So in the old times and now, the glorious road to Jerusalem was both real and also a metaphor for a life integrated into the cosmic cycles, a life functional in a transcendent sense and fully lived in a personal sense. Of that road, Isaiah wrote in both senses:

> There shall be a causeway there which shall be called the Way of Holiness ... it shall become a pilgrim's way. ... By it, those He has ransomed shall return and the Lord's redeemed come home. ... (Isaiah 35.8–10)

The message, in secular terms, is that human life has a purpose. In spite of the ancestral deaths by which each new life is purchased, that life is neither a blind biological adventure nor absurd. The purpose in living is to contribute to the long communal enterprise, for thereby the wheel is turned that advances humanity toward whatever abstract and general destiny it may signify by the simple word *father*.

✦ ✦ ✦

Owing to the multitude of pilgrims who visited it, the Second Temple of Jerusalem acquired world renown. When it had stood for two centuries, Alexander visited it and was struck by the sight of the priest in Mosaic costume with a gold plaque on his brow engraved with the name of God. The young emperor did no harm to the place and the routine of ritual went on, though in his wake came Hellenistic culture that would change the world.

In the reign of the Greek-minded Seleucid King Antiochus Epiphanus IV, an attempt was made to bring Jewish rites into conformity with pagan ones. Circumcision was banned and an altar to Zeus built in the Temple grounds. When, in 168 BCE, Jewish worship was declared illegal, the people revolted and won back their rights. The Temple was purified and the new celebratory feast of Hanukkah was added to the calendar.

But Rome was now on the horizon. Her first armies entered Asia Minor in 190 BCE. A century and a half later, Pompey invaded Palestine and, in 37, Herod was made overlord of Judea and set himself up as king. Jerusalem was his throne-city. With magnificent zeal, until he died, he pushed forward its reconstruction in Roman style. By pounding down and shoring up ruins dating even from Solomon's time, he provided a buildable base of some thirty-six acres, supported by massive retaining walls piled up without mortar, for none was required between stones that weighed tons. Over two great arched causeways, traffic flowed into the city and to the Temple that, according to Josephus, was so overlaid with gold that one who tried to look at it close by would be blinded, while from afar it looked like a snowcapped mountain.

Of stone the walls and shrines of Herod's city were built, but the events that led to their final destruction are still cloudy. A fateful pattern was repeated at least three times. Each time, apocalyptic myth was reinforced, and the city and population suffered again.

In 70 CE, Titus, son of the new emperor Vespasian, marched on the city in response to an uprising. The season was Passover. Memories of Exodus and later escapes and triumphs of a mythologized history kept the people in a restive mood. Titus sent the Romanized Jew Josephus into the city to try to make peace, but his efforts failed. The cordon tightened. Summer drew on and people began to die of thirst and hunger.

In the month of Av of historic disaster, the walls were breached. Some sources say over a million people died in the siege. The city was razed again save for Herod's watchtowers and a few courses of wall too heavy to topple. Titus sailed for Rome and triumphal procession with the treasures of the Temple, including the branched candlestick of gold. The scene of plundering was eventually carved in high relief on his memorial Arch, and Vespasian installed the relics in a Temple of Peace in Rome, all save the Tablets of the Law and the Veil of the sanctuary. These he kept in his palace, from where, in a later time, it is said, they were vandalized and passed out of human experience.

THE collapse of the thousand-year-old axis of Judaism carried the society with it. Taxes, instead of flowing to the Temple, were sent to Rome and the Temple of Jupiter Capitolinus. The bureaucracy that had served pilgrimage was wiped out. On Polestar's field, the jackals that the Prophets always took for harbingers of disaster had free play.[34]

All the same, a remnant regrouped in the nearby city of Jabneh, and though the Pilgrim Feasts could not be observed with joy any more, they still served their end of affirmation of theoretical nationhood, and on these occasions, many drifted back to Temple Mount to lament among its ruins.

Fairly soon in short, recovery, with Roman aid, seemed on the way. Fields were planted, cities rebuilt, roads laid down, and trade with the East, especially India now, brought new ideas and money. The destruction, some might say, had even released productive energy. Yet opposition to imperial law continued, first underground, then in widespread anarchic revolt. In fact, the ancient, iron-hard myth structure of pilgrimage, with its associated faith in the Pilgrim Lord's millennial return, played its part in the deteriorating situation, so that violence mounted and, this time, true apocalypse came swiftly on. To push a question: how far does this myth still affect political destiny, by implanting structures in the minds of millions that must be fulfilled in historical time?

ONE has only to think of Middle Eastern politics today to know how hostilities can mount over small cultish insults. If a Roman idol was installed one day on Temple Mount, zealous defenders of the faith responded with acts of terrorism.[35] When Hadrian came to power there was brief hope of his allowing the Temple to be rebuilt. But while touring Palestine in 130 CE, he decided instead to restore Jerusalem as a center of Roman authority. So he did, making it a showplace of Roman architecture and a center for the forcible imposition of Greco-Roman culture on the region.

Now the end was coming, as Ezekiel had foretold. And it came in part over the same issue Antiochus had raised three hundred years before: the outlawing of circumcision.

To the Hellenistic mind, circumcision may have seemed an oddity, a tribal endurance test. In fact, many Jews were dispensing with it, even undergoing dangerous plastic surgery to obscure it, especially athletes who wanted to compete in nude games without prejudice.[36] But from the time of the stone circles of Canaan, the rite had carried overtones of cosmic urgency. The curve of blood defined a sacred bond, and the act had enlarged into a metaphor for the purification of thought that precedes moral action. "Take away the foreskins of your heart . . . lest my fury come forth like fire," said Jeremiah.

It was at this crossroads of myth and political fanaticism that the famous Rabbi Akiva—then in his ninetieth year—threw in his lot with one among many who called themselves, in those days, messiah. This one was named Simeon, but renamed "Son of Star." Whether Akiva believed it when he said, "This is the King Messiah," he saw come down on his people the final destruction out of the north which Ezekiel had called Gog of Magog.[37]

Long before, it had been prophesied that a saving star would come out of Jacob (Numbers 24.17). So it had been awaited for centuries while, in astronomical fact, a new star had come to stand near the polar north. It is, on my star-wheel, Beta of Ursa Minor, called "mill-peg" by Arab astronomers. But its old name was Kochab. "Kochab . . . at different times in that epoch may have been considered the pole-star" says my astronomical guidebook.[38]

Was it then from Kochab that Simeon took his title "bar Kochba," Son of Star, as well as title to the illusion, and so led Israel on to annihilation?

The zealots were riding the rails of the myth. At first it seemed the revolt would sweep Palestine. But Rome, though distant, had time to spare. Legions were called from as far as Britain and as near as Egypt. At last they moved, and on the ninth of Av again, or so myth says, of the year 135, the revolution was crushed. Bar Kochba was killed with the rest. Akiva was tortured to death. A massacre followed, and a team of oxen plowed up the place where the Temple had stood. In its place was erected a Temple to Jupiter with a monumental statue of Hadrian, mounted on a horse, before it. The rest of the city was razed and its very name blotted out. The new city would be called Aelia Capitolina, and the land of Judea, Syria Palestina.

This time the Jews, under ban of circumcision and all other rites and ceremonies, exposed everywhere to revenge-persecution, were banned also from the city save for that one day of Av that now marked three holocausts. It would remain a day of lamentation, Tishah be-Av, with its linguistic echo of the herald-star that had again proved false. From dusk on the eve of that day till dusk of the next, the religious Jewish world still mourns. In old Russian homes, the mother might paint a black square—a mandala of utter ruin—on the wall nearest Jerusalem.[39] In Orthodox communities, men still read from the Book of Lamentations (1.8–15) lines filled with bitterness, ancient, mystical, and enduring, for the female. In these passages, the city is reviled as a woman raped. She is not, however, a victim to be pitied. She is responsible for her fall and despised for it. She is a "filthy rag," naked and cheap. She is broken and crushed, "like grapes in the press, the virgin daughter of Judah."

THOUGH it is doubtful that anyone in those chaotic days remembered the whereabouts of the tomb of the Jewish Jesus, dead a hundred years before, Christian apologists would eventually say of Hadrian that he built atop that tomb, to defile it, a temple to "the unclean she-devil Aphrodite." If it is true that he ordered a statue of the Seafoam-goddess on Moriah, as well as the equestrian portrait of himself and various Roman cult images, hers would have been a copy of the original by Praxiteles, which by then had stood for almost four hundred years on her island-shrine of Cnidus and which Hadrian copied also for his villa outside Rome. In both places, the marble stood in a small, round, and columned temple, and so it would have in Aelia Capitolina, one of the loveliest images in art history, whose mellow contours and downcast eyes seem still to speak of passing ages.

After the ravaging of the Temple and its environs, unrolled the centuries of intermittent horror that would destroy Hellenistic culture and break monotheistic myth from myth. The Jews, in principle, were still banned from their axial city when a new breed of pilgrims would travel there under a new imperial mandate. The first recorded Christ-worshiper of the new age, remembered only as the Pilgrim of Bordeaux, wrote in 333 that he had seen, "not far from the statues of Hadrian . . . a perforated stone to which the Jews come every year, anoint it, bewail with groans, tear their clothes and depart."[40]

A half-century later, the scholar and translator Jerome, in the contentious diction of one fully turned around by a new myth, wrote:

> On the day when Jerusalem was captured by the Romans, there can be seen the spectacle of the arrival of sorrowing folk—a stream of weak, old men and women, clad in rags and betraying by their demeanor and even by their outward appearance the wrath of God

. . . populum miserum et tamen non miserabilem, a miserable people yet not worthy of commiseration, weeping for the ruin of their Temple.[41]

✦ ✦ ✦

In history, politically important cities controlled the plains around them and so were worth fighting for. Jerusalem was a minor hill town off the main trade routes. Yet because in cosmic myth it affords access to the stars, it has been disputed for millennia by men of pilgrim mentality who sought not power but immortality there. Thanks to them, the city sits on what may be the deepest pit of shards, bones, and crushed illusions in the world.

From the time David danced the Ark into the city, it changed hands over thirty times, never in peace. Along the way, five years after the death of the Prophet Muhammad in 632, the first of his followers entered the city as its conqueror. It is still Islam that, by agreement with Jewish administration, holds jurisdiction over Temple Mount today, basing its claim to the site on old cosmic myth. The Prophet's horse—El Baruk or "Lightning"—carried him in a dream to the mountaintop from where he leapt up the seven spheres to Allah's very throne. Hoofmarks are visible on the Foundation Stone, say the Moslem keepers of it, and nearby, framed in gold, are hairs the Prophet let fly from his beard that night. Not far off, by the old double-arched eastern gate to the precincts, is the place where Muhammad is to meet with Christ on Judgment Day, whereafter the two in friendly cooperation will string a pulley up to the Mount of Olives, bring the dead down from their graves there, and weigh the souls in a set of hanging scales.

On the other hand, if numbers count, Jerusalem has always been only third in holiness for the Moslem, inasmuch as one prayer to Allah in that city is equal to 25,000 elsewhere, while one in Medina counts for 50,000, and one in Mecca, 100,000. In the cosmo-geography of Islam, the latter sacred city of course takes precedence over all others, for there Abraham and Ishmael installed, in the huge square Ka'ba, a smaller stone the angel Gabriel brought down from heaven. It was red at first and blazed like fire. But pilgrims' tears have turned it black, or else it was its night flight down the seven heavens that did that, for it is generally known to be a meteorite.

FED by turbulent social forces that fed in turn on their own myth, the Moslem tide—as it is justifiably called—rose with awesome speed. In 634 Damascus fell. In 638, Antioch. In less than a century, Egypt, North Africa, and Spain were under Moslem rule and southern France was being harried by invaders.

In 638 Jerusalem too fell to the Prince of Believers, Caliph Omar. He cleaned the sanctuary area of a couple of Early Christian installations, built a small mosque on the site of sites, and gave permission for seventy Jewish families to resettle in the city. Some fifty years later, Caliph Abdul Malek did what no Christian had presumed to do. He raised "seven times the revenue of all Egypt" and built a magnificently refined structure, the Dome of the Rock, over the Foundation Stone. His son would erect a smaller mosque, El Aksa, "the far-off place," a little beyond. Still today, Malek's eight-sided, mosaic-rich shrine gives place to as many myths as the Temple did, providing niches for prayers to be sent skyward to Abraham, David, Solomon, Elijah, and Gabriel.

From time to time, depending on the benevolence of Moslem—and later briefly Christian—overseers, shards of the nation Israel would reassemble in Jerusalem, then be broken back and banished from it again. So during the Diaspora centuries, the myth of the high and gold-crowned city survived as a distant dream and an unending longing. A Jew dying far away might ask for a few grains of Jerusalem earth to be sprinkled in his coffin, and some people went into their graves with twigs tied into their hands that might take root and grow out the other way. The medieval Sephardic poet Yehuda Halevi spoke for many who harbored the wish to go back to Jerusalem if only to die there.

> Who will make me wings that I may fly,
> That I may take my broken heart away
> And lay its ruins where thy ruins lie?[42]

Nowhere in the Diaspora had the Jews more cause to feel secure both in their attachment to mystical Jerusalem and also to actual place than in Spain. So when in 1492, on the day of the ninth of Av of dread memory, the last of them bowed to the order of Expulsion, they experienced again the fundamental trauma of their history. Nor was earthly Jerusalem open to Jews under the Ottoman Empire save for occasional visits. It was a Turk, the last of the strong Moslem rulers of Jerusalem, who in the sixteenth century erected the walls that ring the Old City today and, over Jaffa Gate, the stone that announces, "There is No God but Allah."

During the last four hundred years until the present half-century, Orthodoxy in Europe grew inward in its hold on Torah and synagogue, while in Palestinian Safed and certain eastern European ghetto communities, the movements of Kabbalah and Hasidism, one esoteric and cosmological, the other popular and ecstatic, would provide forms for the longing for transcendence that rabbinical codes might fail to satisfy. Surely the alienation of the Jew from his sacred shrines and the frustration of his historic desire to go on pilgrimage enforced his bent toward mysticism. Already long since, subtle transformation had been worked on Jewish thought by Platonizing influences, so that it was said that that wonderful Temple, so distant in actual space and time, had existed "prior to all created things," that it still did exist in a timeless mode and so could never be truly destroyed.[43]

It had also entered Jewish thought that, from the beginning, there had existed an essence or form companionable with the Lord that was called Wisdom, feminine and beloved. This Wisdom was "so pure." She was "like a fine mist." Passing everywhere, she possessed

> true understanding of things as they are: a knowledge of the structure of the world . . . the beginning and end of epochs and their middle course; the alternating solstices and changing seasons; the cycles of the years and the constellations; the nature of living creations and . . . the thoughts of men. (Wisdom of Solomon 7.17–20)

This Wisdom, was she not an imaginative gloss on the ancient perception of starlight—love for which the people had been exhorted to cut out of their hearts—here reentering consciousness and language, eventually to be given the name Shekinah?

THE present nation Israel was born in blood as if again out of Exodus, and for two decades after its establishment the nation was partitioned off from its holy center. Then came bloodshed again, and on June 14 of 1967 Jewish military smashed through the surrounding gates and, in hours, word broke over the radio, "Temple Mount is ours! Repeat . . . the Temple Mount is ours!"

To this day, Orthodox Jews won't set foot there, however, because, politics aside, the turf is polluted by Moslem and Gentile presence. The Government of Israel has resisted pressure from extremists to take over the site, restricting itself to statements that the Temple will be rebuilt when the Messiah will have come. For fundamentalist Moslems and Christians, however, that first-light has already dawned, and what lies ahead is high noon and Holy War, when the Sons of Light and the Sons of Dark will fight in the Valley of Jehoshaphat till Adam's sin and Pilate's error are wiped out and the Age of Perfection returned.

When I was in the city, a berserk American Jew attacked the Moslem shrines on Temple Mount with a rifle. Over the citywide amplifying system that carries the muezzin's cries to prayer came a shrieking howl translated into my ear as, "You Moslems come! They are burning our Mount! You come from the streets, you come from all sides and protect it!"

That evening I sat in the garden behind the bone-white Crusader church of St. Anne's to hear vespers sung. I listened to the haunting vocal changes that, by ancient belief, drew down the setting sun and brought out the evening star. Nearby lay the Pool of Bethesda, where the suffering once gathered and there was, sometimes, says John (5.1–9), a "moving of the water" that brought cures. The sky was turning ever a darker blue when, suddenly, the cry of the muezzin came pouring out of the dusk. In Turkish times, every synagogue and church by law had to be vertically dominated by a nearby minaret, and many still are. Mournful and commanding, the cry fell through loudspeakers as if out of the stars into every corner of the shrouded city.

The following year, another party of zealots tried to blow up the Moslem shrines; they were financed by American evangelical Christian groups.

PERHAPS because of these tensions, collective myth and subjective experience seem to meet in this city as in only a few places on earth, one of them, Benares. For back when the field behind the Wall was filled with architecture and fire, it symbolized male and female in union, as does, in Benares, the play of light over the Ganges. Then out of the Jewish sages' long rumination on that union, ruptured, came recognition of other forms of rupture on the human scale and also how to heal them. The means, as the Hindu knows, is to grow together. "If your soul is to grow it must become a woman," says a midrash addressed to Jewish males.[44] To women the message is to receive the male in loving-kindness. Sexual union is a metaphor in Jewish liturgy for the Shekinah's reunion with the Lord. The coupling of brides and bridegrooms in Jerusalem spreads perfection, it is said, through all Zion.

When the seventh day comes on, the Jewish woman prepares her house and her body. When the sun has set and the evening star shines, the Shekinah comes out of hiding and waits. Then the woman takes a flame and lights the Sabbath candles, hiding her eyes from their unearthly gleam, and at that instant the Shekinah enters her house. Then the wheel of secular time ceases to move. The Jewish house is in eternity. Then man and wife are King and Queen, and their lovemaking that night is a religious act.

On Sabbath morning, the men depart the house for the synagogue. The double doors of the Ark, on the wall nearest Temple Mount, are opened. One man takes the Torah in his arms as if it were a woman and carries it around the congregation.[45] Other men reach out to lay a hand on it, for the upright wooden roller has the name Tree of Life.

At last the Torah is lifted onto a platform in the center of the synagogue. A man from the floor mounts the steps toward it. That religious act is understood to be a metaphor for the pilgrim's ascent to the original Temple. During all these hours of the men's attendance on the Torah, the women sit high up in their balcony as if hidden in clouds.

But afterward come the joinings of families again. And when the sun goes down on Sabbath night, silver incense burners and spice boxes in the shape of temples may be brought out. The incense drifts through the house and fades slowly, savored with regret for what is ending but with perfect confidence in its return.

That incense-laden smoke is Wisdom.

I would follow it now.

PART FOUR

Interregnum

◆

She said poetry and apotheosis are one . . .
Each matters only in that which it conceives.
Wallace Stevens:
THE PASTORAL NUN

◆

◆ ◆ ◆

Continuing my research into the roots and forms of pilgrimage, always following the lead of Shiva or Wisdom, I proceeded toward a crossroads, unknown to me yet, where my own subjective quest would merge with collective myth—the place and moment of revelation.

THE two centuries or so on either side of the year One are, by biblical scholars, called the Intertestamental Period. That transition was also, as my astronomy books and star-wheel affirm, "the interregnum as regards Pole-stars. Alpha Draconis had ceased to exercise that office. Alruccabah or Polaris had not yet assumed it."[1]

Then, stars turning on the great wheel were assuming positions with meaning for those who could read such things.[2] Then by the autumn equinox it was the Virgin's house that stood in the rising-sun position. "Now the Virgin returns," wrote Virgil. "A new generation descends from heaven ... a new golden race [shall] spring up throughout the world." Pagan antiquity saw Isis in that constellation, holding a corn sheaf in her hand, and Virgil saw her as herald of the primordial Golden Age, returning.[3]

Spring equinox too had moved now from Lamb to Fish, *ichthys*. Before long there would be those saying it was cosmic law that had brought up *Iesous Christos Theou Huios Soter,* Jesus Christ God's Son Savior, while letting the lamb-slayers, celebrators of Passover, sink into the past.

During these years, the Greek historian Plutarch set out to inquire "Why the oracles have ceased to speak." In the course of his essay, he recounted a tale current at the time. A ship at sea drifted by an island from where an unknown voice hailed the captain, saying that when he passed the next island along he must shout, "Great Pan is dead!" So the captain did, and at once there came from shore the sound of loud weeping.[4]

Scholars say the story only echoed common rites for the dying field-gods, though later it was picked up by Christian apologists to prove a point. Yet truly it has an eerie sound. The death of a world is being announced. The word comes out of nature, and is sent back into it, as an event in which humanity has no other role than transmitter.

It is true that the passing away of rites of paganism, including pilgrimage to the old shrines and oracles, was as much a sign of change as the destruction of the Temple in Jerusalem.

In pagan antiquity, the Cosmos spoke to pilgrims out of a multitude of mouths. It spoke to them in star-diagrams and smoke and fire, in the helical entrails of animals and the flight patterns of birds. It spoke through the human voices of oracles, east to west. Ishtar spoke through a mouth near Nineveh and Apollo through one near Didyma. Orpheus spoke in Thrace, where his dismembered head lay caught between some rocks, and Osiris's dismembered head spoke in Egypt. Amon spoke through mouths in Egypt, Ethiopia, and Libya. The sibyls spoke in Italy, where one of them, the Cumean sibyl, also wrote her words on leaves. South of Naples, voices came out of a maze of underground tunnels so tortuous they were said to have inspired Homer's account of the underworld. In all these places, the oracles taught natural philosophy: subservience to time, fate, and the devouring earth, to the creation instead of to a Creator, as Christians would hold against them.

There are still places on earth where it seems impossible the ground shouldn't suddenly roll and groan, where a bird cry in the distance seems a fluted signal and the miniature intricacy of wild pink petals seems coded speech. From such a place in Greece, from the heights called Parnassian down into the zone of the Delphic Oracle, there flows an underground watercourse that surfaces in springs and pools along the way. One of these is the famous Castalian spring out of which the Muses were born, to which pilgrims have come for inspiration for millennia. Down and down the water flows into the awesome gorge with its thousand-year-old olive groves running like a gray-green river to the sea.

The myths of Delphi concerned the opposition nature propounds between dark earth and illumined sky. The opposing divinities were deep-breasted Gaia, universal mother, oldest of gods, and Apollo, who slew her serpent Python with his fire-beams. An ancient cult object in Delphi was the Omphalos, a beehive-shaped stone that stood for the base of the cosmic axis. The axis itself, Greek philosophy gave to a goddess, Dike.[5] Around Dike turned the oracle-bearing earth and the Apollonian skies. From Delphi, the center of the Cosmos, spoke the Pythia, whose dominion, symbolized by her sacred tripod, was the Triple World of world myth.[6]

She came into possession of her power in the eighth century BCE, that is, while Solomon's Temple was standing in Jerusalem. Her voice was that of a long line of women raised from priestess to the Pythian throne. Was she, as the Christians would say, a trumpet of irrational frenzies under the influence of narcotic fumes? Scholars say not. She was generally a balanced, even worldly, woman whose sayings might be obscure but were open to meaningful interpretation and touched, even conservatively, on political and social issues, not metaphysical ones. She was a realist, too. When an old man came to learn how to father a child by his young wife, she told him to "put a new tip on the old plow-head."[7]

Great men—Socrates, Plato, Cicero, and Plutarch—considered hers a more moral voice than most human ones. Others—Aristotle, the Cynics and Epicureans—had scorn for her. But she seems to have effectively promulgated the Stoic philosophy that humanity is bound by existential limits and that adaptation to them is its only mode of freedom. Plutarch, who was a priest of the Apollo cult in Delphi, declared that the god of clarity "puts the visions in her mind and the light in her soul."[8]

As the oracles, so the Mysteries. These were pilgrim-initiation events correlated with the seasons. The spring Mysteries of Egyptian Osiris were celebrated in Abydos around his tomb, possibly the very sarcophagus that stands in the Cairo Museum today. There he lies yet, beside the Nile, Lord of the Vine and of Corn, of Poetry, the City and Death, held down by the granite wings of four hawks. Pilgrims came to Abydos as elsewhere to die beside a "heavenly river," and after the god's death had been enacted, the cry "Osiris is risen!" rang out along the banks.

The cult of Osiris's sister, mate, and savior Isis also drew crowds to her sanctuary at Philae on the Upper Nile. The Roman writer Apuleius joined her cult and described the rites, enacted at the full moon of the autumn equinox. The pilgrims dipped seven times in the sea and called on her to appear in the sky. Forthwith she sailed into view in a silver gown with overmantle black as night, and at every thread-crossing was a star. Patron Goddess of the seafaring Greeks of Alexandria, her cult spread up the great rivers of Europe. Her dark-eyed, erect image became a form-center that drew other goddesses into it until she absorbed them all, only in turn to be dissolved herself in a newer form. And always she was identified with Sirius, "the bright star of Isis . . . the true Stella Maris, Star of the Sea."[9]

The Mysteries taught submission to death in expectation of transformation that would likely bring loss of memory. Initiates into the Orphic cults, for instance, went into their graves wearing amulets of mystical hope.

> I am a child of the earth and the starry heavens . . .
> I have flown out of the sorrowful circle of life . . .
> I am dying of thirst. Let me drink the water of memory . . .

and

> Great circular mysterious form of the universe . . .
> Fire-walker, creator of light, fire-breather,
> Open the doors to me![10]

But of all the Mysteries, the autumnal ones honoring Demeter, Goddess of earth and corn, at Eleusis on the Greek seacoast were most magnetic, for they provided a natural epiphany that was apparently so striking it elicited not sadness from the participants but exalted wonder.[11]

Three days before the equinox, great crowds of pilgrims bathed together in the sea outside Athens and sprinkled their bodies with animal blood as if to take upon themselves the sacrificial role. Then, dressed in saffron robes with crowns of evergreen myrtle, they set out for the shrine, a day's walk from the city. The site of the occasion was a cavelike theater carved out of a cliff.

In two thousand years, no one has given away the secret of the Eleusinian Mystery. It's only known that somehow, forms were witnessed in actual process of change. But perhaps a modern pilgrim arriving at this place in time may be forgiven for an unprovable suggestion: what took place at Eleusis might have been related to the Asian shadow play. On a thin screen of silk or cotton stretched across the cave's mouth, silhouettes—like black figures on vases—could have seemed to lie down in death, then sprout like new corn, bearing in their leaves a child; for at the climax, an infant's cry was heard. Then cymbals clashed, a blinding light went up, and the congregation broke into jubilation. A powerful theatrical event it must have been to interest men and women of worldly experience, including emperors and philosophers.

Whatever in fact occurred at Eleusis, the evening of the next day there took place a rite of cosmic adjustment and settlement like the Hindu Kumbha-mela. Two urns were filled with water and spun like tops, one eastward, one westward, as prayers were said to the sky for rain and the earth for bounty. When the urns fell, spilling water across the ground, new prayers were made for a "foaming over" of benefits in the year to come.

On the last night of initiation, a torch dance was performed by the pilgrims. And what was the nature of the dance performed on this equinoctial night? Various types of ancient dance are known—fertility and battle games, and routines in imitation of totem animals. But according to Euripides, at that point in the Eleusinian ceremonies,

> the starry heaven of Zeus begins to dance, also the moon and the daughters of Nereus, the goddesses of the sea and the everflowing rivers—all dance in honor of the golden-crowned maid, and her holy mother.

In the light of this description, it would seem the torch-bearing pilgrims may have followed choreographies mirroring those of the stars. Then such dancing would have been an initiation ritual, as was the Eleusinian theatrical performance, and both would have advanced the same science of the Cosmos, of turning cycles, changing but continuous forms, and returning measures. As the Greek writer Lucian put it, "dancing came into being at the beginning of all things, with Eros the ancient one, for we see this primeval dancing set forth in the choral dance of the constellations, and in the planets and fixed stars, their interweaving and interchange and orderly harmony."[12]

And such a dance, as Lucian suggested, would have come out of the incalculable past, performed in the mouths of earlier caves and around the tumuli of forgotten kings.[13] It may have been danced among the standing stones of Britain "beyond the north wind" or else "among the Hyberboreans" in the direction of India, places where Greek myth had it obscurely that Apollo spent the winters.[14]

In either case, the arts of clarified intellect based on star-counting, like architecture, musical harmony, poetry, and choreography, passed from earlier peoples to the Mediterranean. Myth has it Apollo taught them to Daedalus, who laid out the seven-ringed labyrinth in Crete on the basis of such formulae and laid out also a dance floor in Minos's palace on which he taught the life-saving, forward and backward, turning and returning steps to Theseus, who taught them to the youths and maids of Delos, from whom they passed to Athens. From there it would have been but some few steps more to Eleusis.

The secret was to keep the connecting forms in order as the feet turned, like the planets and stars as they rise, turn, and sink in the great wheel around Dike. This was the dance of dances, that brought wisdom and peace. "Happy is he who, having witnessed such things, goes under the earth. He knows life's end and its god-given beginning," the Greek poet Pindar said. "Thrice happy are those who have seen into the Mystery," said Sophocles.[15]

✦ ✦ ✦

Once in Jerusalem, a man I was talking with turned abruptly and asked my religious affiliation. Since, like many Westerners, I was raised in a secular home among works of art, books, and talk about all the faiths but instruction in none, I uttered a conventionality that, even as I said it, rang hollow in my ears: "I'm nothing."

Passionately, the man raised a hand and cried, "I feel sorry for you!" But I was already shocked, though I had no idea what other reply I could have given.

What I had communicated was a sense that—like a lone Hindu woman—I had no intrinsic function in this world; that it went on its way unchanged by my life. In a literal sense that may be true. I needed a myth to support a sense of my functional existence in it. But I did not know the nature of such a myth. It could not require worship of any of the male gods: they were illusory and apart from me. To adopt a worshipful relationship to one of them would have deepened my sense of nothingness.

Then I must proceed like an Asian temple-builder: lay out a blueprint of basics, that it may reveal its center.

Nothingness is real; so Buddhism teaches. But there is both an imaginative (Hindu) and a social (Jewish) procedure by which the lone individual may achieve a sense of functional reality in the world.

Now as I moved through the pagan fields of the interregnum in my readings, I was nearing the crossroads but not there yet.

An early mystery god of paganism was Asclepius, the healer, who knew the relationship between cosmic and human systems. He was said to appear to pilgrims in his shrines at Epidaurus or Pergamum, after which they woke cured of their ills. Once, however, he prescribed that the very bones and nerves of a sufferer's body must be pulled out and then put back. But they must not be simply replaced, new for old. Instead, there had to be "a certain change of those existing, and thus there was need of a great and strange correction."[16]

What secular pilgrim can be even now in Jerusalem, the very operating theater of that correction, and not be shaken by the strangeness of what happened there?

THE approaching Christological myth, then, would be not new but rather a change with corrections of one existing. And like its predecessor, the new myth can be read in terms of pilgrimage in the Cosmos.

Scholars have traced chains of typologies through the two Testaments that are the bones and nerves of a cosmic body. For example, the old covenants had been of light or blood, while the new one would be openly of immortal life—which in the equivalences of myth is "the same." The place in the River Jordan where "the destined Elijah," now John the Baptist, would baptize Christ was the very spot where the waters had stopped for Joshua and the tribes. Only in the new myth, the skies were "torn open" while a voice announced the new line of descent: *"this* is my Son" (Mark 1.10).

Then Christ, in the footsteps of pilgrims from Tereh to Joshua, must set forth to learn how his life-course was bound into the cosmic whole.

Northward he traveled, therefore, and entered the mode of miracle, *limina,* as social scientists call the pilgrims' mode of experience.[17] At Cana water became wine, as wine would soon be blood. At a Greek pilgrimage place called Seven Springs, he fed many on a couple of fish. At Migdal, he had a meeting of deep portent. He met there the Magdalene. She had been evil but he healed her of seven devils. Then she was corrected, turned around to good.

He traveled on north to where the Jordan enters the Galilee, preaching in the hills and valleys. He continued north into the foothills of the Mount Hermon range, one of the globe's great snowcapped, myth-breeding ranges, where three rivers have their confluence in a savage landscape. Like many such regions in the eastern Mediterranean world, it was sacred to Pan, the goat-footed pagan son of Polestar, brother in myth of a like creature in India.[18]

As Polestar's offspring, Pan should never die. But here again, while the Hindu gods live on in transformation, the Western mind forced myth and fact together, condemning even Pan, like the field-gods and natural man, to death. In spring, when the slopes were red with anemones and the rushing water with iron ore, a living boy would be flung into the whirlpool. In the zone where Pan met annual death, Jesus met knowledge of his like fate and named one of his friends to stand on for him after his death. It was Simon, now renamed Peter, the Rock.

But still the place of encounter lay ahead. Truly the summoning star stands in the farthest north, beyond reach. Then suddenly, even as he climbed, Jesus was struck in the face by a tremendous light. That light, that must have come from Polestar, did not bicker like Sirius's wild fire. Instead, it flowed steady, cold, and white, the source of all fractured colors seen on earth.

The geometry of the vision was consummate. The Son stood on a peak in perfect triangular conjunction with Moses and Elijah, two mountain-climbers of the past, while the Father of all myths spoke again, "This is my Son . . ."

There were another three witnesses to the event, a second triad. These were the Rock and two fishermen-brothers from the Galilee, John and James, whom Jesus had just named Sons of Thunder. Thus on the mountain were six men in all, half a zodiacal wheel around Polestar, for the wheel had yet to turn full-revolution. Christ's death had not yet taken place.

FROM the vision on Mount Hermon, Christ's road sank back toward the grotto darkness out of which it had come. South the Jordan sinks below the Galilee into the Sea of Death. The rest of the way was given. The pilgrim had only to follow it.

Only, at some time between his entry into Jerusalem and the night of Gethsemane, he broke the pace of his descent to take his twelve friends into a courtyard and stand them around him like a circle of stones, holding hands and answering Amen to each line he sang, while all of them danced the star-dance of dances, singing,

> I will be born/and I will bear . . .
> I will be saved/and I will save . . .
> I will pipe/dance, all of you . . .
> To the universe/belongs the dancer . . .[19]

✦ ✦ ✦

Again it has to be said: there can be no pilgrimage without a Cosmos in which to enact it. As the world knows, the violent correction of the old cosmic structures—its axes, hinges, planes, curves, and confluent systems—is assigned to the season of Passover around 33 CE in Jerusalem. At the moment of Christ's death, a convulsion shook the Three Worlds. Overhead, the sun went out. In Herod's Temple, the Veil that Vespasian would soon display in Rome ripped from top to bottom. And deep under Golgotha hill, the bedrock under which Adam lay asleep split, and blood seeped down to wet his face.

READ as purest metaphor, scripture the world around holds no greater leap of unconscious intention than Christ's resurrection.[20] What really would be enacted was this: the one who had gone away as if forever would be found and repossessed by one left behind. The choreography of the miracle would be a sheer creation of uncontainable human will. And in regard to the finder's identity: a question that has troubled Christian apologists, male, for centuries is simply this—why was the person who first saw Christ risen, that one?

The answer to that question, as to other related ones in myth, I propose to discover in that light like burnished copper or ruby red that rose ahead of the sun in the Near East, in that time, from midsummer on into July. Jewish myth had made it the signal star of rejection of the Goddess and anticipation of the Messiah. And now indeed it led the Magi to Bethlehem.

The star whose ancient function had been rejected and forgotten became the leading one.

That fact is clue enough. The person whom myth joined with Christ in that early rising could be none other than who she was: the one known first as a sinner, who later wiped Christ's feet with her hair and then was good.[21]

Indeed, her significator in art is also the carrier of her astronomical identity, so that her famous reliquary in France displays her cranium with red hair streaming. Yes, it is her flaming hair that finally sets the Magdalene in her place at the very pivot of myth.[22]

It had to be the Star-queen, returned to life with a new name, who saw Christ first, for she was already "out in the sky" ahead of him. Wherefore those Christians closest to the origins of the myth in place and doctrine, the Russian and Greek Orthodox, still greet one another on Resurrection morning with the gift of one red egg in a swirl of shiny bread.

So one arrives at the further thought that the Polestar-father, gone, leaving behind him only the residual part of himself that was his Wisdom, was, by the miracle-work of imagination firing a new development in the myth, brought back into conjunction with her in the person of his son.

And she, in the same movement of the myth-makers' imagination, turned around to greet, with disbelief but then welcoming amazement, that miracle-presence back with her.

The secret metaphor for transcendence of death, then, in the Christian myth—the perihelion of the Christian pilgrimage trail—isn't Christ returned, alone, from the tomb but the Magdalene's going forth and finding him, just as the secret Jewish metaphor-held-in-reserve is to be the Shekinah's discovery of and by the Lord. And the Hindu metaphor is the perpetual releasing and gathering-in of light by water in Benares. And behind them all—for those who like to look for primordial sources—may have been the beautiful star Sirius drawing up the sun on late-summer mornings back in time.

By extension: the past can be possessed and let live-on by the imagination, or Wisdom. And a function in the world, metaphysical, imaginative, and social, is revealed for the human individual.

And that flickering "red" was the very flame that led the way, as Rilke said it would.

After that apotheosis, Christ's appearances on earth were recorded as if through broken glass, partial, uncertain, fragments of a mystery in the minds of those who tried to remember, later, what such a one might have been like, had he been.

You are from below,
I am from above.
You are of this world,
I am not of this world. (John 8.23)

If they say to you, where did you come from,
Say to them, we came from the light. (Gospel of Thomas)

Before Abraham was, I am. (John 8.58)

When he first appeared to the disciples, all were present save
Thomas, the one whose feast day would be the winter solstice,
who was even called his twin, and who would be sent later to
India. The hidden suggestion in that geographical connection for
Thomas may be this: that between Indian myth and the original
Christian apotheosis—a divine Dancer in the aura of a Goddess—
there was influence the Church won't acknowledge openly.[23]

Later, Christ appeared to his old friends of Mount Hermon, the
Sons of Thunder and the Rock, together with, again, the Twin. By
these four he was not recognized, though he spoke in tropes of
pastoral tenderness. *Feed my lambs. Feed my sheep.*

There was little here on which to build a cosmic Church, only a
vague presence, some movements of intelligence seeking him while
still on earth. Once "out of nature," to use Yeats's words, the
Christ would vanish into forms of "hammered gold and gold
enamelling."

Now into such forms the twelve Apostles moved as well, as the
twelve tribes had entered the Jordan, and of their mixed-up lives
and legends, time would soon make hagiography. Of them, who
can say who really lived or died or where or how? In Jerusalem
around 35 CE, Stephen was stoned to death, perhaps. In 44, James,
Son of Thunder, to be Santiago, was perhaps beheaded there.
Thomas may have died in India. Did Matthew go to Ethiopia?
Jude to Persia? Bartholomew to Armenia? Did Peter go to Rome
at all? Or James or Matthew or anyone else of the twelve, to Spain?

In Jerusalem, the midsummer Pilgrim Feast came around. It was
Shavuot. But it was not rain the flamboyant rain-star let down this
time but fire. And that day, Peter warned the gathered Jews to
"save yourself from this crooked age." The Age was to be straight-
ened and reset, and in the new Age, the Feast would be Pentecost.

In these convulsive times, one last Jewish prophet came forth to work himself the Great Correction. By change of name from Saul to Paul, he signified his role in that cosmic labor. So he sailed off in a ship flying the standard of Castor and Pollux on its bucking mast, heralding as clearly as Noah had a change in Ages.[24]

In historic fact there were already small seed Messiah-cults around the Mediterranean. In Antioch for the first time, one was named Christian. In Athens, Paul met with the Stoics and rejected the cult *To the Unknown God*. He traveled to Ephesus and on to Rome where he found a group whose "faith is spoken of throughout the whole world." Excavations in Herculaneum have revealed the existence of one there too before the eruption of 79.

In Rome as elsewhere, Paul spoke of death. Death and Cosmos are locked like ten fingers intertwined, for only in the Cosmos of myth is there eternality of place. Christ's followers, baptized, were drawn "into his death" and "buried with him by baptism into death," "planted together in the likeness of his death." But the acknowledged Pauline creative stroke was universality. All people in the Cosmos were, as logic would suggest in any case, bound into the same salvation. "There is neither Greek nor Jew, circumcision nor uncircumcision, Barbarian, Scythian, bond nor free, but Christ is all and in all."

Yet, his vision fell short. For he shifted the ancient concept of divided union onto the individual person and preached that "nature sets its desires against the spirit while the spirit fights against it," and that to follow Christ one must crucify "the lower nature with its passions and desires." In the future, the Christian and eventually Islamic concept of human nature polarized would project itself in venomous attacks on women as on Jews. The campaign against women borrowed the language of certain Asian—and old desert—sages, so that, for example, the fourth-century Doctor of the Church, John Chrysostom, might work himself up to his notorious description of woman as "nothing else but phlegm and blood and slime and bile . . . how can you be in a flutter about the storehouses of these things?" And in much of Islam today, as we know, women are wrapped in cloth like swaddled infants or wound corpses and forbidden to eat with, speak with, or exchange looks with men.

So the old image of rupture between male and female, too briefly healed by the Magdalene's role in the resurrection drama, was reaccepted as an aspect of natural psychology. Meanwhile, the theme of male and female in perpetual longing for unearthly union survived in Christian romance and pilgrimage literature of the future and in time would generate the passionate Gothic cult of Mary-veneration.

PAUL was killed or may have been in Rome in 67. His head—"antitype," as biblical scholars put it, of Orpheus's and Osiris's mantic skulls and many others yet to come—struck off with a sword, fell three times, liberating from the ground three healing springs, the Tre Fontane, visited by pilgrims to St. Paul's Outside the Walls in Rome today.

Three years later, Titus marched on Jerusalem and broke it down. That is fact, not myth. Sixty years after that, the stones still standing after the even more terrible war against Bar Kochba were thrown over by the troops of Hadrian.

✦ ✦ ✦

The social and cultural forces that began to work together in these transitional years may never be agreed on by historians, but what writer, turning to the scene, can resist trying to give such momentous development expression?

There is, for instance, in the museum on the Greek island of Rhodes, a late-Hellenistic head of Apollo that conveys the new spirit. The god's hair streams back in a wind that blows straight at him. His eyes are stretched-wide and anxious. If they look toward anything in nature it is only a point on the horizon. This Sun-god harbinger of the coming Christ is rushing toward a tumultuous death and knows there is not in the natural world the resurrection he despairs of. Instead of Gaia's or Demeter's dark calm, he has caught the scent of immortality and has already left behind the counsels of the oracle that bore his name: *Nothing in excess . . .*

and *Know thyself.* He is no more the god of plainsong but Phoebus Apollo of the blinding rays of light.

FROM the time of the early Republic on through three centuries of Empire, even while supporting certain of the oracles and Mysteries, Rome had tried without success to quash the bloody transcendence-seeking cults coming out of the east.

It had itself to blame, perhaps, for ecumenical liberality had been the republican point of view about the gods. Back in 205 BCE, in a season of storms and also threat of invasion by Hannibal, an oracle had said the Phrygian mountain-goddess Cybele could save the world. Therefore a ship was dispatched to bring her west—the black-stone sister to Kali-Durga that she was—and, after Hannibal's retreat, the rock was installed in a temple on Palatine Hill that became a cult site for pilgrims for centuries. On into the reign of Claudius, death- and resurrection-rituals were held there to her doomed mate, Attis. A pine tree was cut, wrapped in wool and violets, and buried. Then bulls were slain and their blood splashed around, while frenzied lamentation and self-mutilation went on among the participants. The pine tree's resurrection was enacted on the day of equinox, with rites of "hilaries" to follow, soon after which the pilgrims carried the stone to a running stream at the foot of the Via Appia to dip it in and so renew the bloodstreams of the Cosmos.

It was ever the immemorial longing: *"by the slaughter of the bull and the slaughter of the ram, born again into eternity."* In Rome alone there were some four hundred bull-slaughtering altars to Mithra, the Warrior-god who slew the cosmic bull and so let evil into the world. One stood on Vatican Hill. One was in a house now deep underground beneath the church of San Clemente. It can be visited there in its niebelungen darkness, fifty feet down in the archaeologists' excavations. The house still fronts on a cobbled lane. Its blind windows are filled with rubble and the sky is usurped by tons of earth. But the altar stands, as does the stone ceiling, pierced eleven times for the seven planets and four elements, through which blood of the bulls was poured onto the initiates. And these were joined by more bull-slaughtering shrines throughout the

Empire, up the Rhone into further Gaul and up the Ebro into Spain and up the Danube and up the Thames.

For blood it was that ran in the veins of the Cosmos and must be added to at the equinoxes especially, when the wheels must be given transfusion to churn on, churn the living to good death and the dead to life everlasting—blood let out of throats and veins, blood poured over altars and heads of pilgrims, blood spilled on cornerstones and thresholds of new buildings to make them stand forever. Was there somewhere the idea urging itself into consciousness, that this ages-long red tide might have an end, or if no final end, a terminus where its sheer appalling profundity might find a symbolic representative to shed blood once for all?

Yet that would have been mostly a popular groundswell of a longing, comparable to the helpless wish people today have for an end to wars, while its unpatriotic quietism—just as today—went against the imperial grain. So when the Christ-cult, with its expiatory wine rite and its denigration of emperor and Rome, began to spread, the Empire turned full force against it, trying by means from torture to mass execution to turn people from it toward Mithra or that *Sol* who could not be conquered, *Invictus*.

AT the same time the very globe was shrinking thanks to traveling pilgrims, merchants, and soldiery, so the image of One World enclosing all nations began to generate other universalist ideas. Scientists, for instance, had long sought universal descriptions of the world—as water or fire or atoms or the frozen forms of geometry. Now general laws and principles about nature were being discovered, for example the lunar source of the ocean tides and the cause of the precessional shift.

Also the multiple gods of paganism had begun to merge and absorb one another and, as if by the fission of their accumulated energy, inflate into vast transparencies, so that the old Storm-ba'als of the Near East, for instance, dissolved into a Lord of the Universal Skies and on into vaster metaphysical concepts like Great Time that Devours all Being, akin to the Hindu Mahakala.[25] Out of such procedures of thought, St. Augustine would soon draw his great meditations on Time, with their echo of ancient Indo-Aryan texts:

> Your years neither go nor come . . . they do not move on because they never pass at all. Your today is eternity . . . You made all time; you are before all time; and the 'time,' if such we may call it, when there was no time was not time at all.[26]

Gradually too the self-images of the emperors in Rome expanded beyond nature, as their gigantic statuary and sky-scraping triumphal columns show, and individual ones were apotheosized as Lord or Your Eternity, while their personal cult gods retained such titles as Savior of the World, or Lord of Past and Future, or Hercules, who is Polestar in a zodiac of labors. And the capital city Rome itself was no earthly city but simply one transcendental *Urbs in Orbe.*

It was the cosmic vision burgeoning, demanding to be born, that could not be held back. Like a living enlarging organism, it seems to require new space continually as if it generatively lived "in us," as today certain creative workers say of their dominant themes and many people say of their obsessions. Into what would be Christian consciousness, some scholars believe, that vision entered from further east via Plato and the Greco-Jewish philosopher Philo, who had it from forgotten teachers of what Babylon had known for millennia. In time to come, "losing Philo, [Judaism] lost . . . the cosmic sense which the Greeks quickened in Christianity," until, with the cosmological systems of the Kabbalah, the vision would be reborn in some 1,300 years.[27]

THE age of Christian apology abruptly replaced that of Christian pogrom in the fourth century, and for the lingering pagan world's benefit, there began a practical labor of back-inserting false messages into the records of the oracles to make it seem they had foretold their own eclipse. One of the first such fraudulent statements was probably prepared in the fourth century but back-dated to the time of Augustus. When he sent to Delphi to ask who would succeed him, the defeated Pythia was made to say,

"A Hebrew boy, a god who rules among the blessed, bids me leave this house and go back to Hades. So go in silence from my altars."[28]

The most haunting of false oracles was back-dated to the time of Julian the Apostate who, succeeding Christian Constantine, tried to re-redress the crookedness in things. He planned to use soft means, however, for "in my opinion, one does not punish but instruct the insane." He would be the last ruler of antiquity with love for the old gods, for whom he said "I feel awe. . . . I love, I revere, I venerate them." To the Jews as well he made promises of rebuilding "the holy Jerusalem which you have for many years longed to see." But a spear wound in Mesopotamian battle ended his life, and the stones the Jews had begun to upright were laid down, perhaps for all time.[29]

The oracles, as it turned out, had been against him. The sibyl had foredoomed his eastern campaign. That same year, Apollo's temple in Rome burned down. Christians in Jerusalem saw fiery crosses in the sky. "The Galilean has won," were last words laid in his mouth by others, and it was soon written how he had sent a messenger to beg the Pythia to speak again. But she had sent only a piteous reply.

The bright citadel is fallen.
Apollo lives here no more.
The sentient laurel is gone, the prophetic fountain.
The murmuring water has stopped its flow.

By then, the time of barbarian terror had come. Theodosius the Great managed to hold the eastern and western flanks of Christendom in uneasy balance, but in 390 he conducted a revenge-massacre considered savage even for those times, and the Bishop of Milan, Ambrose, laid on him a penance. He must silence the Delphic oracle. The final tearing-down of the thousand-year-old complex of temples, treasuries, shrines, and sculpture on the mountainside was left for Theodosius's son—whose name was Arcadius.

The Mysteries passed out of being with less notice. The rites had expanded in late Roman times, and Eleusis had been enriched by several emperors including Hadrian. There is no record of a last ceremony. It is only known that, in 395, the troops of Alaric, king of the Goths, who in fifteen years would overrun Rome, threw down Demeter's walls and no one came to build them up again.

During these same years, Ambrose's greatest convert, Augustine, was penning his *Confessions,* in which he was moved to write, "This most beautiful order of things that are very good will finish its course and pass away."[30]

A few microcosmic spores of Greco-Jewish-Christian culture would float the Mediterranean like little Arks riding out the centuries. The notion of a social capsule to outfloat floods of war and chaos may have come west from India, where the "sangha" or enclosed community of like-minded people, usually male, had been advocated by the Buddha. From western India to the Essenes to medieval Christian brotherhoods would be but a series of little leaps.

The first such cell in the West is said to have been set up in the third century in Egypt by a converted ex-soldier, trained to the authoritarian rigors of military life. The idea was carried west by one of his student-monks, John Cassian, who spent the rest of his life setting up such cells around Marseilles. Nearly contemporary was Augustine's brotherhood in North Africa.

Only spores they were, but once implanted, they would provide the model for a Christian Cosmos, with religious pilgrimage, as ever and everywhere, at the service of transcendent cause.

PART FIVE

SON
OF STAR

✦

Paradigms gain their status because they are more suc-
cessful than their competitors in solving a few problems
that the group . . . has come to recognize as acute.
   The success of a paradigm . . . is at the start largely a
promise of success. . . .
                 Thomas Kuhn:
        THE STRUCTURE OF SCIENTIFIC REVOLUTIONS

✦

IN THE CENTER : JERUSALEM

✦ ✦ ✦

Christian Jerusalem's history may be said to have begun when Constantine converted in 313, and the cult of supernatural return was granted official privilege. At once, what may have been the first archaeological dig in history was initiated to draw out and reset the bones of a new pilgrimage center. It would be a methodical labor to initiate a thundering revision of culture.[1]

Every artifact of sacred Jerusalem must be corrected. The old Temple had been the hub of a horizontal system drawing Jewish pilgrims across land and water. By the end of the fourth century, new Jerusalem would also be functioning as the nexus of a web of lesser shrines through which Christian pilgrims approached "the fire which is in Zion."[2]

The old Temple had also functioned as a joint in the vertical structure connecting Eden with Polestar. Christian Jerusalem would also provide ascent to the heavens but at a clear remove from the old site, indeed "outside the walls" of the old Temple.[3] So that spinal cord, the cosmic axis, would be changed while the body, the Cosmos itself, would survive. The literary critic Northrop Frye has suggested that "Christ" is a "secret presence" in the Old Testament, revealed in the New. I would say it is not Christ, but the vertical geometry the mind craves to lock itself into Eternity, that is the unacknowledged presence in both Testaments.[4]

THE fire over Zion, the ancient summoning star, had been of feminine gender. A woman had borne and a woman greeted the returned Christ. The flame led still. It would be Constantine's mother, Helena, whom legend would credit with most of the archaeological finds in the Holy Land.

In 326, Helena and Bishop Macarius of the city still called Aelia Capitolina arrived there from Nicea, where an organizing council of the new religious-political program had just been held. With them was the bishop of the Palestinian city of Caesarea, Eusebius, who would be ever on the spot to document the miracle-finds as they took place.

The Emperor was not. He never came. And certainly Aelia Capitolina was not high on his list of priorities. Rome was, however. There he ordered the building of three big pilgrimage churches—a basilica where the stables of the rich Lateran family had stood, a cruciform church on what was believed to be Peter's tomb on Vatican Hill, and a basilica where Paul was supposed to have died. And in his "new Rome which is Constantinople," he ordered a Forum that would stand for centuries, dominated by a column topped with a statue of himself as Apollo.[5] That city of his heart, he dedicated to the Trinity and also to the Mother of God. In this last designation, he could be said to have jumped the gun on theology, for it would not be till the Council of Ephesus in 431 that the Virgin would be formally nominated Theotokos, not Christ's but God's own Mother.

What went on in Jerusalem around Helena and her helpers, however, is hopelessly colored, for mythologizing intelligence was seeking orientation in the new Cosmos and would be served by fantasy or fact.[6] For example, Helena, newly arrived, went straight to the "unclean marble" of Aphrodite standing west of the old Temple and knocked it off its base. So says legend. Then she set her workmen to digging, and in no time a large rock with a carved-out hollow was unearthed. It was of course Christ's Tomb.

Next Helena discovered a twelve-foot-high rock lying southwest of the Tomb and called it Golgotha, "Skull-hill," even though from the start it was remarked an unlikely execution site. Indeed, it was "in no sense a mount . . . it bears no resemblance to its name, for it is not situationed on any height." So said the Bordeaux Pilgrim when he came. The argument would not be soon settled. Defenders of Helena's Skull-hill claimed it was so called not because it looked like a skull but because Adam's lay under it. That very notion was a flight of imagination by the early theologian Origen, who proposed that Christ's death had "brought life to Adam who was buried beneath the place of crucifixion." One image brought on the next, so that pilgrims were presently being shown "blood-staines" there, and so they are today in Jerusalem's Holy Sepulchre Church that encloses Golgotha hill.[7]

However, doubt kept recurring, and in the nineteenth century, English diplomat and amateur Bible scholar "China" Gordon, in the spirit of modern empiricism, went hunting one day in a part of Jerusalem he figured more likely to have been outside the old walls. There he came upon a cliff with skull-like features. Best, it was big enough to hold three execution-size crosses on top. There was excitement when, some time later, an authentic tomb of the first century was excavated at the cliff's foot. Protestant pilgrims still consider "Gordon's Tomb" to be genuine and hold their Easter services there. But recent archaeology situates the Herodian execution ground somewhat southwest of Helena's site, near the present Lutheran Church of the Redeemer.

HELENA'S son died before New Jerusalem could be fully laid out, but he left orders for a basilica to be erected on an axis pointing toward the Tomb and fitted out with columns, mosaics, and paintings. When it was done, it had a gilded roof coffered within. Eusebius marveled that it "stretched over the whole basilica like a great sea." Oppositely to later Christian style, this basilica was entered in Roman style from the east so its altar end might abut the "hillock Golgotha" only "about a stone's throw from the Cave where they laid the Lord's body." That significant west end of Constantine's basilica contained also twelve columns that stood for all twelve ever has. And in Christendom "twelve" would go on generating transparencies into the time of Charlemagne's peers and Arthur's knights and even the twelve jurors in American courts today.

The basilica was named the Martyrium. At first it was the only roofed building on the site. Later it was enlarged and enriched. But it fell prey to violence and, in the eleventh century, was burned and razed by a fanatic "mad caliph," El Hakim.[8] The church that stands in its place, built by the Crusaders, contains not a trace of Constantine's, any more than the Second Temple probably contained of Solomon's.

✦

THE Tomb, however, was the place of deepest mystery. Like the human umbilicus it was not the most beautiful part of the organism's anatomy, but it encoded the natural miracle of its origin.

Probably as soon as the rock with what looked like a burial niche in it was cleared, the ground around was leveled so that it stood alone. The cavity, some seven feet long, was aligned east-west. Sometime after Constantine's death, the contour of the rock was shaped into a beehive round, and columns were cut into its northern flank. In a mosaic map of the sixth century, it sported a gilded dome.[9] Eventually, it acquired its own twelve columns and later was enclosed in three circular walls with doors. By then it was officially known as the Anastasis or Resurrection.

So it was that the beehive-round architecture, employed from prehistory for both matriarchal omphalos-stones and shrines to Aphrodite, and also for patriarchal tombs—in Buddhist Asia for the stupa and in the West for the noble male dead (Menelaus in Mycenae, Augustus in Rome, Hadrian by the Tiber, and Herod in Jerusalem) and given its most beautiful formulation in Hadrian's Pan-theon in Rome, that sky-turned eyeball dedicated by him to *all* the gods—was given new life as the symbol of the resurrection of the one and only Christ.

Thus into the Christ myth poured genetic riches in symbolic form, from ancestry both female and male. For his myth is as much enmeshed with Aphrodite's as with Polestar's, in that both hers and Christ's concern the mystery-birth of love out of brutishness. She was born, we remember, out of the Sky-god's dismembered phallus flung into the sea, out of which she rose straight up in majestic verticality, a whole-body erection that replicated the member of her father and so the axis of the Worlds. Up she rose out of the deeps on a shell with her red hair flying, no "she-devil," as the Christians labeled her, but an authentic "*She-god.*" And in that role, as I see it—*pace* Catholic dogma—she merged and merges with other earth-transcending, sky-reaching goddesses past and to come, like Isis on one hand and on the other, the Virgin of the Assumption. These transformations in myth and art of course reflect transformations in thinking. They rise out of a well never to be exhausted—human incomprehension before the facts of human generation—and bind the Christian mysteries to their antique sources.

In time, the round and centered blueprint, that in the iconography of cosmic myth signifies both the deep sea and the dome of the sky, would generate many new usages, for geometry, as I've tried to show, is a form of myth.

It was taken up in European Christendom for baptistries, generally attached to but not inside their mother-churches. Such a structure might, in practice, be round or else octagonal or dodecagonal, but dead center in it stood the stone basin filled with the sweet holy water that, again in the terms of myth, flows in the Jordan and, sprinkled on newborn flesh, ensures its return to paradise. So death, by means of geometry, was turned around to birth.

Or, when the circle-shape was overlaid by a cross, it signified victory over death. So it was used for their domed churches by the Knights Templar, and so it was most nobly called on by Emperor Justinian for his Church of Holy Wisdom—of the gender feminine—whose domes seen across the Sea of Marmora provided Yeats with his image for the unattainability, save by artifice of imagination, of eternity.

And so whoever drew a rough circle on the ground with a dot in the center might be writing out a whole cosmology and theology, as well as drawing a map or a graffito for "woman." In the Gothic Lady Cathedrals of France, circular mosaic labyrinths were laid into the nave pavements for a penitent unable to make the trip save on foot or knees in a rite like the little Brahmin boy's "Going to Benares." Here it was called "Going to Jerusalem," and the labyrinth might be actually called "death" or "heaven." In the Church of San Savino in Piacenza, Italy, one of these floor maps even includes the wonderful statement, "This labyrinth reveals the structure of the world."[10]

In the seventeenth century that greatest of sky-watchers, Galileo, would call the circle a metaphor of Being, and to what he meant by that, there has not yet been put an end by science, philosophy, theology, or art.[11]

✦

IN Christian Jerusalem there were two other major round buildings, both built in the fourth century. The Church of St. Mary Ever
Virgin, which enclosed her own tomb, lay in the Valley of Jehoshaphat, even though Ephesus, where the pagan Temple of Great
Diana had stood, also claimed her sepulchre. And at the very top
of the Mount of Olives was the "great round church . . . from
which the Lord ascended into the heavens." It was the logic of
cosmic geometry that required the Church of Christ's Ascension
to sit atop the ever-building "column" of sacred Jerusalem even
though scripture located the Ascension up north in the Galilee,
possibly on Mount Tabor. But by this translocation, the Three
Worlds of tomb, womb, and heaven—or abyss, earth, and sky—
were corrected and set into vertical coherence.

That remarkable building had an empty oculus at its crown,
perhaps in imitation of, and so triumph over, the pagan Pantheon.
Under the opening, the earth was left unpaved, for Christ's footprints there wouldn't sustain weight but "cast back the flagstones
in the face of those who herein lay them." Nor would any amount
of tramping wipe them out. The round plot was railed, and pilgrims knelt by it to wonder at the marvelous marks and, through
the railing, gather handfuls of sacred dust.

The column of emptiness rising from that dust to the sky signified, like a Linga of Light or the Borobodur's shaft, the axis of the
luminous sky-dome that curved out from and around it. And in
actual fact, whether by unconscious or deliberate sense of cosmological theater, just such a dome of light shone from that building.
For a large candelabra hung over the footprints, and through eight
lofty windows facing the city, eight more lamps beamed. In the
seventh century, the pilgrim-bishop Arculf of Gaul saw them sus-
pended as if miraculously in space,

> positioned so that each one of them seems to hang neither above
> nor below its window but just inside it. These lamps shine out from
> their windows on the summit of the Mount of Olives with such
> brilliance that they light up not only the part of the Mount to the
> west . . . but also the steps leading all the way up from the Valley
> of Jehoshaphat. . . .[12]

✦

MINOR corrections to the Jerusalem sacred axis continued to be made over the centuries. The spot where Jesus cleaned the money-lenders out of the Temple was pointed out to Christian pilgrims near the Anastasis. The old Altar of Incense of the Temple was now said to be the stone in the Anastasis whereon the Angel sat on Resurrection morning. But two translocations were of critical importance. To the end of one, a little chapel was hollowed out of Golgotha rock and, sometimes, the True Cross was kept in there. That Cross, in a narrative of awesome intricacy, had been hewn out of an apple bough in Eden. Then it had been a beam in Solo-mon's palace until Sheba saw it and foretold the death of the World's Savior on it. So Solomon had it torn out and buried in the watery pit under the Temple where the animals for sacrifice were washed. In time it floated up, and was shaped by the Jews into the Cross of death and afterward sunk in a pool again. But it gave off such sweet perfumes—like Osiris's body tombed in a tree and many a holy Christian relic to come—that Helena went straight and fished it out.[13]

However it really came to be, the fragment of Cross, actually a bit of the cross-beam where it met the post, was mounted in silver and kept under guard because, as an early pilgrim reported, "on one occasion [someone] bit off a piece of the Holy Wood and stole it . . . and for this reason the deacons stand around and keep watch."[14] The rock-cut chapel where it was kept was christened the Altar of Abraham, and by such linguistic means the Christian axis reached out and drew in Abraham to hinge Adam to Christ.

A final invention completed the new mandala. Christian Jeru-salem must be shown to be the center of the earth-plane, as the 74th Psalm had affirmed: "God is my King of old, working salva-tion in the midst of the earth."

And so that place was located in an open area bordered by the Tomb, Golgotha, the Martyrium, and a fourth church that stood south of the others for a while.

These four churches [wrote Bernard the Wise in the ninth century] have between them a garden without a roof, with its walls sparkling with gold and a paved floor of costliest stone. From each of the four churches runs a chain, and the point at which the four chains join in the center of the garden is said to be the center of the world.[15]

✦   ✦   ✦

Even before the Christian shrines were consecrated, a few hardy travelers made their way there, breaking trail for thousands to follow. First, maybe, were some Armenians, who got there in the fourth century and scratched a little boat on a rock with the words "We went to the Lord." Others soon came from Egypt, Syria, Greece, Rome, even it is said from Ethiopia. The first to leave record was that Bordeaux Pilgrim, who came three thousand miles on horseback. It was still the third decade of the 300s, and he made note of fountains where women became pregnant, the field where Goliath fell, and the almond tree where Jacob fought the angel. Next with a notebook, a half-century later, came a woman of Spain named Egeria. She took the Egyptian route to satisfy her wish to follow the Israelites in their ancient wanderings. At the end of the century, Jerome chose to settle in Jerusalem out of disgust for the Rome he called the "house of Satan," and in his wake came a flock of noble Roman women to "the village of Christ [where] all is rusticity and, except for psalms, silence."

For these pilgrims in a newly consecrated space, time too was reconsecrated, so that the small and large wheels of hours and days might churn their souls to their reward. Daily services revolved among the Anastasis, Martyrium, and Golgotha and were continual, passionate, and participatory, probably like evangelical meetings now. The mysteries of the cult were expounded by a priest standing inside the Tomb and speaking through the walls. Mass was performed in the Martyrium. Golgotha was the lamentation place.

Prayers began at dawn when the cocks crowed. Twilight brought Lucernare, the Service of Lamps, when the bishop went into the Tomb and lit a taper from an eternal vigil-lamp there. "Great glass lanterns are burning everywhere," noted Egeria, "and there are many candles in front of the Anastasis and also Before and Behind the Cross. By the end of all this, it is dusk. . . ."[16]

But the major corrections were made to the annual round, once loaded with the old gods' festival days, now reset to the single narrative drama of Christ's pilgrimage.

The year still peaked as nature requires at the equinoxes and broke at the solstices, with fire-festivals celebrated at those points, now with Christian names. Midsummer solstice that had been water-goddess-time and Shavuot now held the Baptist's feast and the fire-fall of Pentecost. July, when blazing Sirius had long reigned as sun-riser, now held in one mystery-embrace—whose elucidation must await the next lap of my own pilgrimage—the feasts of red-haired Magdalene and the dazzling fighting St. James of Compostela.

Then August would bring Mary's Assumption on the same day that had been Artemis / Diana's feast, followed two days later by the anniversary of Helena's fishing the Cross out of its watery grave.

In December, when Dionysius had been born of a virgin in a cave, and also Osiris and Sol Invictus, and Mithra and Isis's son Horus, now Christ's birthday was celebrated. And still the enormousness of winter solstice was sufficient to support as well the feast days of his doubles, Thomas and John the Divine.

In spring Holy Week, the two fundamental Christian mysteries of Incarnation and Resurrection fell together in the period that had held Cybele's feast and Attis's death and reappearance as an evergreen tree. The deepest Christian mysteries were enacted as theater in which the pilgrims were participants.[17] On Good Friday, the bishop read aloud to the congregation, and "you could hardly believe how every single one of them weeps," wrote Egeria. That and the next two days were full of rhetorical exchange, some of it drawn little changed from pagan lamentations:

> I am overwhelmed o my son
> And I cannot endure
> That I should be in the chamber
> And you on the wood of the cross
> I in the house
> And you in the tomb.[18]

Holy Saturday alone of all the year, there was no mass, for Christ had not yet attained to heaven to invest the bread. At Lucernare that day began the paschal vigil till midnight, when the pilgrims went to sit around the Tomb till dawn. And then on Easter day, an antiphon would be sung between bishop and people in hastening imperative rhythm,

> Whom do you seek in the Tomb, you Christians . . .
> Jesus of Nazareth, crucified . . .
> He is not here, He is risen . . .
> Go, proclaim the good news, He has risen . . .[19]

And a wood cross wrapped in cloth, decorated with flowers and hidden in the Anastasis, or a piece of consecrated bread, would be discovered as if by miracle and brought to light.[20]

✦　✦　✦

The cult spread so rapidly a modern Catholic writer even refers to the phenomenon as *"la contamination évangélique. . . ."*[21] And as dogma was carved out of myth, it became both more specific and also more prone to folklorish and propagandistic enlargement. Soon it would be said, for instance, that Constantine saw a silver cross in the sky and from it took his bellicose motto, *in hoc signo vinces.* And so a cross anywhere in Christendom would stir men to fantasies of empire.

Yet even while the artifacts of the new Cosmos were being invented, the concept "Christ," like that of the Buddha in Asia, gave evidence of weakness along the very fault line it had come into being to heal. Polestar's western son had emerged from thought as one more of those hinges to lock heaven and earth together, the unnatural with the natural, the unseen and longed-for with the inevitable. But the stumbling point for the monotheistic mind was certainly this, that the creature was not to be let live in the mode of mythic illusion but had to be accepted as a literal individual with head and feet, "Son of the Living God" and "Son of Man" imploded.[22]

However, the dialectical gap remained, and therefore the question kept returning. From which part of the Cosmos did this Son of Star come: from the Sky-side or the Earth-side? That is to say, was he made of spirit—*homoousios*—or of spirit-in-matter—*heterousios?* Two hundred and fifty bishops at the Council of Nicea strove to solve the paradox but could not end the argument. How could they? For contradiction is implicit in the myth.

Already by the fourth century, in fact, a third element, the Holy Ghost, had been introduced into the dialectical gap to fill it with an exquisite haze.[23] But so powerful is the mind's drive to make images of ideas that that Ghost would sometimes coagulate into a traveling spark with wings, in which shape it pierced the Virgin's womb, as Renaissance painters delectably described.

In the end, of course, the contradiction led to rupture between the two sides of Christendom. The Orthodox East would continue to stress Christ the incandescent Pantocrator, Creator of the Cosmos, and dread Judge of human souls. The Catholic West would tend to stress Christ's organizational influence on earth through kings, popes, bishops, ministers, and other worldly governors. Thus evolving Christian doctrine followed the course of bifurcating Buddhism. And the paired symbol of mystery-reunion so briefly glimpsed in the morning-light of the myth vanished, leaving behind only its hammered, enameled traces in dogma and its shadows in the protean forms of art.

However, fundamentalist Christians East and West retain the imagery of Polestar's pilgrimage around the top of the sky. So that they, like fundamentalist Jews and Moslems, preach the Eschaton, the apocalyptic End of Days, with varying degrees of enthusiastic expectation.

✦ ✦ ✦

After the Moslem conquest, Christians, like Jews, generally could visit and maintain their shrines, though under Moslem custodianship, and this joint protectorate was extended by Charlemagne.

All the same, as Christian empire coalesced in the Middle Ages, drawing strength and unity from myths of Holy War, the recapture of its east flank, Jerusalem, and its west flank, Santiago de Compostela in Spain, presented themselves as efficient political causes.

Like other wars, the Crusades were preached by theorists and fought by the obedient. An inciting act, in 1010, was "mad Hakim's" renunciation of the agreement made with Charlemagne. Five years later, his mobs torched the Martyrium. Though that caliph soon after changed his mind and gave permission for the shrine to be rebuilt, the rationale for war existed. In November of 1095, Pope Urban II broadcast the "horrible tale" that "the Moslem race holds Jerusalem" and evoked the glories of dying to retake it. At the end of his address, he handed out crosses to an audience raised to fever pitch by his words, and the idea of Holy War took hold. In the heat of mid-July of 1099, the first Western troops appeared below the walls of Jerusalem, many barefoot, carrying palms, singing and praying at the top of their voices. On Jerusalem's ancient day of catastrophe, the gates were broken in. Once again blood ran ankle-deep. That one day, at least says legend, ten thousand Crusaders cut down forty thousand Moslems and Jews and claimed the city for the Prince of Peace.

For all that, the Crusader Kingdom survived but seventy-eight years. The Holy Sepulchre Church was built during those years, enclosing under one double-domed roof the two separated sacred places designated by Helena and her advisers. In its cavernous gloom still stands the humped rock of the old Anastasis, where it has for two thousand years. For structural reasons, the church is entered from the south through a double-arched portal in the Romanesque style, based, as medieval legend knew, on the Temple's twin portal, Mercy and Repentance.[24]

The Crusaders took over the Moslem shrine on the old Temple site. Inevitably, therefore, the sacred axis had to be corrected once more. The dent in the rock that had been called Muhammad's footprint was now said to be Christ's, and the Islamic lamp above it was said to hold Christ's blood. The fact that the Crucifixion, according to theory, had taken place half a mile westward was, apparently, not so compelling as that the blood should now hang vertically over the rock from Eden. The shrine itself was renamed the Templum Domini. It would in time lend its blueprint to Temple Church in London, thence one day the Middle and Inner Temple Law Courts in that city.

On this mountaintop now again generative of myths of glory won and suffering rewarded, the Knightly Orders were born that would carry the cult of chivalry west. First in 1070 had come the Knights of St. John Hospitaliers. They wore black tunics with white crosses and served a Jerusalem hospice where two thousand sufferers from battle wounds as well as all the plagues of the medieval near-Orient, from leprosy to parasitical diseases, dysentery, and emotional breakdown, might be helped to die. This place, for all its sounds and smells of horror, was called one of "three columns built by God for the support of his poor people," that is, access routes for pilgrims upward toward heaven. The other two columns stood by the Great St. Bernard Pass in the Alps, through which pilgrims made their way to Rome, and in the Pyrenees on the way to Compostela. The three columns bound into one orbital tour the High Complete City, and City in the Orb, and the Spanish place called Field of Stars. Trudging the circuit, Christian pilgrims, like their brothers and sisters elsewhere around the world, lent their momentum to the turning of the Three Worlds and the increase of empire on earth.

Next to come, in 1120, and most renowned of the Jerusalem Orders were the Knights Templar, gorgeous in white chemises with red crosses. Rule 57 of the Code of the Templars—drawn up by the great Bernard—specified that "The faith, enforced by knights, should advance and destroy the enemy without remorse." On their model, in 1175, was built the Order of St. James of Compostela, mandated to clean the Moor out of Spain. Then came the Teutonic Knights, with the black cross on white that one day Prussian troops would wear to war.

THE faith, enforced by knights and fed on myth, was no match, however, against a force just as fanatic but better witted. In 1187, the Crusader army was engaged by the Turks led by Saladin, one of the renowned tacticians of history. The season was again deep summer. The armies took their positions outside the ancient city of Tiberius on the east bank of the Jordan, below the Sea of Galilee.

In some time past, the True Cross had brought victory to those who carried it. Indeed at Easter of 629, the Byzantine Heraclius had come riding with it through the Golden Gate after retrieving it from those who had earlier sacked it. This time the Bishop of Acre, in armor on an armored horse, bore it aloft to lead the way as the Ark had once led the tribes, and it led the men straight into strategic grassfires set off by the foe. In smoke and flame, the Crusaders went down, and the Turks marched on toward Damascus with Christian heads on their spears and, at their lead, the famous Cross with an icon of Christ's head nailed onto it, upside down.[25]

News of the loss of the Cross made its way through Europe and inspired the Third Crusade. The thirteenth century was spanned by the worst of the Christian military adventures, turning on Constantinople and on the Albigensians in France and engaging children in a suicidal march. Meantime, the Inquisition made its own use of Moriah, Mountain of Light, by sending heretics toward it in irons.

Despite military reverses, during the High Middle Ages Venice and Genoa rode high on the seaborne pilgrim trade controlling every aspect of it, even providing advocates to help travelers make out their wills. For though jolly a pilgrimage may have been to Canterbury—so that a Wife of Bath might go in "gay scarlet clothes" as if to a marriage—there was hardship aplenty on the Jerusalem trail. But possession of Christ's death-place and the right of free, safe access to it had by then become the "collective myth," some have called it, of the West. The failure of a military program could not shake the myth. Only then the city became for Christians what it already had been for centuries for the Jews, "more and more dreamlike and inaccessible, the symbol of a great longing."[26]

Therefore, when in December 1917 the British Protestant field marshal Sir Edmund Allenby arrived to take command of the city, he entered its gate not on horseback but, as he said, on foot like any humble and reverent pilgrim.

❖

THE majority of the pilgrims who went to Jerusalem in the late nineteenth and early twentieth centuries were Orthodox Russians, often poor peasants who may have walked a thousand miles in birch-bark shoes to an embarkation point on the Black Sea. Some of them came burdened with penitential irons around their arms, legs, and necks, talismans of a faith that was truly an opiate. One sees their faces in early photographs, lined by age and hardship but wide-eyed with astonishment to have arrived at all.

After visiting the shrines in Jerusalem, they walked on to the Jordan, in which they bathed fully dressed in the black death-caps and white burial shrouds they would doubtless soon put on forever. And in testimony to enduring cosmic myth, they carried bells that, dipped in the river, would be charms forever against thunder. Then many took, and take still, the long road south, following the star of myth, Canopus, or the Star of Sancta Catherina, all the way to her shrine at the foot of Moses' mountain.

One sees these rural pilgrims today, garbed in country black, on their knees in the Holy Sepulchre Church before the Stone of Unction on which, by tradition, Christ's body was laid to be wrapped. That slab of stone is kept awash in holy water. With shaking hands, these old folk pull out of their satchels rosaries, family photos, prayer cards, and dip them into the water. With rags, they sop it up, dumping the soaked cloths into plastic bags to take home. They press one cheek to the Stone, then turn and press the other, then the forehead, with such grief that they seem to be rehearsing their own deaths soon to come.

For these are of the race of passionate pilgrims who in Greece at Pentecost are known to court epiphany by dancing on beds of embers. First they pray, and then they sing to the music of lyres and drums. Then Saints Constantine and Helena whisper in their ears, and they walk across the coals that feel, one of them has said, "like walking on green grass."[27]

✦ ✦ ✦

So much blood had been spilled through history to gain access to the Holy Sepulchre, it must have amused its Turkish overseers, then shocked the Protestant British, to watch the Catholic and Orthodox sects scrap for footholds in that church.

In 1757 the Turks even drew up a contract of privileges between the main contestants, the Latin West, the Greek Orthodox East, and the Armenians, the last claiming first-rights because their forebears fought the Jews under Titus. In fact their Cathedral was built for them by the Crusaders and has the name St. James for two good reasons. Buried under its pavement, supposedly, are two of Christendom's principal relics, the whole body of James the Lesser and the bodiless head of James the Greater.

When the British came in, they adopted the Turkish contract and published it in a booklet, "The Status Quo," which also paid honor to what the crown took to be permanent political status quo: "the world-wide domination of Great Britain, the Turk pushed back far beyond reach and, most important perhaps of all, Russian influence extinguished."[28]

The contract applies still to all parts of the church, whose floor plan is the Crusaders' of 1149 but whose superstructure is a motley jumble, jerry-built after 1808 when a monk reportedly tried to douse a blaze in a gallery with brandy.

The apportionment of privileges begins with the courtyard before the main doors. It may be used by all the major rites save the Ethiopians, though only the Greek Orthodox may clean it. The major denominations and also the Copts have right of entry through the doors, but the Copts have no claim to altars or chapels, though they may swing the incense censer at certain places. The same goes for the Syrian Jacobites. Neither Copts nor Syrians, however, may march in formal procession into the church unless they go with the Armenians, except on Good Friday when each sect can make its own procession, except the Ethiopians.

The "Seven Arches of the Virgin" are argued over by Latins and Orthodox; the Chapel of St. Nicodemus, by Armenians and Syrian Jacobites. None will allow the other to clean or lay out altar cloths except as written in the Status Quo. The Armenians own St. Helena's chapel; the Orthodox, the choir of the Crusaders; the Copts, a tiny chapel east of the Tomb; the Syrians, a still tinier chapel; and the Franciscans, who have been in Jerusalem since the twelfth century and run most of its Roman Catholic shrines, a big Chapel of the Apparition of Jesus to His Mother.

Just inside the main door is a steep staircase leading to the top of the rock called Golgotha, passing on the way a glass through which the famous bloodstained fissure can be seen. At the top, two smallish chapels have been hollowed in the enclosing wall. One, the Latin Chapel of Calvary, marks two events: where Christ was stripped of his garments and where he was nailed to the Cross. The other is the Greek Orthodox Chapel of Calvary, where the Cross was erected. The sites of these three terminal events are aglow with lamps and icons, with ornaments of brass and silver, gilt and marble, ex votos of wax and bejeweled gifts of rich pilgrims.

But in between, as if in the cleft between two peaks, is a tiny Latin altar of deep and solemn sanctity, where the Virgin is said to have stood when she received her son in her arms. The double image of sorrowing woman and dead man, itself a cross-shaped icon, inspired the liturgy Stabat Mater that has been set to music many times and helped inspire the passionate Mary-cult of the Gothic Age. It is the dark preamble to the radiant reunion between Christ and the Star-goddess, whose meeting is, however, not commemorated in any corner of the church.

The events marked atop Golgotha form the next-to-terminal Stations of the Cross today. The last is the Tomb, which belongs to all the rites—save, again, the Ethiopians.

The some twenty Ethiopian Coptic monks in Jerusalem, like their brothers the Ethiopian Jews, trace their lineage back to the lost tribe of Dan and the Queen of Sheba and represent one of the oldest pilgrim presences in the Holy Land. Down the centuries, in their mountainous homeland, they have kept alive their claim to the myths: Adam, they say, sleeps under a stone in the nearly inaccessible city of Lalibela. The Ark from Solomon's Temple is said to be hidden nearby. When the Lord abandoned Jerusalem, they say, he moved not north but south toward Ethiopia. Yet for whatever cause—one hesitates to suggest, skin color—they have been excluded, as are the Fallachin Jews from free acceptance by Jewish Orthodoxy, from all privileges in this or any other Holy Land church. Instead, they have contrived to set up an African village that perches fantastically on the roof of the Holy Sepulchre, where between the warped old domes and the stars they enact their strange and sumptuous Easter vigil called "Searching for the Body of Christ."

It only remains to say that in the exact place beneath the great dome where a thousand years ago two iron chains crossed in an open courtyard, there is a modest marble urn that marks the center of the world.[29]

IN spite of so much discord, the Holy Sepulchre Church is home to one of the oldest equinoctial ceremonies in the world, going back at least four thousand years to Indo-Iranian fire worship and, behind that, to the very origin of consciousness of the natural miracle of fire.[30]

The Holy Fire Ceremony that culminates at noon on Saturday before Orthodox Easter opens with a stunning procession of bejeweled and robed ecclesiastics.[31] One of them is then stripped of his finery and goes alone into the empty Tomb. Its door is sealed and all lights in the building, vaults, domes, and galleries are doused. For an hour or so then, a band of excited youths whirl, leap, and shout around the Tomb, Christ's dervishes churning life back into it. When they finally bound away, silence falls. Not a soul stirs among the hundreds of pilgrims packed in and waiting. And then suddenly, fire is seen to pass out of two portholes in the Tomb wall onto torches held by two deacons, who turn and rush it off to the local churches. In the old days, the fire was sent off in clay pots all over the world, and even now a bowl of embers may be pushed into the cockpit of a jet plane for transport to another continent.

At the same moment, in the church itself, fire seems to leap—or to *have leapt*—from candle to candle in people's hands until it fills the whole church with its miracle-light.

The trick must be worked by someone who climbs into the sealed Tomb through an underground tunnel. But when with a sudden rush the whole basin of the church, every corner to the farthest reach of it, seems to have caught fire at once, thousands of candles flaring up in thousands of hands as if in one stroke, it's impossible not to be shaken. Then people are crying *Kyrie Eleison!* and *Christos Vostrece!* Bells are ringing, chimes and gongs are sounding, and around stand old men and women of the Old World with blurred eyes and open mouths, like children about to cry.

"I have come to set fire to the earth," Luke (12.49) said Christ said. By noon on Saturday in Jerusalem, even a skeptic may feel that some such release of energy has taken place. And all the splendor of robes and gold implements that have filled the Holy Sepulchre Church is but a reflection of what the pilgrims believe they have churned out of the stone.

That fire, scripture said, hovered in the world still, and would for forty days—offspring of Pole- and -Star, their merged, incarnate glory.

PART SIX

FOLLOWING STAR

◆

It was as if the legendary "Cathédral Engloutie" emerged
from the depth of prehistory with its bells still ringing.
Giorgio de Santillana and
Hertha von Dechend:
HAMLET'S MILL

◆

TOWARD THE WEST:
COMPOSTELA

I turned from the fire in Jerusalem and set my course toward the afternoon sun. My pilgrimage was nearing its end. I flew to Paris; from there my road would wind southwards, then west, leading me also through the coils of the myth of the pilgrim St. James of Compostela, fisherman in the Galilee and Apostle to Spain. And I was lucky in my timing, for it was a Holy Year in Santiago's shrine city, out at the northwesternmost corner of that country. When a Holy Year comes round in Christendom, as in the other sacred kingdoms on earth, time and space are timeless and all-enfolding, and *grace*—the sum of Shiva, flame, Wisdom, and luck—shines her light into all places.

Then the Holy Door at the sunrise side of the Cathedral in Compostela, carved with twice-twelve guardian figures of gentle old men, is opened, as the Golden Door in Jerusalem will be open when the Messiah comes, whether at last or again. To that door, many pilgrims still flock at such times. For each one entering it automatically wins the release of his or her dead out of Purgatory and wins also absolution for the living, as if he dipped into the Ganges or Jordan.

But there is more to the Santiago Trail than absolution. The word "trail" itself has overtones of mystery. Its root is "tragulare," to drag. An implication is that someone has died, and the body been dragged on ahead, leaving pursuers to find their way by subtle clues. So alluring in fact are the clues on this Trail that even an art historian's reserve melts before it. "There is," wrote Kingsley Porter, "in the place and in the road, a singular poetry . . . chords in the memory, long unused, are set vibrating. Like a cosmic phenomenon [it] overwhelms with the sense of its force, its inevitability."[1]

DURING at least four hundred years, the Santiago Trail was the most traveled pilgrim system in the West, a continuum through which ideas and artistic styles moved back and forth between the Far and Nearer East and the Atlantic and also north and south across Europe. The system in the old days began with four roads like feeder streams that flowed through France toward the Pyrenees, funneling their freight of pilgrims through two historic mountain passes, Roncesvalles and Somport.[2] Some fifty miles (or "three short days' journey") west of the Spanish border, the two streams merged at an actual bridge, the ancient, arched Puente la Reina. Thence the joined and deepened stream flowed west through Navarre and Castile, through the royal cities of Burgos and León, on through ever wilder, rockier land into the province of Galicia.

Each of the ways drained a different sector of medieval Europe. From Italy and Provence, pilgrims came on the Via Tolosana along the old Roman Road of Hercules past the Rhone delta and the ancient cities of Marseilles, Aix, and Arles. From Germany, they came down the Via Podiensis, through Burgundy with its great abbey churches of Autun and Cluny, on through the Auvergne, the volcanic outcrops and rough uplands around Le Puy and Aubrac, through the gorges of Languedoc, on by the cliffside hamlet of Conques with its fabled treasury, on through Gascony toward the mountains. From Limoges toward Perigord and south, the Via Lemosina drew from west-central France. The Via Turonesis brought travelers from England and Flanders, gathering others from Paris, Orléans, Tours, Poitiers, and Bordeaux.

During the Middle Ages, some half-million people a year trod these town cobblestones and highland footpaths. "Palmers" might go to Palestine and "Romers" to Rome, but according to Dante, "he only is a *pilgrim* who goeth towards or forwards the House of St. James."[3] More accessible than Jerusalem, more revered for its one saint than Rome with its two, its four basilicas and many martyrs' shrines all crying for attention, the Cathedral of St. James outpulled also those of St. Martin at Tours, St. Joseph of Arimithea at Glastonbury, and St. Thomas at Canterbury.

In fact, the saint's bones, purportedly enshrined there, spawned subcults all over Europe. There were two of his heads for a while in Venice and others in Valencia, Amalfi, and beyond. There was a bit of his corpse in Toulouse and another near Milan. Parts of his arms and legs were preserved in Sicily and Capri and various German shrines. When Mathilda, mother of Henry II of England, visited Compostela in 1125, she took home the bones of one of the saint's hands.[4] Yet none of these diminished the drawing power of the center. "May transmontane rivals blush who claim to have any part of his relics," puffed the twelfth-century guidebook to the shrine. "His whole body is there . . . divinely illuminated by heavenly carbuncles, endlessly honored by divine fragrant odors, decorated with the brightness of celestial candles and unceasingly honored by angelic adoration."[5]

In a metaphoric sense, the trail has another shape. In historic reversal, it winds its way down from the Gothic highlands of the Île-de-France, passing then through the lower Middle Ages of coalescing Romanesque empire, then the Age of barbarian chaos when Christianity must struggle with the dying gods of paganism, to arrive at last at the primitive Galician shore, Cape Finisterre. World's End, that means. But sky's beginning. For in the language of myth, the Santiago Trail is, of course, one more of those "heavenly rivers" like the Ganges, Euphrates, Jordan, and Nile that flow down from the sky across the earth to the sea, only to rise back into identity as the River of Stars.

Indeed the cosmic image was evoked with delight in the Middle Ages. Then, as Dante says, the "white circle" of the Milky Way was known "by the common people . . . as the Way of St. James," while in an elegant chiasmus or crisscross, the trail on earth was known as the Via Lacta. And as it was claimed by at least one poet-monk, Paulinus of Nola, that a martyr's grave on earth was a "star" come to rest there, folklore responded that the Milky Way stars were souls of dead pilgrims still hurrying to their destination, and a shooting star was one of those spirit-pilgrims who had slipped.[6] Then, lest he or she fly off the road entirely, someone down on the ground was supposed to say quickly, *"Dios te guia y la Magdalena!"*[7] Which saying, when I heard of it, was a clear sign to me of the rightness of my ending my pilgrimage here. For I had already, in Jerusalem, adopted that Star-creature as my guardian.

THE Milky Way and the Magdalene might beckon from on high, but there were tangible road markers in the old days. One finds them carved in odd places over the doors and atop the columns of churches and on holy-water fonts and the like. In the first place, there are little figures of the Magi, in peaked Persian caps and flying capes, hurrying along toward the great star Matthew wrote about. In an old tale, the Magi lost sight of it when they neared Bethlehem, but they found it again in the depths of a well right beside the holy grotto.

As to which star may actually have been visible around the year One, scholars have argued for centuries.[8] But I take it there was at that late moment in cosmological proto-science not one star that burned itself into the memory of a world to come, nor even one triad of fire-following Magi, but many, though all would have been transparencies of the great rain-star Sirius, which lives in myth as a ray of connective tissue between Polestar and ourselves.

Then as other guide signs for pilgrims on the Santiago Trail, there is the scallop shell with its own pearl of meaning, and the image of "seynt James" himself in his broad-brimmed hat with the shell over the brow, his great-cloak big enough to sleep in, and his staff of oak.

Very solemn he looks in his stone effigies, set apart from his secular brothers by that monolithic costume. In fact, along the course of the twelfth century, ordinary traveling clothes became rigid and formalized to signify the spiritual traveler.[9] The pilgrim might even receive his outfit at the altar in a rite comparable to the investiture of a priest or the blessing of a Crusader. There was overt symbolism, of course: the leather pouch signifying poverty; the staff, protection against the devil, and so forth. But the deeper meaning of the pilgrim dress, I take it, lies in the old idea that human anatomy must be rendered rigid, columnar, and sexually neuter to serve as an architectural beam between earth and sky.

Perambulating columns like these abounded on the roads in the Middle Ages, drinking out of brooks known to be magically life-extending and spreading miracle tales as they jostled with horsed knights and also with beggars and those self-branded or with crosses cut in their flesh, and also with those sent into *limina* by their bishops for crimes from murder to heresy, hung with "iron manacles, fetters, chains, hobbles, shackles, traps, bars, yokes, helmets, scythes and diverse instruments of penance."[10]

All these travelers made their way along a trail of little stone carvings that promised redemption at the journey's end: a Noah in the porthole of his ark; another beside his beached ark, flanked by eager cows; Shadrach, Meshach, and Abed-nego, woeful but confident of rescue, in divers fiery furnaces; and so on. However, two repeated subjects refer, even if in a style of childlike simplicity, to deeper cosmological ideas. One is the Mystical Mill, in which the grain of the old Cosmos is being ground by Christ into the flour of the new. The other is the figure of Father Abraham holding Lazarus straight upright against his bosom. For Abraham was the one who back in the beginning went searching for Polestar. And by this image, a medieval rendering of Luke 16.23, we are informed that in the end the pilgrim from Ur did attain that unattainable star and that his bosom is now the still point in the turning sky.

Yet another rare piece of information is conveyed by Luke. For when Abraham was appealed to by a person down on earth for a sign of his presence up there, the old man leaned down and, for that one and only time, spoke:

> There is a great chasm fixed between us; no one from our side who wants to reach you can cross it, and none may pass from your side to us. (Luke 16.26)

The loneliness of Polestar and the distance of humanity from Him is an ancient intuition perhaps first voiced in Asia, to which world myth responded by breeding the intermediary gods and other double-natured hinge figures.

But Abraham goes on to say there are people on earth with true understanding. But if you will not listen to them, you will not know the meaning of rising-from-the-dead, even if it is shown to you.

✦ ✦ ✦

As for the myth of Santiago, it took centuries to exhaust the energy in the bulb, so to speak, out of which James and his permutations came, like Shiva out of Rudra, increasing in glory in the minds of a few pragmatic dogmatists and the millionfold minds of his devotees. For cosmic myth was drawn on deliberately by those who plotted to advance the dream of empire through this hero. So while his tale seems, on the surface, to be merely utilitarian in serving the Christian Reconquest of Spain, it drew its life from a deep source. The gracious stone figure that welcomes pilgrims to the end of the Trail holds a scroll with the words *Misit Me Dominus,* The Lord Sent Me. And indeed, the Lord sent him a long way, even from what Mircea Eliade called the "time of marvels."

St. James was a product of imaginative invention from the beginning. There is no evidence for any part of the legend that made him the Apostle-missionary to Roman Spain.[11] Not one of the early historians of the Church mentions him in connection with that country. After Christ's death and the breaking up of the zodiacal twelve, there is only one mention of him in scripture: that is, his beheading in Jerusalem in 44 (Acts 12.2) at the order of Herod Agrippa I. However, with his brother John, he forms a hinge-pair of exceptional interest.

The story begins (Mark 3.17) with the two as fishermen in the Galilee when Jesus came that way performing miracles. Their parents were Zebedee and Mary Salomé, but according to Mark, Jesus renamed them the "Sons of Thunder" and in that one stroke swept them out of whatever historic reality they might have had and into the procedures of mythic transformation.[12]

And there at the very outset, one must dredge up the whole structure of the old Storm and Thunder Ba'als of the ancient Near East, and Yahweh himself coming out of storm clouds, and Zeus/Jupiter, thrower of thunderbolts to the ground where they fell in the shape of what we now call stone "celts," prehistoric hand tools dropped by cave dwellers but considered magical by latecomers into rural Europe and, in a wonderful ellipsis of time and belief, called "Zebedee stones."[13]

These two Apostles, then, were close relatives of the principal Son of the Sky. With Christ, in fact, they appear ever in geometric figures: in that semicircle at the Transfiguration and, with Peter, in a quartet at Gethsemane. Indeed, puffed up by these proximities to their teacher, they even asked of Jesus that he seat them to his right and left in Paradise. They were rebuked for hubris, but the geometry stays in the mind: the Sons of Thunder flank the Son of Polestar even as the Gemini lifted the sun in the Golden Age and, in India still, Shiva's two priests flank the linga.

For they were brothers, wherefore the seas of myth must disgorge other siblings, like those Gemini, whose heroism in myth foreshadows Santiago's adventures to come:

> . . . horse-taming Kastor and blameless Polydeukes . . .
> Saviours of men on this earth and of swift-sailing ships . . .
> Having sped through the air with pushing wings . . .
> Hail, Tyndaridai! riders of swift horses![14]

Like Castor, brother John was the earthbound one of the pair. He would live out a human if visionary life appearing now in Patmos, now in Ephesus, serving as at least the source and perhaps the author of the Fourth Gospel, the Apocalypse, and the gnostic Gospel of the Cross of Light.

But Santiago belonged to the sky. A supernatural warrior like Yahweh, he was like Christ a supernatural savior and may be considered one last emanation of Sirius, for out of the cumulative mythology of that star, the appearing and disappearing saint derived his flamboyant character. In point of fact, his identity as one of Sirius's host of figurations was hinted at early on, while Jesus was approaching Jerusalem and stopped, with James and John alone, at a Samaritan village. When they were refused entry, Luke says the brothers flared up on their leader's account, using odd language in his defense: "Lord, may we call down fire from heaven to burn them up?" To which the New English Bible adds, as if we did not know it already, *"as Elijah did."*[15]

The *"astro brilliante de España,"* then, as James would be known until today, is the final appearance at least to date of the astronomical myth-structure that earlier gave forth Elijah. And he would draw into his myth, willy-nilly, the same Star-goddesses whom Elijah repulsed but who reappeared in the person of the bad one turned good to welcome Christ. The forms and meaning of this reappearance are at the very heart of the mysterious glamour of the Santiago Trail. The Golden Legend provides a myth-particle in which the Magdalene was actually in process of being married to brother John when Christ, arriving by surprise in the "midst of the nuptials," broke them up.[16] Jacopo calls the tale "false and frivolous," but it holds as if in amber the idea that a Thunder Brother and a Star-queen belong in union.

In further support of the argument, one has only to consider the steps by which James would be locked into the Christian calendar. His day of actual martyrdom, the Golden Legend says, was the spring equinox, the same as Christ's and several pagan gods'. But later the Church reset his feast to July 25, a date that also reverberates. For late July was, to say it again, the time when for some three thousand years overlapping the year One, Sirius rose brilliantly before dawn along the 35th parallel, which is the very route Santiago's great pendulum of a pilgrimage would take him, swinging west, then east, then back west to his cathedral to stay.[17]

The Magdalene's feast day is July 22.

And to cap the point: in both the Latin and Greek calendars, the feast day of Elijah is July 20.[18]

THE saintly narrative as it proceeds is full of charm even if, like the back-dated death-plaints of the pagan oracles, it's devoid of truth.[19] If Christ died in 33, then according to the tale, seven years later James asked permission of the Virgin in Jerusalem and sailed off with two disciples to convert Spain.

He landed, says the storyteller, either in Galicia, at the Roman seaport of Iria Flavia at the mouth of the Ulla River, or else in Tarragona, at the mouth of the Ebro. If he landed at the Ebro (which he assuredly did not), he followed the river upstream for a while and fell asleep by a woodland canal. He was wakened by flashes of light and angels plunging out of the sky with the Virgin on a column of jasper. In the Cathedral of Saragossa she stands today, the little Madonna *del Pilar,* black as the night out of which she is said to have come in a star-fall two thousand years ago.

If he landed around Iria Flavia (there is no evidence for this place either), James wandered along the coast to a place called Mugia, where the Virgin came by water to ask him to build the chapel of Our Lady of the Barque, which still draws pilgrims today. Offshore is a rock with her footprint on it and another that shifts in the tides, and that is the keel of her ship.

All versions of the story, however, agree that James had little luck making converts and after four years sailed home, where he met his fate when either Herod or—as Gothic fabulists had it, a Jewish mob—struck off his head. He caught it in his hands and carried it to wherever it is now. Some twenty years later, James the Less, who had become the city's first bishop, was either thrown off a wall or beaten to death. In the Middle Ages when Santiago's remains would be glorified in Compostela, James the Lesser's head would also turn up there, paraded to this day on a silver platter at festival time, though both heads are also in the Armenian Cathedral in Jerusalem—or nowhere.

If in the tale of the traveling Apostle there was any vestige of fact, it ended there and imagination took off in spasms of invention, working transformations on sea-, star- and sky-myths of the whole Mediterranean basin. To begin with, the saint's disciples stole the body to return it to Galicia. An angel led them to Jerusalem's seaport, Jaffa, from where they set sail with the body along the route of Jonah and Ulysses and how many others, toward the Pillars of Hercules that in pagan cosmic myth guarded the gates to the unbounded beyond. And as the boat passed through those mystical narrows, it itself turned into stone like Osiris's granite sarcophagus and sailed on without wind or favorable tides to its destination.

Eventually the ship neared land, and as it drew to shore, the disciples saw a man in wedding clothes on a horse, galloping along the beach. Suddenly the horse bolted into the waves. People on shore cried out that the bridegroom like Great Pan must be dead. But the horse surfaced with the rider still on his back. And when it stepped out of the waves, horse and man were hung with scallop shells. Wherefore the saint wears a shell, whereby the trail-follower comes into possession of one more of those clues that point toward the journey's end but must wait a while for interpretation.

But the rising out of the sea of the bridegroom and—even though still in his casket—Santiago himself brings one more structural timber up from the depths. For all the drowned gods of the Near East had ended their lives washed down the rivers into those deeps—Pan, and again Osiris, and Dionysius who then drifted ashore in a box "out of the depths of the sea." So now had come the time, as Ezekiel foretold (26.16), when "the sea-kings will come down from their thrones" to be refashioned for a new age into one more like "a man rising from the sea."

To continue the tale, the saint's disciples landed at Iria Flavia, tied their boat to a stone mooring post, and, in one version, carried the body ashore and laid it on a rock that folded around it as the tamarisk tree enfolded Osiris. By another version, burdened with the bier, the disciples asked the local Queen of Wolves, Lupa, for the loan of her bulls to pull it to safety. She agreed, knowing they were savage, and also sent them straight toward a dragon's lair. But the Christian men made the sign of the cross over the dragon and it split down the middle. The bulls grew tame and led the party into Lupa's courtyard, whereupon she converted. The coffin was then buried or hidden under bushes. The disciples died, and the place was forgotten.

At this point, the narrative pauses for the wheel of myth to interlock with that of fact. While the bones slept, history spun on. Seven hundred years passed, during which time Rome fell, half the world became Christian and much of it was lost to Islam, before the cycle of Santiago was taken up again. But then it would be forced into life as an instrument in divinely justified military strategy.

✦ ✦ ✦

In 711 the Caliphate of Spain was established in Cordova, within a century to become the richest and most civilized city in the Western world. The Moslem flood moved on across the Pyrenees and in 732 was stopped before the city of Tours, where Charles Martel had the help of St. Martin, dead four centuries but still a wonder-worker. The Moor then withdrew behind the mountains where he had free reign save in pockets of Christian resistance. One of these pockets, says legend, was ever-wild Galicia, and there a Christianized Visigothic King Pelayo, barely recorded save as "the contemptible Goth" by his enemies, reportedly won a battle and initiated the line of kings of Asturias that would span the centuries of the Reconquest.

Pelayo's perhaps great-grandson came to the throne in 791, the second Alfonso called also "the first Pilgrim King" and also "the Chaste," whose chastity smarted under the obligation, recorded in Christian texts, of donating annually to Cordova one hundred Christian virgins.

A good fright had been given the enemy twenty years before when Charlemagne crossed the Pyrenees and drove them back as far as Saragossa. There they regrouped and drove him back again. In August of 778 his company was cut down in the gorge of Roncesvalles. Hero of this defeat, to receive full treatment in eleventh-century epic poetry, was Roland of the magical sword and horn and the triumphant cry that echoed pilgrims' first glimpse of Jerusalem—"Montjoie!" St. James's pilgrims still compete to be first to utter that cry when they catch sight of the cathedral's towers from a far bluff.

Charlemagne himself survived to kneel to the Pope, God's standing stone on earth, in St. Peter's basilica in Rome on Christmas eve of 800, when the vision of a Christian Empire received blessing. Meanwhile, though in its rush of conquest Islam would obliterate centers of culture, cutting off trade routes across the Middle East, ruining irrigation networks that had supported civilization there for millennia—in chosen cities it would give haven to the survivors of those same holocausts. Moorish Spain would draw into its ecumenical magnificence refugee scholars, scientists, and mystics from many lands, Jews with their salvaged Torahs, Arabs with their Aristotles and Euclids. The renowned Moslem annihilators—Aurangzeb in India, Mohammed Gran "the Moslem Attila" in Africa, Almanzor in Spain—when each had realized his dream of conquest, could manifest a refined nature. It is well known, not without irony, how these men loved the arts.

Then in Cordova's Mosque, with its twelve times ten columns of marble sacked from Roman temples, its nineteen bronze doors and 4,700 hanging lamps, there came to rest a world-class relic that for a time gave the city an eminence second only to Mecca. It was the Prophet's very arm. If it is true as some say that concepts break into consciousness in binary opposition to others, then it might be said that Muhammad's arm gave rise to Santiago's bones.

POLITICS, then, was the cause that brought Santiago's bones westward. The bones had to come west so they would be there to be found when politicians would need them to stimulate traffic to Galicia as the first driving shaft in the Holy War to come.[20]

Their discovery, their authentication and framing in fiction, spanned at least three centuries and was back-dated to Carolingian times. Though Charlemagne anticipated the future course of empire, he certainly did not travel the barbarous northern route as far as Galicia. However, in time pseudohistory would say that in the year before his death, that is in 814, he heard a voice come out of the Milky Way saying, *"This is the path of St. James and I am that Apostle.* My body is in Galicia, but no man knoweth where, and the Saracens oppress the land. The starry way . . . signifies that you shall go at the head of a host, and after you, peoples in pilgrimage till the end of time. And I shall procure for you from God a crown in heaven."

At this news, the Emperor set out at once for Galicia, always following the Milky Way till he came to the sea, nor did he stop then but walked straight out on the waves. There came up then a boat, the same that had brought James from Jaffa, which carried him out onto the open water where he stood up straight at the prow like Gilgamesh or Ahab and hurled his spear down into the depths.

So artful a joining of symbolic structures of World axes, seas, and spears did not come into being spontaneously. The fiction was contrived, it seems, by one who goes in scholarship only by the name "pseudo-Turpin." Well hidden is his identity for good cause, for he had a Cosmos to bring down by his skill so he could help build up another.

WHAT the contrived texts next introduced was a Galician hermit, living inland of Iria Flavia, feeding on honey and grasses and praying for deliverance from the Moor.

Praying one night, the old man saw an unusual star. He checked with shepherds, who confirmed strange sightings in the bushes and music in the sky. Together they visited their bishop, who told them to pray for three days. The third was the eve of the day that would mark St. James's feast.

When the lights did not leave off their blinking, the bishop called out the citizens of Iria Flavia. Armed with shovels, they foraged around and found a cave. In it was an arch, under the arch an altar, under that a stone casket. Within was a body, head intact, sweetly perfumed. On the ground lay a letter, saying:

> Here lies Santiago, son of Zebedee and Salomé, brother of St. John, whom Herod beheaded in Jerusalem. He came by sea, borne by his disciples to Iria Flavia of Galicia. . . .

What year it actually was that the relics turned up is impossible to know.[21] It is only certain that they were not "found," since they had never been. On various grounds, various scholars have mentioned 808, 835, 860, and 899. Some put the date as late as 1077, though pilgrimage to a shrine in Compostela seems to have gotten under way along in the tenth century, for in 950 a bishop leading a party of French pilgrims made documented arrival.

In any case, those who made political use of Santiago's myth back-dated the first of his famous miracles to the year 845, which would have been even before the discovery of the bones by some accounts.

That year would have seen Asturian forces besieged by the Sultan of Cordova.[22] His army in disarray, the Asturian King took refuge on a hill called Clavijo. There in the night, Santiago appeared to the King and offered help. The next day, while swords clashed, down he came out of the sky on a white horse, brandishing a flag with a red cross and a sword with which he cut off the heads of 60,000 men.[23]

Again in 939, when Asturian forces under Ramiro II, with the combined help then of Castile and Navarre, fought 100,000 Moors, James came out of the clouds. Thirty years later he appeared once more to help the Galicians throw off an attack on Compostela by the Normans. He returned in 1064, when Ferdinand I, then of León and Castile and helped by the famous hero the Cid, marched on Coimbra. All in all, James came out of the blue some thirty-eight times, almost always on a white horse. On into the Age of Discovery, he would appear to help Catholic forces in the Lowlands and also overseas. In 1519, Cortés, needing help against the Indians, reportedly cried out, "Santiago, to the rescue!", and he came. Pizarro, clanging swords with Arahuadpa, called for his help too. Eventually in Chile, Cuba, Haiti, Argentina, Peru, Colombia, in California, Australia, and Catholic Scotland, cities would, by bearing his name, invoke or recall his protection.

It should be known, however, that Santiago's help was of no avail against the great tenth-century conqueror Ibn Abu Amir, Almanzor Al Allah, "Victor by the Grace of God." In 987 he began to look covetously toward the Christian shrines in the north. He took León and carried the booty to Cordova to adorn the Great Mosque there. A decade later, he turned his sights on Compostela itself. When he arrived, so the tale goes, the city was abandoned. Everyone had fled save one old monk still in prayer over the saint's tomb.

"I am a devotee of Sanct Yakob," said the graybeard to Almanzor, who stood over him with drawn sword. "I am saying my prayers."

"Pray on," said the Moor, and left him alone.

However, historic report says rather that he broke into the city by force and destroyed it utterly. One has to suppose that, if the relics were indeed in place when he got there, Almanzor would have taken them to Cordova as battle-prize. However, since they had to be accessible for later miracles, legend must provide for their remaining in the ruins. Therefore, the story was spread that, when Almanzor approached the reliquary, the saint cast a spell of blinding light around it, and when the infidel horse drank from a holy-water font, the beast exploded, and the Moor fled.

IN point of fact, Almanzor took away everything of value and pulled down the church. Onto the backs of prisoners went the bronze doors of the shrine and the bells that had called the people to worship from the outlying countryside. The bells went into the Mosque, upside down and filled with oil, where they burned as braziers for Allah during two and a half centuries till Ferdinand III liberated them and sent them home on the backs of Moors. But it must be supposed that, by then, the bones were no more in the shrine of St. James than the Tablets, the Urim and Thummim, and the Shekinah were in the Second Temple in Jerusalem.

Nor are they now.

For all this drama was, as the wealth of sea and sky imagery in it has suggested, a pure revival of cosmic myth and drew its resonances therefrom. Of that first Asturian Ramiro who supposedly won epic victory with the saint's help at Clavijo, there are almost no contemporary accounts. His reign was short and troubled, and it was not until a century later, when Alfonso the Great consolidated his grip on Asturias and set out to reinvent a mythologized history for his dynasty, that the miracle folktale was spread. In his time, the year One Thousand, whose mythic repercussions so many feared and prepared for, still lay ahead. When it came, it passed like any other year, releasing Christians and Moors together into the millennium from which we are now departing in another wave of myth-generated crisis and fear. Two years after that turning point, in 1002, as later Christian texts rejoiced to say, "died Almanzor and was buried in hell."

THE city of Compostela's modern history, however, can be said to have begun a century later, in 1100, when it was made an apostolic see and Diego Gelmirez, a sagacious and ambitious Benedictine monk trained at the monastic Abbey of Cluny in France, became its first archbishop. Just the year before, the first eastward Crusading army had bloodied Jerusalem. By that triumph, the Holy City would be briefly won. But Turkish advance threatened the easterly trails, and it was understood that western Christendom must be cleansed of alien presence, first Moslem, then as it would turn out, Jewish.

In years to come, between Gelmirez and certain shadowy figures in the Paris-Cluny-Rome axis, the Santiago pilgrimage system would be formalized. Cluny would adopt the scallop-shell insignia for its widening empire and the great Crusading-missionary enterprise would begin to move west in tandem as it moved east. Soon, as Kingsley Porter says, Cluny would hold "in her grip the entire lower and consequently richer course of the gold-scattering stream [of the Santiago way], as well as the strategic points of the headwaters." And the city of St. James would be "the fulcrum of the strategies of Reconquest."[24]

There is currently disagreement among historians about who actually achieved the Reconquest, whether Benedictine Cluny and later French royal power, the papacy in Rome, or a popular movement of Christian colonists and Moor-slayers like the Indian-hunters of the American frontier. The answer is surely that, as ever, the powers made use of the people and the people lent passion to the powers. In the old world, the Homeric myth cycles were put to use to prove, by reference to Troy's destruction, that some events are fated, and death is good that leads to their accomplishment. The Indian epics served the same end for Hindu imperialists. In the same way, in Europe, popular songsters and tale-tellers, the famous jongleurs, kept alive from Carolingian times a flow of epic narrative, including Santiago's cycle, that was used by the powers to show they were conforming to divine cosmic law by obliterating the Moslem.

The same friction of fire-stick in propagandistic tinder won for modern nations their great plains and sea-route empires and is of course carried on by the superpowers today.

✦   ✦   ✦

Some more history is required in order to see, later, how the myth of Santiago was made use of.

The Benedictine Order of monks that, first in collaboration then in contest with Paris and Rome, shaped the Santiago pilgrimage was itself shaped on the ancient, still generative template, living in the mind since before Babylon, of the enclosed, centered, and everywhere interconnected Cosmos.

Its first expression in the Middle Ages was attributed by the seventh-century Pope Gregory to his predecessor, the spiritual father of Cluny. That monastic, Benedict, had been at prayer by his window one Umbrian twilight when suddenly, as Gregory wrote, "the whole world seemed to be gathered into one sunbeam and brought thus before his eyes."[25]

Whether Benedict saw the vision or Gregory in his zeal to bring it into reality thought it up, it is full of the old meaning. It says the mind sees more truly than the eyes do. A single Order underlies all nature, all its variety and capacity for mutation. In line with this theory, a natural man submitting himself to Benedictine monastic rule would give up his individual identity but gain instead, by taking part in hourly, daily, seasonal, and annual rites and ceremonies, a feeling of sharing in larger ritual rhythms.

As for one man, so for global society. Gregory sent out radiances of monks into the hinterlands where they labored for Christian union. Gregory himself took interest in crafting doctrine out of pagan myth, for example, amalgamating the pagan goddesses and their Early Christian sisters the several Marys into a single God-bearer with only one darkling shadow-sister, Magdalene. Moreover, not only liturgy, rite, and scripture would be made uniform to forms provided from the center, the Papal Chair, but European society itself would be shaped to the same template, or cut to fit it.

An earlier model for social unity had been the Roman Empire. Constantine and Charlemagne, each one in turn, tried to restore that model, but each time it failed. What then ensued in terms of social anarchy, some historians feel, stayed in the collective mind as a nightmare vision and made new efforts in visionary social planning welcome to the people. So it was that Cluny, with its theologians, its architects, artists, and geopoliticians, its "army of monks working quietly and strenuously," could lead a coalescing European society "out of the smoking ruins of war, out of social chaos."[26]

Phase by phase thereafter, the clear visual image of a Christian Cosmos would enlarge, assuming, by the thirteenth century, the aspect of a vast glass-windowed balloon. And in this Cosmos, comparable in function to the Ganges in India, ran Santiago's Star-river trail, by which the sinner might sail to redemption and the dead to immortal life.

THE laying of the foundation went fast. The first little community was set up in Burgundy some forty-six years after Charlemagne's crowning, the same year that Rome was invaded, Peter's and Paul's shrines destroyed, and the population barbarized. The refuge, in the town of Cluny, was a hunting lodge owned by the Dukes of Aquitaine, itself built on Gallo-Roman ruins. At first the organization was to be a single zodiacal diagram: twelve monks around their friar.

But before two decades had passed, Cluny, with papal counsel, was diagraming wider fields. Politically nonfunctional monasteries elsewhere were let "die of liturgical cancer," as a modern Church historian puts it, while power and gold would be deployed upon the French-papal axis.[27] In 1049 a twenty-five-year-old Burgundian monk, Hugh, became Cluny's abbot, to hold that seat for the sixty years of its greatest glory. It was during his regime that, in 1073, another Cluny monk, Hildebrand, became Pope, revived the name of the great amalgamator, Gregory, and proclaimed that the kingdom of Spain belonged *in toto,* not just the still half-savage North but the rich and civilized Moorish South as well, to St. Peter. And Spanish knights would be exempted from service in Jerusalem if they applied themselves to Moor-slaying at home.

Spain was locked into the Cluny-papal axis when Alfonso VI of León and Castile was wed to a daughter of the Duke of Burgundy. The Castilian king henceforth would send to Cluny an annual tithe of two thousand gold pieces, which he exhorted in turn from the

Moorish South. In Burgundy, the Spanish gold would fund Cluny's ambitious building programs. Cluny in return would sow monasteries, priories, and hospices along the Santiago Trail, assign Spain as a special field for its missionaries, and find and promote new relics along the way: in other words, give full treatment to the cult of St. James.

OVER the course of the eleventh and twelfth centuries, over a thousand Benedictine establishments were sown by Cluny from Portugal to Poland, and among these, relics were installed, exchanged, sent on fund-raising tours, and relocated for reasons both economic and political.[28]

Such objects, notably the bones of Christian martyrs, had been hidden in places like the catacombs around Rome, from where they were gradually disgorged. Also two relic-bearing waves passed over western Christendom from the East, one in the Carolingian era and another when the Fourth Crusade plundered Constantinople. Eventually along the Santiago Trail, each village would have its ornament, and Compostela, the crown. And each of these waystops for pilgrims became in time, as a historian says, "a political and economic center as well."[29]

Still, could the trade of relics have worked so well had there not been psychological and conceptual appeal to the objects? After the Reformation, to take an opposite example, Puritan graves might be sad reminders of "grim death," but the old martyr's grave or reliquary never was a sad place. It offered to all who came to it the sweet grace of heaven, and arrival there was occasion for joy.

As to deeper meaning, it's strange how after Paul lifted the requirement of circumcision from Gentile males, the cult of violent martyrdom, what one might call whole-body circumcision, and then mystical repossession of the saintly parts through communal worship of them, grew. The trail of meaning is interesting. The word relic derives from *relinquere*. To eternity the soul is relinquished. The flesh decays. But a particle remains, a little hinge between living and dead, a point of dialectical implosion corresponding to the Diamond Point of Buddhism.[30]

Santiago's bones, then, were in the same class as the hair and milk of the Virgin or the umbilical cord and foreskin of Christ, said to have been brought, packed in oil, to Rome from Jerusalem by an angel. In the Lateran basilica, those of Christ's parts were displayed but not to women, for "uphap some woman in the press, eithir for sikness or with child, be in grete perel there."[31] Other foreskins turned up in Poitou, Boulogne, Antwerp, and at Charroux, where a famous one went on display each seven years in arcane planetary connection. In the sack of Rome in 1527, the original is thought to have been lost, though it is in the nature of such things to reappear after centuries of concealment in some remote nunnery. In comparison to these multiplications, the spread of Santiago's parts seems less astonishing.

CLUNY thus worked its will through the magnetism of relics and also through doctrine embodied in that Cosmos of stone, the Romanesque church, that gave quintessential form to a policy of social correction. The great abbey church at Cluny, now destroyed, was more imperial in scale and sculptural ambition than any Gothic edifice would be, and its offshoots were bound in filial relationship to the Mother- or, more appropriately, Father-church. Examples along the Santiago Trail, in Vézelay, Autun, Le Puy, Tours, and so on loom on their elevations like the fortresses they were, with massive, piled-up walls, small doors, added-on cellular sanctuaries, and space inside for whole villages at times of festival or siege. These structures hold the pilgrim in muscular embrace. They lord it over his longing for sensuous experience and make of that hunger the reason for his fall from grace.

Then in the sculptural ensembles of these churches, that became the spinal-cord of Cluny's Cosmos, one sees the propagandistic use of art on which the empire grew. The ocean of pagan mythology was trolled for scenes, just as Santiago's myth was absorbing antique literary tropes, while from the barbarian farther east came decorative patterns that engulfed the stone surfaces. Here, fish-tailed, lion-pawed, double-headed beasts, birds, and other fantastic compactions were shown twined in foliage in which, from time to time, a tiny human figure could be seen struggling for breath. That bestiary in its tangle signified humanity's pre- and non-Christian condition. The lions, griffons, chimeras, and cherubim that, for antiquity, had illustrated the miracle-forms of creation, here represented untamed nature despised and rejected. And Christ, each pilgrim understood, was ever at work on that rough substructure to remold it.

But the core teaching of Romanesque Christianity was announced with skull-breaking force over the main door on the sunset or death-acknowledging facade of the church, or else on the same wall of the covered porch or narthex just inside, where lepers, penitents, neophytes, and others excluded from the sanctuary would sit to beg, pray, groan, and often die.

Visited *seriatim* along the Santiago Trail, these arched over-doors provided a narrative with crushing impact, always centered on the splayed figure of Christ, the shattered axis and paradoxical instrument of cosmic stability. Over the door of Vézelay he hangs in the Pentecostal fire-fall, when he sent down lightning bolts onto the Apostles and the Apostles out to conquer the world. His body is bent as if prepared for an act of shamanism. Were he to straighten up, his feet would drive into the abyss and his head break through the roof. Below him the Apostles twist, leap, and dance on the seven seas, while around the whole collage runs the great arch of the zodiac.

Autun's more terrible Christ rears back in his mandorla as cosmic Judge, while the damned, whose bodies are twice snapped-off, at knees and neck, are labeled with the one word an illiterate might read: HORROR. And over the great west portal at Cluny, Christ loomed in Majesty backed by nave arches nearly one hundred feet tall.

Each of these and other churches on the trail churned the pilgrim on to the next where he would offer up more prayers—and leave more gold—while those in disgrace dragged their chains they might shed only at the end or if they died on the way. It must have been something to walk underneath those figures in their seething auras. But once beyond and in the sanctuary, the pilgrim would be drawn toward the flames on the altar, one among them the red eternal-vigil light that says, with the Magdalene, *Hope lives.*

✦

ONE of the seemingly minor tasks undertaken in the early twelfth century was the preparation of a popular text advertising the Santiago pilgrimage and confirming the authenticity of the bones there. It was part of this manuscript that was falsely signed with the name of "Turpin," a legendary bishop-knight in Charlemagne's company. The object of that forgery was to force the Emperor, dead three hundred years, into the Santiago cycle. The whole manuscript was titled, again falsely, the "Codex of Callixtus." Pope Callixtus too would have been dead, some twenty years, by the time it appeared, but a papal byline lent the work authority.[32]

Several versions of the codex survive, one in the cathedral archives. Its parchment pages have grown soft over these eight hundred years and the colors of the illuminations are dulcet. It contains a Mass with antiphonal choruses still sung on feast days; miracle tales about ordinary pilgrims, Santiago, and Charlemagne; and a travel guide advising where to sleep, which inns were bug-infested, what to eat, what waters were poisoned, and which relics were worth making detours to see. Finally, the French author warned his countrymen against lascivious Spaniards they would meet on the way.

Gelmirez surely sat in consultation over the project. So would have a geopolitician from Cluny. Abbot Suger of the Kings' Royal Abbey of St. Denis in Paris may have, too, and would have argued for French centrality to the scheme. So may have Bernard of Clairvaux, whose Cistercian order was just beginning its struggle with Cluny that would end by the replacement of Romanesque aesthetic and political theory by the Gothic.

These men—one among them "Turpin"—would breathe life into apocalyptic fire that would burn on for centuries. It would take two hundred years, but Islam would be routed from Spain. A unified Christian front of Castile, Navarre, and León, with the support of France and the papacy, would succeed in capturing Cordova in 1236, then Seville in 1248. A vassal kingdom would hang on in Granada for two waning centuries until, in the 1490s, the Catholic Majesties would tire of that tag of an infidel empire and drive out the last of the Moslems and the Jews.

✦ ✦ ✦

Now comes the mystery: a miracle-appearance complementary to the one beside Christ's tomb. There, a male, dead, was welcomed back to life by a woman. In Santiago's myth, a woman emerges from obscurity to take dominion over the world.

No female impinges upon Christ's myth as it is embalmed in the Holy Sepulchre Church. He is alone there save for the flicker of the Magdalene's candle, the ghost of Helena, and the shadow of Stabat Mater. Perhaps for want of a consoling female presence, that sanctuary is so childishly scrapped over by male faithful. Santiago's myth likewise looks, at first glance, to be characterized by a dominant, combative masculinity. That saint was not famous for consoling or healing, nor for taking interest in people's conjugal lives. Therefore, it is puzzling to find, in the symbols of the military Order of St. James, founded in the twelfth century to police the Santiago pilgrimage, signs of the immanent presence, in conceptual union with the death-dealing warrior, of the life-supporting Goddess.

A curious strain of sexual self-consciousness ran through the order from its inception. Membership was open only to males who fulfilled three requirements. They must observe chastity and be free of Jewish or Moslem ancestry, in other words, be uncircumcised. Thirdly, they must accept the doctrine of the Immaculate Conception of the Virgin. That tortuous proposition, that the Virgin herself was conceived mystically without sexual sin, was so undermining of the critical Christian argument for Christ's natural birth that it was not admitted as dogma till the nineteenth century.

Also, though the slogan of the order was militaristic in the extreme—*Rubet Ensis Sanguine Arabum,* Red is the Sword with the Blood of the Moor—the insignia worn by the knights was Santiago's graceful scallop shell, marked with a red cross whose nickname was *el lagarto* or lizard. That symbolism is as encoiled in the larger myth as a bit of DNA in a cell.

The scallop's relevance to a death-cult is obvious: the shell survives the seas. Therefore, the dead even from Paleolithic times were sometimes buried with shell ornaments, in shell barrows, or with shells on their eyes. "Coquilles St. Jacques" grew abundantly offshore of Iria Flavia, inspiring the famous dish and sold as souvenirs. Many are found in graves along the trail, mixed with bones that failed to make it home safely. But still, this particular shell would not ordinarily be thought an appropriate sign for a male warrior, a chaste one to boot. For the scallop was of course a symbol of the pagan Love-goddess, and its flesh was even dried and sold as a love philtre. For that reason, the Vatican reasonably objected to its association with the saint. But the bond could not be unmade, for it served myth, not dogma.

Wearing Aphrodite's emblem, James took on her female ontology as, from Zeus, he took his maleness.

And a lizard, as anthropologists have shown, represents in certain tribal myths the anatomical part excised in circumcision.[33] The implication is hard to avoid. *El lagarto,* blazoned on the emblem of this Christian male sworn to asexuality, represents the female element cut out of his ontology yet imperative for him to take back, in this unconscious fetish form, if he is to have a numinous guardian in war. Thus by that red-slashed shell that he wore on his person, James, Son of Thunder, bonded already to a Star-goddess, was bonded again to the one who rose out of the Sea.

ALL this is arcane symbolism, to be sure. But two cults that appeared in close association with the pilgrimage to St. James suggest that the Goddess had been with him from the beginning, even if in disguise. One is the cult and myth of the Three Seaborne Marys, and the other, what Marina Warner calls the "mysterious and exotic . . . special cult" of the Black Virgin.[34] To follow these clues to their sources, I must go down for the last time to where the roots of Christian pilgrimage lie tangled among earlier strata of human experience.

While the process of Christian conversion was proceeding in Europe, worship of the old gods, in this case the primordial Goddess, persisted especially in portions of the Santiago Trail washed by the great rivers—the Spanish Ebro, the Rhone with its lunar sweep of delta, and the Rhine. For here during the Greco-Roman era, powerful cults of Artemis, Aphrodite, Cybele, Isis, and others had been implanted, drawing vigor from prehistoric cults of water- and cave-spirits and the Great Mother.[35]

The transmutation of these chthonic and classical divinities into Christian Mary took place gradually, as cycles of Mary-stories spread westward from Palestine and Egypt.[36] One by one, the old shrines were exorcised and made ready for their new resident. One of the first to be so corrected was an Isis shrine in Marseilles made over to Mary by the early monastic, John Cassian.

For a while, then, there existed a near-polytheistic "muddle of Marys," as Marina Warner describes it, embracing so many abandoned older sisters. It was to clear up such a muddle that a later churchman made up a document in which one of them tried to amalgamate the others:

> I am Mary Magdalene, because the name of the village wherein I was born was Magdalia. My name is Mary of Cleopa. I am Mary of James, the son of Joseph the carpenter.[37]

Small wonder Pope Gregory tried to meld them. And in the tenth century, it was another Benedictine monk, Odo, Cluny's second abbot, who tried to combine Mary the Virgin and Mary Magdalene into a single Star of the Sea, and so she entered Western iconography in the form she had already had for ages.

But the triad that clings like sea foam to the figure of Santiago were called the Seaborne Marys or the Holy Marys of the Sea when they entered the myth around the eleventh century. Queen of the triad was the Magdalene, a serviceable model by which celibate monks might preach Christian sexual mores to heathen women, since she who had been so proud was so honored after turning humble.

The Marys' tale brought them westward from Jaffa, in Santiago's wake, in a boat without sail, rudder, or oars, tide-borne to a remote point of the Rhone delta still known as Les Saintes Maries de la Mer. The region is the Camargue, famous for gypsies, who enact a pilgrimage each spring to the crenellated fortress of a church marking the place of mythical landing and, not incidentally, also the southernmost limit of Cluny's empire.

In the boat with the Magdalene were her brother Lazarus and sister Martha, and Mary Salomé, Santiago's mother. Some versions add a holy man named Maximinus and, as baggage, the head of James the Less. Lazarus would become the first Bishop of Marseilles and, because of his gruesome past, patron saint of lepers. Martha would calm a dragon by wrapping her scarf around his throat. Maximinus became Bishop in Aix. The Magdalene preached thereabouts, then withdrew to what the Golden Legend describes as a "frightful barren wilderness of horrid rocks and caves" where she lived as an anchorite, but not alone. Seven times daily, angels came to lift her to the sky where she experienced transports of bliss. The Victorian writer on biblical iconography who signs her books simply Mrs. Jameson says these flights caused the Magdalene to be "ravished by the sounds of unearthly harmony," but the Guide Bleu puts it that *"chaque jour, la penitente était ravie par les anges,"* which is quite another thing.[38]

THE Magdalene served Cluny well. When the pilgrimage churches were being plotted along a line to Galicia, her bones turned up near Marseilles in an old chapel to Maximinus. At a propitious time, they were taken to Vézelay and installed in the hilltop church there that was a setting-off point for Santiago-bound pilgrims and also a center for crusading propaganda. As part of the same program, Lazarus's skull and bones turned up in an old chapel in Autun, once sacred to a Saint Nazarius, and were taken with great publicity to a new Benedictine church in that town. The Magdalene and Lazarus then entered on careers of politically expedient glory, while Maximinus and Nazarius sank to the sea bottom of defunct myth.

For a while, the siblings worked wonders. So famous did the Magdalene's body parts become that in the late thirteenth century one of her ribs was broken off to be sent to the city of Sens north of Paris. However, that deconstruction was a portent of more serious change to come. For her fortunes shifted as Cluny's sank and the Virgin-venerating Cistercians' rose. In 1283 the supposedly empty sepulchre outside Marseilles began to exude perfume. Soon clerics announced that the relics taken north had been false ones. The Magdalene's true bones had never left the place.

For a time then there were two shrines to the Magdalene. But she lost Burgundy, or won the South. The official relics are down by the Mediterranean in a church in whose crypt is the famous Neo-gothic reliquary with an opening, in the back, to display the Star-goddess's red hair.

As a product of mythic imagination, the Magdalene represented the contradiction between wild and controlled nature. Her conceptual home was the Middle World where sinning and forgiving human beings try to do their best, fail, and try again—the dialectical bridge-span where appeared also the phantom male she could not live without and so drew back to a kind of life.

But the Virgin's mystery is at once deeper and wider. Its measure is taken by that dogmatic oddity forced on Santiago's Crusaders: belief in the Immaculate Conception of the Virgin. For to push that idea to its logical—or illogical—conclusion, such a Mary would be the offspring of the same Sky-god who would later impregnate her. Like many a primordial cult-goddess in antiquity, she would be the fruit of incest, projected by Christian myth-generating imagination into an ever enlarging, ever higher-reaching role in the myth of Cosmos. Bearing a son to Polestar who was her own progenitor, she would be shaped to the ancient end of cosmic geometry: to lift the dead to His dominion.

In fact, she had been destined for cosmic instrumentality from the time of her fourth-century designation as Theotokos: generatrix of God himself, the Father. And during the early Middle Ages of male dominance and struggle, belief in a female personification of cosmic power survived as popular tradition. One of its manifestations was the cult of the Black Virgin, whose images in sculpture cluster in striking numbers along Santiago's Trail.

How many is a phenomenon never explained nor even much investigated by art historians until recently. There are paintings under the same rubric, whose landing ports are far-flung, ranging from Guadalupe in Mexico to Kilnacanough, Ireland, and Czestochowa in Poland, where stands the one venerated by Pope John Paul II. These paintings are mostly Byzantine and were sacked out of Constantinople by the Fourth Crusade. But the sculptures are older, and their relevance to this narrative greater.

On terrain sacred to St. James, there are famous examples in Chartres, Orléans, Le Puy, Rocamadour, Marseilles, Estella, Saragossa, and Monserrat. Some are dated around the end of the tenth century and are thought to be copies of even earlier works. But beside their sacred venerability, their extraordinary formal sameness is striking. They are black and rigidly vertical, like many figures of pagan Isis, and hold the infant Christ upright and stiffly parallel to their spines, precisely as Abraham, in many a stone-carved image, holds Lazarus. And as if in deliberate enhancement of that vertical geometry, the statues are often displayed on a pillar. Moreover, many arrived on the scene with just such a fireworks of folklore as brought the *Madonna del Pilar* to James's attention outside Saragossa: angels sang, music was heard, stars flickered in bushes, and lo, the figure was found lying on the ground or by a pond or stream. One modern Black Virgin in Loreta, Italy, by virtue of such a wonder-story of origin, has as wonderfully been named Patron Saint of Aviators.

There are puzzles here that tempt me beyond the limits of conventional art history. Some technical explanations for the blackness of these figures are their old age or exposure to smoke or oxidized silver on their surfaces.[39] More romantic theories have them blackened to recall the Song of Songs ("I am black but comely ...") or even to look like sunburn the Virgin might have suffered in Egypt. But none of these explanations, as Marina Warner agrees, "illuminate the mystery of their origins."[40]

When technical explanations fail, meaning may be sought through the substructures of myth. If James is the Son of Zeus, then his sister is Athena, who was, like both their fathers, a storm and lightning divinity, even represented on earth by stones fallen out of the sky, in her case statues of herself, "palladia," the same objects that were called Zebedee stones elsewhere.[41]

Nor of course were Athena and Zebedee / Zeus alone in being

represented on earth by stones fallen out of the sky. Artemis / Diana, that black meteorite, was known "by all the world," as the New Testament says (Acts 19.35), to have fallen out of the sky. And so had Cybele.

Looked at this way, the next step seems obvious. The Black Virgin's blackness, I suggest, carries the information, fiercely combated by the Church, of both her descent from pagan Sky-queens and—in dialectical balance—her ascent from chthonic Earth-mothers. Like Kali-Durga, then Sati in India, she has survived a flaming plummet to rise out of the dark fields and so evokes our awe and also, perhaps, our horror. And the pillar on which she sometimes stands is the fossil of her track along the chute of night.

Her stiffness too is in the genes, for like all participants in cosmic architecture, she had to be shorn of natural grace to function in that role. The Lord of the Animals taught as much in Mohenjo-Daro, and wrapping and stiffening was the secret of immortality taught by Isis's mate Osiris. In the Gospel of that Thomas who died in India it is written that "only the woman who will make herself male will enter the Kingdom of Heaven."

The Black Virgin, then, as I see it, shares with her Father and son the vertical geometry that is the "secret presence" in the history of cosmic myth and religious art and rite, and the axis around which these human endeavors turn. Geometry, again, is myth: the myth that there is an ultimate form of human reunion that supports the Cosmos.

THE image of the Black Virgin put forth new formulations evoking new mysteries, for example the implication that, in standing on after her child dies, she *is* the Cosmos that survives the correction of its bones and nerves. And precisely such a mystical Virgin as iconographic type appeared in the Gothic era in the Rhineland: a sort of columnar cupboard shaped in rudimentary female form that opens to reveal a tiny Christ between her knees, sometimes holding a small cross of twigs. Then Christ is of course the Tree of Life to be cut down while she, his container, will stand on: *Stabat Mater*. In the case of the Black Virgin of Monserrat in Spain, the child holds a pinecone while his Mother, again, is the enclosing form that will not feel the ax. Her surgical transformation came earlier when she was broken into human shape out of pure abstract geometry—the circle that encloses all being—and her next transformation will be her ascension straight back up to that paradigmatic circle of the sky.

In any case, it should be no surprise that these Black Virgins, so heavy with time and suggestion, were considered to be, again as Warner says, possessors of "hermetic knowledge and power."[42]

GOD'S Mother's cosmic ontology was, in any case, openly accepted by the Gothic era when the great Mary cathedrals were completed. Such a role then was claimed in hindsight for the little pearwood goddess that had stood from prehistoric times in a grotto later engulfed by the Cathedral of Chartres. Christianity, taking her in, renamed her *Notre Dame Sous Terre*—Our Lady Under the Earth. Several times destroyed by fire like most wooden images, she was always copied and replaced, black, as she is today. Her true character is disclosed when she is envisioned in place, between the two towers of the cathedral. For they are named Sun and Moon, and she stands between them as the downward point of a huge triangle that locks the spheres together, its linchpin as long as she stands— *Stabat Mater* again. By then only a subordinate actress in the cosmic drama, the Magdalene, in a stained-glass window at Chartres, performs the ancient rite of dipping water out of a stream with an urn.

By the late thirteenth century and on into the Baroque age, the Ever-virgin, Immaculately Conceived Mary was openly granted the stature of more than mediating star, instead the cosmic polar axis.[43] As that, she was represented in painting ringed by the twelve stars of the zodiac. She by then had broken out of her black husk, and her color was blue. Rising over the earth, her blue cloak spread, her eyes shining like sun and moon, she was a genuine Sky-queen, regent over the Gothic highlands, *"Vergine chiara stabile in eterno,"* creature of ultimate contradiction and transcendent reunion in Bernard's great prayer,

Vergine madre, figlia del tuo figlio . . .
Umile et alta piu de creatura . . .

and the sublime myth-shapes of Dante's poem, "clothed in living flame," standing amid the "eternal wheels."

And those wheels, I'd learned in the course of this pilgrimage so far, turn universal skies that turn over all our heads, so that no single priest or pilgrim, shrine or temple, is more illuminated than the others, nor any one form of myth, poetry, or rite the only one to give their true description.

◆ ◆ ◆

The Gothic Age saw the cosmic vision lifted to supremacy in the religious and political mind and enlarged from the primitive template of Cluny's twelve monks around a friar to twelve bishoprics around the hub of Paris.

Paris was the center of the new empire that was to correct and encompass not only all Europe but, theoretically, the whole earth, even if to do so it would be necessary to "eclipse the great pilgrimage centers of western Europe" previously set up by Cluny. Architectural and ceremonial symbolism would be compounded at the center of the rose, as it were, while "armed pilgrimages" would carry terror and death to whoever obstructed its expansion. In this scheme, the Mary cathedrals of France, like the Trail of Santiago, provided pilgrims with a living experience of political mysticism.[44]

The cathedral as sheer structure in space announced the world-engulfing ambition of the Universal Church. If the Hindu temple stands on ground purified of contaminants, the Buddhist stupa on a seed that will burst into life and die, and the Romanesque church on a hilltop, the cathedral stands on history. All foregoing stages of evolutionary culture are its foundations, bent under its weight but also redeemed by bearing it, for the old world had to have collapsed for the new to rise up.

Ne had the apple taken ben,
Ne had never our lady a-been heavene queen.

Blessed be the time that apple taken was.
Therefore we mun singen *Deo gracias!*[45]

The crypts in a cathedral reveal old walls, old roots of shrines and graves, and, below those, natural watercourses, wells, and fissures used for prehistoric spirit-worship. Under Notre Dame of Paris are traces of a Roman temple to Jupiter Great and Good, while a few feet off was a shrine to the Star-boys and river-guardians Castor and Pollux, endowed by the Seine boatmen. Underneath Chartres was the grotto with its pearwood goddess. Santiago's cathedral stands on vast Romano-Iberian and Visigothic graveyards and the walls of pagan temples.[46] Furthermore, each Gothic cathedral also devoured the Early Christian, then the Carolingian, and finally the Romanesque shrine that had come after.

THE entryway into a cathedral, that embodiment of time, is called the *Porta Coeli,* Heaven's Door. But it is not the heaven of story-books one finds oneself in when that portal is passed but a sense-obscuring gloom more like Dante's woods.

Down at the foot of these metaphoric woods, as beneath them, the past clings to life. Smokes of old Masses hang in the air. Echoes off the vaults bring voices from distant corners. Squat shadowy columns belie their own loftiness and hint how clandestine politi-cal cause has shaped the structure they uphold—those cross-vaults in which "monarchical and theological spheres . . . converge."[47] The only clear-cut form the eye can find at first is the nave or "pilgrims' causeway," which runs straight east to where it meets the north-south transept. That crossed floor plan describes a per-son dead and also an instrument of death, a model that indeed gave privilege in the thirteenth century to the Inquisition to use comparable torture machines. So architecture served as both promise and warning to the pilgrim.

Standing looking east in this Cosmos of stone, the pilgrim imi-tates Christ who when he died, as the Golden Legend spells out, "was taken up toward the East, and we turn toward him waiting for his coming."[48] But another implication is there too. For while in Asia the pilgrim enters the sacred space from the east, sharing the sun or planet's ontology as a natural inhabitant of his cosmic home, the Christian comes in the west door as out of exile, seeking the remote source of light as his salvation.

And his longing is answered. For as the pilgrim enters the dark woods in the morning, the sun rises before his eyes beyond the choir windows in dynamic welcome. Then it swings to the south to pass along the clerestory windows all day, casting shining trapezoids down onto the nave pavement. And as the hours inch by, these bright flagstones inch in the opposite direction to the sun's own flight, moving easterly and so leading the pilgrim to his destination, while through the hours, the sun submits to its daily aging till it dies in the west, even then leaving behind a promissory glow through the western rose window, that lifts toward the vaults and fades, leaving the whole interior dark.[49]

Light in the Gothic cathedral is the lesson—does not teach but *is*. It is Wisdom and Shekinah, imagination and grace, and it fades out of the cathedral each evening with solemn sadness, as the incense fails in a Jewish house at Sabbath end or as a man—any person—dies.

YET here, just as I saw happen in the Hindu temple, Proteus will not die but must do his changeling dance. For the cathedral has other ways of being. It is Christ on his feet, his head its pinnacle, his body from feet to crown the standing axis through the Three Worlds of water, earth, and heaven. Standing so, he is his Father Polestar's double, while around them both swing the stars: *Stat Crux dum volvitur Orbis.*[50]

The mystery here is that Christ in the image of man is, like his transcendent Mother, also of cosmic extension. This contradiction, embodied in the cathedral-body that encloses the body on the Cross, baffles logic ("the idea . . . appears paradoxical to us," says historian Otto von Simson) unless it's accepted that He, God, had in mind what that historian calls an "ontologically transparent" model: exactly my golden Piranesi, in which a vertical form supports an interconnected transparent system of curves, planes, wheels, and embounded space.[51] Indeed, the very name of this stone Cosmos is now Christ, his Body, in which in some mysterious way his Father Lord Polestar, God, is enclosed, just as in nature, the parents live on in their offspring's genes, and the child is their preserver, their vessel of futurity.

What was sought in Gothic architecture was an essential geometry that would render its gross material irrelevant, just as in a thousand years Modernist steel and concrete frames would rise a hundred storeys without supporting walls. Immanent in the completed building, then, are the balanced cross-points and thrust-conveying lines, exactly like the pilgrim trails that abstractly course the suffering, clamoring, skeptical populations of the world.[52]

As for decoration, Early Christian and Romanesque churches treated the apse end of the church naturalistically with paintings or mosaics of trees and foliage rising up to rainbows and starry skies. In some cases, actual constellations were shown, with the stars Procyon, Sirius, Aldebaran, whose risings in the Middle Ages were watched for, though their comets' tails of pagan reference were gone. But the men who shaped the Gothic were bent on more intrinsic descriptions of nature. As a characteristic "correction" on too-literal matter, a Romanesque solid half-domed apse might be worked as if with scissors, the walls cut into pointed fingers letting in, most properly, pure white light but sometimes light stained cherry-rose red or sky blue. Such minimal harmonics again state the claim on totality: that by a few, the All can be shown. White stood for purity and the death-rites of children, for instance. Red, for blood and fire, green for hope, black for death of the adult. These events and states of mind were singular, plainly what they were.

But the conflicted human condition "sorrow," exemplified by the rupture of community between man and woman, must have a mix of tones to describe it, and so it is symbolized by purple, a dye extracted from the glands of shellfish—a method the ancients may have dreamed they had from Aphrodite.

So the Gothic cathedral was an "earthly counterpart of the various regions and spiritual gradations of the supernatural universe,"[53] in which, as the pagan inspirer of Gothic metaphysics taught,

The true order of going is to use the beauties of the earth as steps along which one mounts upwards for the sake of that other beauty . . . until he arrives at the notion of Absolute Beauty and at last knows what the essence of Beauty is. (Symposium)

The vision had engulfed the past and filled the mind and was furthermore so fully mapped internally that there was a proper slot in it for every angel, blade of grass, musical mode, and human skill. The modern mind, I think, reels with the precision and wholeness of it and also with the further projections it would give rise to in a thousand years—One World, One Peace, One People— until the globe would seem to manifest One Consciousness, as Emerson would say, "by one music enchanted."

But there was and is the flaw.

My pilgrimage of thought brought me now to a new reflection.

The enclosed Christian Cosmos was an illusion forced out of imagination building on innocent perception and held aloft on popular longing for its propositions to be true. But embodied— that is, established on earth as dogma, architecture, or political empire—it revealed itself unable to stand except on propositions that were evasions of the natural law of cause and effect.

Here is a famous example.[54] In the quarters of Paris around Notre Dame, there was in the Middle Ages a ferment of debate of a kind considered normal in free societies today and intolerable in controlled ones. The debate concerned the substance of the Cosmos—whether its Platonic forms were simply ideas or actual entities. A deviant from orthodoxy was Peter Abelard. At the outset of his career, for deviance of another sort, he had been subjected to surgery fitting him for a pillar of the Church. Nonetheless, he was bitterly attacked for his ideas by Bernard, that same Doctor Mellifluous—as he was called for his honey-sweet rhetoric—who preached the Second Crusade at Vézelay and a little later lent himself to Provence to warn the Albigensians what heresy would bring down on them.

Bernard's style of mind characterized and created the Gothic. He excoriated the art and architecture of Cluny, its "supervacuous" scale and the "ridiculous monstrosities" of animal and humanoid sculpture that drew energy from a barbarous past and deformed the ideal proportions that bound man into the order of heaven.[55] He accused Abelard of "intellectual mania" and "chimeras of reasoning." In theory, Bernard sought universal peace. But it was a totalitarian peace he sought.

I began now to see the logical end of my trip.

The flaw in the Myth of Cosmos, I reflected, is that any deviation from its order must bring on the collapse of the whole. From that imagined construct derives the expanded mode of consciousness, sometimes ecstasy, of those who share it. But one lapse in the logic—one rebel in a family, one infidel or heretic in the world—and the whole is lost. And as in the course of time many people will naturally deviate—for the imagination takes its course regardless of instructions—so the rigidity of those who hope to see their heaven built on earth in their own time will increase, until violent confrontation is inevitable. Then must follow the collapse of the vision, beautiful as it was, whose existence was only as geometry in the mind.

This is the meaning of Henry Adams's foreboding passage on the fragility of Chartres Cathedral.[56]

Yet the pity and sorrow of it is that it's in just such contradictions in art as in theory that the formulations of metaphysical longing are to be discovered most authentically. And in that respect, no architecture on earth, not the linga-containing sanctum in India nor the breast-shaped domes of Jerusalem and Byzantium, is more expressive of the desire for reunion in resurrection than the Gothic, in which rising imploring shafts lift groined vaults in which they probe and lock in crossings marked by wide-open flowerets of stone. But these joinings take place high above the weak standing walls, that have to be held upright by buttresses.

✦ ✦ ✦

History proves the point.

South across the Seine from Notre Dame Cathedral is the tiny cavelike church of St. Julien le Pauvre, where poor pilgrims in the old days stopped to light a candle to their guardian saint. They then walked straight along the old Roman way, renamed the rue St. Jacques, toward the Porte d'Orléans and Burgundy. On the way, however, at least from the fifteenth century on, they passed a Renaissance palace graced with carved scallop shells that was the Paris headquarters of the Order of Cluny. By the time it was built, Cluny's power was eclipsed, and it now houses a museum of medieval art, some examples of which have relevance to the later fate of St. James's Trail to heaven.

It was in Santiago's festival month of July 1793 that revolutionary mobs turned against the five-hundred-year-old cathedral that stood for all that was hated in the old regime. That day, the statues of the kings of Judea on its facade, mistaken for kings of France, were "guillotined" with ropes and mallets. The heads fell to the ground where, two months later, their crowns were beaten off. A month after that, the headless torsos still standing were hauled down.

A few years ago, some of these heads were found buried around the precincts and put on display in the Musée de Cluny. One had taken such a hammerblow to the face that an eye, the nose, and one cheekbone are gone. Each mouth is broken back to the jaw and caught open as if in a scream. Such are the ghosts of Clovis and Charlemagne, the Henris, Louis's, and Philippes whose dreams of global Christendom produced also the Santiago Trail.

All down the Trail in the 1780s and '90s, especially in that terrible year of 1793, the wave of violence broke. Black Virgins were burned and cathedral bells melted. Sanctuaries were stormed and then opened to the people to use them as quarries for building material. Chartres was torched. Vézelay was torn apart. The great abbey church of Cluny was knocked stone from stone save for a portion of the transept and two towers. And then the shrines all the way from Paris to Souillac in the far south were purified of Christ, corrected and reconsecrated to the Goddess of Reason or the God of Universal Order and Law.

And these ruins form only one layer of what a scholar of the Trail calls its "petrified lament," which has its latest echo in war memorials along the roadside informing motorists that *Ici est tombé pour la liberation* . . . and also *Ici été fusillés* . . . such and such a youth, or men women and children together—while along the Spanish roads the dead of the Civil War lie among the bones and shells of old pilgrims.[57]

IN fact the Renaissance when Cluny's Paris quarters were built saw the beginning of the end of pilgrimage—though not of missionary work—as an instrument in Western empire. A growing skepticism about the papacy and its trade in relics and indulgences undermined the pilgrimage business. On the other hand, the humanistic metaphor of the pilgrim—temptation-prone animal on his perilous way through life—began to generate new works, by Langland and Chaucer and Cervantes and related novels to come, still coming, all exploring the proposition that "we all ben pilgrims since that we ben borne"—as a Lollard hymn put it.[58]

Langland's Plowman for instance, after meeting a Santiago pilgrim of the old type in "shells of Galice and many a crouche on his cloke," proposed that it was hardly truth that that type went in search of, and Erasmus came home from Santiago with a dry attitude toward "feign'd Miracles and strange lyes," for he'd heard an apostate cleric there telling one and all that "We haue not one heare nor bone of Saynct Iames. . . ."[59]

Under Ferdinand and Isabella, inspired by the Lord's Dogs, the Domini Canes, the Inquisition would reach new heights of efficiency and their Majesties respond with grateful benefactions to the Shrine of Shrines. Indeed in 1492, in thanks for the success of the Jewish Expulsion, they granted a bushel of grain to Compostela for each pair of oxen put to the plow in Spain and underwrote the enrichment of an old pilgrim hostel abutting the cathedral, which still receives travelers today. Still, though sixteenth-century Spain rode dominant over the Age, drafting fanatic soldiery to fight Turk and Protestant with equal zeal, and though gold from the New World flowed in to gild its altars, and though initiative was kept at a boil by Loyola's publicized pilgrimage to Jerusalem, Santiago's career was over. Gradually he appeared out of the sky less often and then no more, and his significance narrowed to a purely nationalistic symbol. After the Battle of Lepanto in 1571, Don Juan of Austria gave the flag from the flagship to the cathedral where it hangs in gray-green tatters to this day.

By that time, religious wars were keeping pilgrims off the road, and churches were being pillaged and burned as in the days of Normans, Vikings, and Huns. If a whirlwind was loosed on land then, the English loosed it at sea. In 1589 Francis Drake, whose aim was to wipe out Santiago's "emporium of Papal superstitions," arrived with his fleet along the Galician coast, and Santiago's bones were spirited away not to turn up again until 1878. Sir Walter Raleigh may have been one of the last Englishmen to die with thoughts of Santiago as metaphor for saving grace. His poem "The Passionate Man's Pilgrimage, Supposed to be written by one at the point of death" speaks of scallop shells and pilgrim's staff and voices hope that when the poet's head falls off, he shall find a new one to walk to heaven in.

But in fact, the Spanish empire was going down, crushed under the burden, some historians say, of its some nine thousand monasteries and a full third of its population in servitude of some sort to the Cross.[60] Industry and trade declined, agriculture suffered under the huge tithes drawn off for Santiago's house, and the cultural flame passed to Italy.

In the seventeenth century, under Philip IV, the shrine had a brief revival of glory. Much of the city was then rebuilt in Baroque style, and by 1750 the Churrigueresque facade of the cathedral was finished. Yet a new affront was endured in that century by the old Moor-slayer, for a movement of the Discalced Carmelites succeeded in having Theresa named co–patron saint of Spain, until such an outcry came from the male side of Christendom that Pope Urban IV canceled the nomination and let Santiago reign on alone.

Probably such a multilayered myth-system as the Santiago Trail could not have come into existence after the Reformation. For new approaches to science and philosophy in the seventeenth century ruptured the ages-old image of an ideal Cosmos and gave prophetic vision to another order of nature. As sky-watching sages had for millennia, Milton brooded even blind on the imperfection of this earth's alignment vis-à-vis the solar axis. Some hand had lost us Paradise,

> turn[ed] askance
> The poles of Earth twice ten degrees and more
> From the Sun's axle . . . push[ed]
> Oblique the centric Globe . . . (*Paradise Lost*, lines 668–71)

And though he still wound his poem to a victorious end in *Paradise Regained* ("the Son of God our Saviour meek, Sung victor . . ." [lines 636–37]), and though John of the Cross achieved the straitening he sought through nights of fire and nights of dark,[61] the pilgrimage as a literary trope would not again deliver its transcendental endings, that "abyss of radiance" Dante found in his *Paradise*—

> Three orbs of triple hue clipt in one bound:
> and from another, one reflected seem'd
> As rainbow is from rainbow; and the third
> seemed fire . . . (Canto XXXIII, lines 116–20)

—or the "Shining Men" Bunyan found at his road's end, in "Raiment that shone like Gold" in a "City that shone like the Sun."[62]

NEW horrors and new realism came with the late eighteenth and nineteenth centuries. In the Napoleonic wars, Compostela was raped again, so that when the Protestant Bible salesman and journalkeeper George Borrow went there in the 1830s he had to go under armed guard, and, arriving, found the shrine abutted by a leper colony.[63]

It might be argued that German and American nineteenth-century Romantic landscape painting projected the last authentic glow of Christian pilgrimage in the West. For though the Transcendentalists cared little for shrines as such, they did conceive of the nature tour as a quest for revelation of the sacred. In Germany the Rhine valley and in America Niagara Falls, the Rocky Mountains, the

Hudson River valley were pilgrimage places (still are!) where a traveler might lose the sense of discrete identity in the "oceanic feeling" Freud called the equivalent of religious belief.

So the expedient "rediscovery" of Santiago's bones in 1878 and their authentication by Pope Leo XIII in 1884 did not affect the world any more than the closing of the books of the Spanish Inquisition, in the year 1820. The twentieth century opened on a Spain left backward by the war with America, so the forces of feudalism, Church, and army aligned themselves and tensions built until the outbreak of civil war just one week before Santiago's feast day in 1936. This time, the patron saint lent neither horse nor sword to Franco, who won on his own at a reported cost of 700,000 dead, 30,000 executed, and 15,000 killed by bombs.

A corrected center of Spanish mytho-geography was then called for. So when the Generalissimo died, he was buried in the Valley of the Fallen in a tomb dead center of a great cross whose arms span the Escorial and the cathedral of Segovia and whose shaft spans the cathedrals of Avila and Guadalajara. Thus was carried out what a historian describes as "the burial of the founder of a 'new order' at his country's omphalos or geomantic center."[64]

It is mostly antiquarian and touristic interest that brings crowds to Santiago today. Still, when the cathedral is full of fire, and a massed choir of hundreds begins to sing a swirling medieval hymn, and the words *pelegrino . . . pelegrino* break over one's head, it is hard not to feel that the place lives still, though not any more in our plane of time.

✦ ✦ ✦

The auto route to Santiago from Paris winds through Burgundy and the heartland of old Roman Gaul, with its dark ochre and tan houses of stone quarried centuries ago.

Overhead the sky is full of light off the river Saône, a tributary of the sky-river Rhone, that brought the old world's culture north and carried back down the mineral wealth of the continent. But despite its fine weather and lush foliage, there is a gloominess to Burgundy. Its past sucks at its roots. Every structure is a restructuring in which the airy Gothic sections of churches may seem to a modern traveler the very embodiment of liberation.

Vézelay, first of the principal step-stones of the Via Podensis, stands on a promontory overlooking farmlands, forests, and the river Cure. Here it was that on March 31 of 1146, Bernard stood to preach the Second Crusade in words like those that fall from television sets tuned to the Middle East today. For now there is no such sound in Vézelay—only wind in the blue-green chestnut trees—but who is to say past events don't echo in the world long after their time? For Bernard's men lost all discipline as they passed through the Rhineland and there fell to massacring Jews just as practice on their way to all they hoped to do to the Moslems further east. And the world, as we know, still shakes to those events.

The road then descends into the plains passing Pontaubert, where the Knights of Malta built a church over Roman hot springs near to a chthonic grotto still called Cave of the Wolves, on through golden fields to Avalon and a holy-water font carved as a scallop shell, and on to Autun, then Cluny.

Leaving Burgundy for the even darker towns of the Massif Central is like going around to the back of the moon. From Le Puy, a dismal dark-red provincial town now, noble Bishop Adhémar left for the First Crusade and death in far-off Antioch. The glory of Le Puy then and until the flames of 1794 was its Black Virgin, a pure Asiatic or African queen in a cap of copper set with antique cameos and an over-robe of barbaric checkerboard. And while her face and her child's were ebony black, their four hands were white, a lapse that supports my argument that blackness in these cases wasn't descriptive but significant.

After Le Puy, the road turns west into the long lonely valleys and windy highlands of the Auvergne to meet the Via Lemosina coming down from west-central France and strike on across moors of glacial rubble, where even the fence posts are hewn of it, and off in the fields stands many a gray stone cross. In one of these bleak towns, Aubrac, when the church bell rings, it rings

J'appelle les errants, et
Je ramene les égarés.

For it is named *"la cloche des perdus."*

FARTHER on is another of the wonders of the French portion of the trail. It is the so-called *Majesté de Sainte Foy,* venerated since the ninth century in the remote mountainside hamlet of Conques in the Dordogne. The object is a reliquary for a bit of the skull of a child named Faith, who, in the pogroms of Diocletian, was slain by decapitation after the griddle she was burning on was damped by miracle rain. Or perhaps this is the truer sequence of events: that there turned up in that region of many cults and their disintegrations, a small, pure-gold Roman or even Celtic head, male, with such mesmerizing personality it had by any means to be worked into a Christian object.

Still, what is strangest about this work of medieval imagination is that the head—surely of a god, emperor, or even military commander—was set on the sculptured torso of a little princess, and at such an angle that it stares off as if in an Apollonian trance. Monstrous-weird in this physical joining as any bi-sexed Shiva or Egyptian or Canaanite god or guardian, it projects all the contradictions in a cult of immortality.

"I would not die," it seems to say, *"and so I died to get to my salvation."*

And beyond Conques is the aerial cliff village of Rocamadour with its hunched black stick of a Black Virgin, in a Neo-gothic entablature of bronze antlers as barbaric in their way as Sainte Foy's jewels.

DRIVING toward the mountains of southern Europe is always the same. You leave vineyards and olive groves and men in sandals and climb into sour wood smoke, a darker higher world where preparations are always under way for snow. White water churns beside the twisting road, fields and stands of fir give way to isolated barrens, then bare peaks. It grows colder.

When the road turns toward Somport Pass, it passes the world-famous old pilgrim hospice, one of the Three Columns built by God, now but a pile of stones in a meadow. And at the high-altitude customs house, a café offers a last French meal, a loaf of bread held end to breastbone and sliced the long way with a long knife, then spread with mountain pâté.

And then the road descends, leaving behind the motionless geometry of the heights, to find its way into Spanish Navarre, whose population, according to the old French guidebook, live like dogs or pigs, fornicating with their animals, whom they strap and padlock so each farmer has privilege only of his own, to apply "libidinous kisses to vulva of both woman and mule."[65]

South the rivers wind then and always westward the road, through sour green and tan valleys, plowed and fallow, and olive groves again, on to the meeting place with the other pilgrim-flow that crossed the mountains at Roncesvalles. The confluence is marked by the Puente la Reina, an old footbridge that rises to a sensuous peak in the middle, so that just to walk its foot-softened old stones up, then down, is to feel a gentle birth-push into the beyond, where the road turns toward the triangular little peak of a distant hill town crowned with a pointed church tower.

Time and again the road takes such a turn, then runs straight as an arrow toward the brown triangle of a far hill where, just at the bull's eye, stands a church. And the arrow's flight continues on into the blue of the sky, drawing the eye forward, while to right and left stand other little brown churches with their west-facing bell towers like sails on ships in the seas of wheat fields that flow to the horizon.

Evenings the globular red sun goes down like a ghost, reminding you of ghosts that lie to the south, at your left, ghosts of Moors who lived and fought in red-walled Granada and Cordova of the Great Mosque, and also in Seville. In that city, in a Holy Week not many years ago, when the Brothers of Light and Brothers of Blood were walking in penitential pilgrimage behind huge gold and silver litters bearing statues of Christ and Mary, suddenly a youth bloodied by his own whiplashes ran and scrambled up Christ's wagon, shouting, "Give me a ladder so I can climb to Christ!" and when he reached the top he cried out for all to hear, "I don't want this Christ of wood! I want the One who walked on the sea!"

There that day was an Indian woman, Hindu, who told me the story in Bombay, and I retell it to show how tales go around the world in the heads of travelers.

BEYOND Burgos and León, the road skirts a gorge and climbs to a windy pass called El Cebrero between circular stone huts with peaked wattle roofs said to date from Celtic times. Then at last it descends into Galicia—Scotland all over again for me—with gray-green heaths, stone sheep pens, gray mist and purple heather. And then one has passed Labacolla, where pilgrims used to bathe, "not just their genitals but their whole naked bodies," before entering the holy city—though a modern airport has swallowed up the place.

And very soon beyond that comes the spot where, in the frame of two hills, suddenly you glimpse the towers that strike the mind like old George Fox's steeples and remind you to say—but your companion will have seen them already and beat you to the saying—*Montjoie!*

AND then at last the road turns up a hill and around a corner and under an archway through a narrow passage right out onto the square before the cathedral, where bagpipes are wheezing and drums rattling and travelers shouting.

Every pilgrimage place has such a collecting pool for new arrivals, where the very air seems tilted by the settling of pavement over centuries, and sounds are confused with echoes off buildings around the edges. So you are disoriented for a moment, even dizzy. And in this case, it is necessary to walk a little farther on to turn around to face the cathedral.

And then you are wiped out by the sight.

The Baroque facade, spouting purple-tinged, wind-seeded vines like seaweed, mounts like breakers, with pilasters and columns leaping upward, each one pulling the eyes up till they reach the froth of the bell towers; and then begins the eyes' flight around the profile of the stones, up pyramids, domes, and pinnacles and over little urns and then up again to the towers where the topmost spires, like frozen droplets, fall upward into the sea of the sky.

Those towers are named Zebedee and Maria Salomé, which is the same, we know by now, as Sky and Star. In Maria's tower hang the embattled bells that came back to Compostela on the backs of Moorish slaves, while in Zebedee's tower hangs a percussion instrument played on holy days. When the hour strikes, there falls from Zebedee's tower a cacophony of crashing sounds. Never came out of the air such wild noise, no ringing or clanging as of bells or even thunder but a banging and colliding, raucous, conflicting and disharmonious, exultant and hungry, as of swords in the sky.

As to the cathedral itself, gone by now are the Chaste Alfonso's walls of 829 and Alfonso II's of 896 that were leveled by Almanzor. Then came a bigger version by Alfonso VI, whose walls still stand, and Gelmirez's Romanesque nave and transept of 1128. Then in the early Gothic 1170s and '80s came the supreme sculptural adornment of the place and perhaps of the Trail. It is the Portico of Glory, which is centered on one of the loveliest figures in stone of the Middle Ages—a Santiago not of thunder and destruction but of sea and blessing, even with a womanly milk-calm and no trace of crusading arrogance, in a halo bossed with petals of a lotus or chrysanthemum, set around with twelve lucent rock crystals.

The figure stands on a Tree of Jesse that grows, as if with no shame about its pagan root-source, from Hercules embracing two lions. At the top of the Tree are the gentle spirits of history: David playing his harp, Solomon and the Virgin, and, at the very top, Abraham with Lazarus in his bosom.

To enter the cathedral is to sink one last time into the dream of Cluny. For though the vaults are ribbed, another hint of the coming new style, the arches are Moorish and the illumination pure Romanesque, glowing and glancing off bronze, silver, intarsia, marble, and painted wood; and the altar is a bonfire of dark gold.

Next to it on a sort of bridge stands another figure of James, rougher and more like the fisherman he would have been, to which pilgrims climb to kiss its stone back.

On high holy days, pilgrims' Masses are sung end to end, with music now Gregorian, now Moorish, now modern and military, in swelling polyphony to the sound of horns and organ, *Astro brilliante de España, Apostol Santiago* . . . and *pelegrino* . . . , mixed with snatches of troubadour songs and hymns that went to war, *Ad te clamamus . . . ad te suspiramus . . . in hac lacrimamarum valle.* . . . And so all day the cathedral breathes light and also breathes sound, drawn-out plaints and howlings, then sweetenings and gentlings so the whole stone house rests, only to begin again with sour-sweet arabesques out of Seville.

AT the end of each Mass is enacted an event long famed among pilgrims to Compostela. It is the flying of the Botafumeiro, King of Incense Burners, one hundred pounds and more of silver full of fire and coals, which hangs on ropes from a pulley fixed to the top of the crossing of transept and nave. It's not known when this appalling demonstration of the laws of flight and momentum was first made, only that some time in the later Middle Ages it flew so high it left the cathedral by a window.

Eight men, trained to the duty, pull on the ropes in intricate order. Slowly, the weight shifts, but quickly it takes on speed till its flight fills the whole transept, north to south then north again. Then to barbaric whirls of music from below, it bucks the rope at each end and hurtles down as if to graze the skulls of people standing below, only to fly up leaving behind its trail of bittersweet smoke.

The Church allows such an apparition into the liturgy by calling it a symbol of God's grace. But I call it Polestar, King of the North, locked in flying embrace with his Shekinah, while directly in the middle of and at right angles to their trajectory stands their son Santiago-Sirius, looking west.

Or let Proteus stand on his head, and it is a sea bell swinging in the *cathedral engloutie.*

◆

EACH afternoon after Mass, in the eastern square beyond the Golden Door of the cathedral, Santiago pilgrims dance to the music of hurdy-gurdy, fiddle, and tambour. As if by long custom, they link arms and form lines that move one way, then the other, then form circles that turn and then open again into lines while the music twines forward its light melodies over a rocking base.

Out of antiquity, out of myth, comes that dance, call it sardena, pasadoble, or farandole, call it Morris dance or what you will. And dance it where you will, in Israel or Greece, Provence or Spain, or in the village squares of England. It was Merlin's wizard-dance around Stonehenge; it was Demeter's in Eleusis and the Apostles' around Christ. It is danced in synagogues around the Torah and by the spinning Hasids. It is danced by Sufi Moslems with their arms straight out and their robes whirling in cones around them. Continually, its waves spread out: Hindus circling their lingas, Buddhists their stupas, Catholics their stations, even the Shakers, almost all spun out of existence by now, who sang as they went,

> They buried my body and they thought I'd gone,
> But I am the dance and I still go on . . .
> They cut me down and I leap up high . . .
> I am the life that'll never never die . . .

ON beyond the city proper lies Cape Finisterre, that seems to hold time pooled, where as the Galicians say, *"la piedra es."* What was the port in Roman times is silted in now and lies back from the shore. There is a little church there. Its sacristan may lift a shutter beneath the altar to let you see an actual sand bank below and, rising straight out of it, a Roman menhir, the very post, says the sacristan, to which Santiago's boat was tied and which, you may reflect, is the true foot of the Eucharistic cup set daily on the table above it.

Under the surface of the place and of this long story lie other truths. One of these has to be that the hope of the myth of Santiago, the reason it held the passionate interest of millions over centuries, must have been deeper than Jihad or Holy War.

Like the myth of Benares, the hope was in resurrection. That from the one great ocean, into which ashes and broken Shiva-lingas go, and from where James emerged, would come walking up the remembered one, the beloved teacher and guide.

But behind this impossible image of a drowned man walking out of the waves, others may rise into the mind: Fire-mountains, East and West; Star-and-sea queens; and John the Divine's Cross of Light, images that themselves rose into our forebears' minds as their imagination played on natural sights—the sun's columnar path, or meteors, or lightning, as the Thunder Brothers would have known.

Far behind me where I stood on Finisterre lay the hill sanctuary of Arunchala in South India. At midnight on the winter solstice in Arunchala, a Linga of Light rises out of a bonfire on the mountain. It rises toward Sirius, then approaching its culmination, and rises on in theory toward Polaris, into which it locks: the great beam of the Cosmos.

In the age to come, I suppose, it will be imagined to rise on beyond Polaris into the immeasurable unknown, where, even then, the voyaging mind will be afforded the grace of the illusion of possible return to its home, the solar system, on that beam of light.

The images of Mountain and Linga, Cross of Light and Star of the Sea, are one and serve to support and orient the mind in space and also in time. For in the language of myth, they are the "same as" the mill staff that stands in the center of the earth, turning amidst the ancestral rivers that flow both toward it and away.

THE END

◆

"Where the journey begins,"—again.
Hortense Calisher:
MYSTERIES OF MOTION

◆

✦ ✦ ✦

In some Spanish town along the Santiago way is preserved what one writer calls a "curious relief" of St. James's tomb being pulled over the waves by a web-toed and winged bird-woman.[1] The creature I suppose is a Siren. Their rookeries lay offshore southern Italy where, to the peril of sailors, they sang of "the mighty deeds of the Greeks beneath the walls of Troy" and "all that happens on the fruitful earth." That is to say, all human history was known to them, but of it the Sirens made only an eerie plaint, so disorganized that even Ulysses was afraid of foundering in it.

The myth of the Sirens, as I read it, concerns the difficulty of making art out of the random events of the past. Their myth flowed into that of Orpheus who, with his lyre, made lyric their confused song, and into that of Apollo, the lucid, brilliant one. With the development of historical scholarship and structured religious and social doctrines, it might have seemed the Sirens' weird oceanic threnody would lose its relevance to the human situation. But that was not to be, not then, perhaps not ever.

We are still what our ancient brains make us be. In the sea basin where Apollo as dolphin swims and sees, the shapes of past beliefs survive to be born again into formulations without measure, as fit the needs of the ages. No form is ontologically single and so goes into oblivion alone forever. But by the same token, no one form is so perfect it can contain the others in perpetuity. What the old world envisioned would have to be envisioned again in the new, including each pilgrim's gathering-in of what lies at her or his trail's end and each society's enlargement toward the end implicit in the form of its founding. Such is the fate of the living imagination, whose dynamics are less understood than the planets' flight we see from earth and seem to mirror, instead, the fires beyond the limits of Cosmos.

And so the Siren passed by sailing from Jaffa to Galicia, drawing

229

behind her the entombed body of the old world's longing and philosophy to the new, and into present meaning.

THE meaning for a world suffering a possible breakthrough from sectarian myths to global consciousness—what Eliade has called a "new planetary humanism"—is that the burden is on the living to suffer the change but preserve the continuities.[2] For a reverent consciousness of the social and imaginative continuities is our inheritance from those who envisioned them within the Cosmos of old.

Now looking back, for instance, we see that those old myths and practices had a function in human survival. Surveying the world and formulating the cosmic image, men and women acquired the will to overcome their fear of the unknown, to migrate vast distances and in time build a world network of cultures with interwoven languages of form and symbol. And cosmic myth continually enlarged humanity's sense of itself by engendering the pilgrim rites— like dipping into "heavenly rivers," orbiting shrines, doing the star-dance of dances and so on—that echo those of other beings from migrant birds to planets.

The myth survives in the popular imagination. Mystics still hold to the idea of escape from corruption through structures that lead from earth to sky. Comparable structures are found in Hindu ashrams and Buddhist zendos, at Lindesfarne in Scotland and New Alchemy on Cape Cod, Arcosanti in Arizona and Taizé in France, and, for that matter, at Graceland, Elvis Presley's home in Tennessee, which draws such crowds for candlelight processions around the axis of the singer's house that a spokesman says, "there's no precedent unless you want to talk about Mohammed or Jesus Christ." People make different value judgments, but the imagery lives, old beyond tabulating: a Yellow Brick Road leads to the sky, and a businessman will mark the miles with Shell Oil scallop shells.

In the end, one has to grant the mind its hunger and conclude that many high-minded programs for social reform and global union have failed because they offered no such imagery as the beautiful Cosmos with its interrelated causeways to paradise.

✦

BUT if the magic of the myth remains, the associated fear of its collapse has resurged in recent times.[3] The warning image of the Domino Theory, that echoes old cosmological prophecies, was proposed in the early twentieth century by a man of religion, a Christian missionary to China, and shapes military strategy still.[4] And on the argument that the Cosmogonic Egg needs blood infusions to survive, political visionaries still promote their death-requiring utopian constructs, in which pilgrimage serves totalitarian ends. Today the immemorial vertical geometry in its reductive male aspect—the Platonic form of the terrible Shiva, Yahweh, the militant Christ, and Muhammad on his war-horse Lightning—has found new embodiment in the nuclear cloud boiling skyward while devouring the earth-plane.[5] People who live in the myth of Cosmos, where it is always ecstatic sunrise or apocalyptic night brought on by their own acts, are susceptible to the inverse grace of fanaticism: to be "inspired by a god, perhaps to madness." So pilgrims and tourists stand in fear together by the valley, call it Jehoshaphat or Kidron, where the Good will meet the Despised and, in one or the other's achieving victory, no doubt destroy this "most beautiful order of things that are very good."

The sense of disorientation, again, sends the mind out looking for permanent attachments, as it sent the minds of the builders of stone circles out along their trajectories toward the ever-stable stars and planets. Something of the ancient urgency may be behind the popularizing of space exploration by some politicians today. But let the mental veil that hides infinity dissolve, and the picture is not so enchanting. To contemplate the frigidity and violent collisions of space without the old supporting structures is not to be enchanted. So much the blacker is the night that falls between oneself and a point of light with which one has no felt connection. It is in our consciousness of the frailty of life and its apparent rarity in the universe that we find ourselves allied, today, to our most remote ancestors, who questioned the sky for the very coordinates of being and concluded that it ended at the limit of what they could see.

Even to find expression for our actual loneness-in-emptiness may not be possible now. By default, it has become the style to deliver such thoughts in a humor called black. "The universe gives me the creeps," Willem de Kooning, the surviving Abstract-Expressionist painter, has said. And nihilism has its own pilgrimage center now, the Rothko Chapel in Texas, where huge black-violet canvases hang on cold gray walls, cut off from all sight lines to the world, soaking in what weak light filters through hidden apertures. For me at least, the place is a crypt of unredeemed death.

THE human mind, it seems, needs an embracing form within which to orient itself, and within that form, a Polestar or "controlling destination" by which to plot the life. A thoughtful mind reaffirms its commitment to that destination or guiding principle many times in a lifetime, in metaphors of transformation.

Indeed already as the millennium comes on, many people sense a new myth surfacing to answer that need. Already we know its shape, lifted from the depths as the vision brought home by astronauts: no egg of stars but a small blue-green floating spore across whose surface an edge of sunlight races, right to left.[6] Then this mutant myth will be a "certain change . . . a strange correction" of older ones. Like earlier myths in their borning phases, this one too embodies sexual union: earth in the arms of time might be its metaphoric image, and its icon the double helix that supports not super-nature but all natural forms of life.

This myth-form still in a state of genesis is still a place of crystal streams, only now not Pison, Gihon, Hiddekel, and Phrath but Yangtse, Volga, Amazon, and Mississippi. It is a garden adrift without guard rails somewhere between Polaris and Canopus. It is the only sacred space where pilgrimage can now unfold, across hills shaped like ribs toward brooks like open veins, to end back in "that gentle brown humus, where the journey begins"—again.[7]

The implication of the new myth is still that the organic body in question—only now not Cosmos but the life-sown planet—counts for something in the sum total of the universe, that it is important for the global community to join in ecological, social, and political measures to rescue it from sickness—as Hindus join in the Kumbha-mela.

This is the implication, though we have no way of knowing whether it reflects an actual condition of the universe. In other words, we are back with the conundrum I began with: Does our sense of things reflect their nature or only the nature of our need? For all we know, organic life is the offspring of a misalliance of protons in the primordial mist, and human hunger for form, a later misalliance of neurons in the brain. But people need to feel they are on a journey that rises out of the past while preserving its connection with it, in order to rise out of the way of hopeless death. So this new myth may enable humanity to survive another age.

THE mutant myth has generated a mutant genre of art, called "Earth-works" by its practitioners and appreciators. Its stylistic predecessor is sculpture by Modernist artists like Calder, Kiesler, and Miró: abstract mechanical and biological forms celebrating industrial man and benevolent nature. That work was imbued with the authority and optimism of an earlier time. The new idiom is vastly more austere and lonely: quasi-architectural forms constructed in remote sites in the American West. Its conceptual predecessor is the anonymous work of ancient and tribal peoples around the world. Like Stonehenge; like the "walkabout-trails" Australian aborigines follow across terrorizing wastelands they call "Eternity";[8] like rock-cut tunnels in Egypt and Ireland and Arizona, into which the sun drives on certain days to light carvings on the far walls;[9] like the "hitching post of the sun" atop Machu Picchu; like the Big Horn Medicine Wheel in Wyoming, oriented to certain star-risings; like stone circles and kivas, ziggurats and temples and cathedrals; like—yes even!—the great linga of the Pan Am Building in Manhattan, with heli-copters buzzing its tip; like all these, Earth-works perform the immemorial job of orienting and stabilizing a conscious body in space.[10]

The body is now not a single sage or people but Earth itself; its consciousness is the collective earthling's.[11] Earth-artists, like astronomers monitoring radio telescopes and astrophysicists examining the interface between physical and organic nature, are the globe's eyes, mouths, and ears fixed on what is still silent inanimation, but with the collective human emotion called *hope*.[12] Merely to engage in such work is to establish orienting axes between ourselves and the beyond, whatever it may turn out, centuries ahead, to hold in the way of knowledge or environment for our descendants. And those who travel by jeep to see the Earth-works are, as surely as was Melville climbing the Acropolis, pilgrims.

THE endings of pilgrimages are both sad and, like their beginnings, strange. The vision fades. Yet there remains the question whether there was more to it than the traveler has understood. Imagination knows more than we think.

From where does it get its instruction? From the stars, said the Orphics. British astronomer Sir Francis Crick, who holds a theory he calls Panspermia, says the same in scientific-materialist terms.[13]

Then, to engage in a mode of thought I call "Visionary humanism"—that is, to ask the outlandish question as to travel to the out-landish place—did there fall to earth, laced in the double helix, a glint so ordered it would seek resurrection here, not in the labyrinths of illusion but persistently, with each new burgeoning, in nature?

When along the course of these journeys I'd visited Lourdes and stood watching the flames of thousands of candles turn in rain and darkness around the water source that is the axis of that shrine, the well-known words had come into my mind, *Eppur si muove*— and still it moves.[14]

And what was most painful at Lourdes was what was most revealing. For I asked myself as I stood by that procession whether it was morbidity that kept me fixed to the sight of so many individuals there in extremes of deformity and fear. But I thought, it was not.

I was transfixed at Lourdes because through those imprisoning bodies, some entangled yet separate *will* had glinted out with shocking immediacy—the same that I had witnessed elsewhere along the course of these travels, pressing toward its own extension and so giving rise to what humanists call the mysteries: religious myths and rites, and philosophy and art.

What law or force it is that bound those pilgrims into their travail and orbit seemed to me then as unarguable—yet still as mysterious—as was, to Galileo, the turning of the earth around the sun.

AFTERWORD

◆

I turned from side to side, from image to image, to put you down . . .
And it is my virtue that I cannot give you out,
That you are absorbed into my strength . . .
Louise Bogan:
JOURNEY AROUND MY ROOM

◆

✦ ✦ ✦

The content of a form, then, is the mystery to be pursued. For example, I've tried to show how collective imagination worked in history to bring back to transformed life certain figures of myth—the teacher lost to death, the bad woman turned good, the love-goddess whose geometry is large enough to encompass both death and birth—so that pilgrims of new ages could have them for guidance. And I now understand it was my own need to invent, first, a form generous enough to contain it and then, within it, a comparable reunion of my own, that drew me into the pilgrim flow in the first place.

In fact, it was while I was driving the River of Stars through France that I began asking myself what I'd been doing on this long journey, traveling roads, some new to me, some I'd traveled before, pulling sights and memories together until the image of a life-preserving Cosmos had come breeding out of my head. The more I'd pressured myself to accept the finality of life in a Buddhistic sense, the more, the very next day, my thoughts had striven on to discover more life in things—as my father strove through his voluminous readings toward the image in Lucretius of the living gods.

And then it struck me all at once that I had contrived—by a metamorphosis I was unaware of at the time—to turn this whole project of travel, research, and writing into just such an exercise. For like those who go down the river toward the ocean that rises to the stars, those who go down the intricate and unbroken continuities of scholarship, art, or memory will arrive at their destination, which is their destiny.

They too will draw in the nets of transformation, enacting for themselves the promise of Christian water-burial: "the sea shall give up the dead to the resurrection."

Then this whole construct I had so reveled in—the celestial sphere holding the earth in its arms—was my own sky-brain bringing itself into expanded being to hold onto what it holds dear.

239

So I'll insert here a memory of how, when we were children, on some summer mornings, my brother and I would fall into line behind our father, who would bring us along a path out into a meadow all bronze with last year's sumac, and lead us then to a dogwood that was a tree of life not death, for under it he and our mother had been married, and then lead us—he ever the Indian chief, swatting at vines with his cane, holding back ancient leaf-cover to show us the buried wintergreen—all the way up to the cliff, hanging, as it seemed, over the world, where he would take up his pose on the brink of nothingness but pointing with his cane east, south, north, toward fields giving into fields, brooks into rivers into the sea beyond, there to declaim, drawing our minds out even farther toward the future so golden to us then,

> I shot an arrow into the air!
> It fell to earth I know not where . . .
> Long, long after, in an oak,
> I found the arrow still unbroke.[1]

How many cycles of years later would I still be coming back toward such places and to the men and women who opened me to the world, showing me how I fit into it, annihilating my loneness because they—we—were, I was, so ringed with *being*—tales, myths, art, lives of people, houses, lands, world . . . until I would come around to say, *all these* are my strength.

AND now, since the mind is restless, never satisfied, where will it take me next?

I go to the beach these winter days to get away from words and back to things. In things seen bare, the unknown still lies tombed. On a cold Cape Cod day, a beach is as bare a place as there may be on earth. Nothing is there but what is inanimate, not a tree, no grass, no other being in sight. Not even, if the swell is running high and the wind offshore, birds.

It could be outer space is like this, cold spinning stones and blowing sprays.

Still it's strange how often on such a day, like others who go to beaches, I'll take home memory of a footprint seen on the sand.

In actuality, there are many of them always, overlaid and contradictory, some going off, some coming back, as fishermen will. I see them all, but I'll take in mind just one to reflect on as I walk home. I see it pointed off away from me, a shaped and tilted plane of light, northbound, rimmed with an edge of shadow.

Cape Cod
1986

Notes

Epigraphs: Jorge Luis Borges, *Labyrinths* (New York: New Directions, 1962), 212, footnote 2.
Temistocle Solera, Libretto for Giuseppe Verdi's opera *I Lombardi,* Act II, Scene 1 (based on Tomasso Grassi's poem).

PREFACE

1. *World Christian Encyclopedia.* ed. David B. Barrett. Nairobi: Oxford University Press, 1982. Global Table no. 4, page 6.
2. The artist's life too can be considered a secular "pilgrimage." See Eleanor Munro, *Originals: American Women Artists* (New York: Simon & Schuster, 1979).
3. See Vincent Scully, *The Earth, the Temple, and the Gods* (New Haven: Yale University Press, 1962), 7.
4. The Crusades, obviously, but more beneficently, the Puritans' pilgrimage to America, the Chinese Long March to Yenan, Martin Luther King's walks for civil rights.
5. At Kataragama, cult site in Sri Lanka for the war-god Skanda, rites are performed that correspond with the American Apache Indian sun-dance: the worshiper is attached, by hooks and cords, to an axial sun-pillar or tree in the center of the sacred space (Black Elk, *The Sacred Pipe,* University of Oklahoma Press / Penguin Books, 1971, 95 et passim). Other mutilations performed by pilgrims in India are: branding, "piercing cheeks and tongue with silver needles," cutting out the tongue, amputating fingers, measuring the body's length through successive prostrations (one Buddhist shrine in Lhasa requires some 4,000 prostrations for a circumambulation). Agehananda Bharati, "Pilgrimage in the Indian Tradition," *History of Religions,* Vol. 3, No. 1, 1963, 140–41.
6. Can generalizations be made from discrete cases, i.e., *is there* influence and continuity between separated cultural groups? Nowadays, in reaction to misuse of general psycho-social theories by politicians, many social scientists

restrict themselves to local phenomena and their roots in local circumstances. By contrast, anthropologist Lévi-Strauss argues (*Myth and Meaning*, 26–27) that cultural structures, like art styles, "seep through" their containing membranes to influence neighbors.

7. See *Archaeoastronomy: The Journal of the Center for Archaeoastronomy* (University of Maryland), Vols. I–IX, 1978–present, and *First International Conference on Ethnoastronomy: Indigenous Astronomical and Cosmological Traditions of the World*, Program and Abstracts (Washington, D.C.: Smithsonian Institution, 1983).

8. Mircea Eliade, *The Quest* (Chicago: University of Chicago Press, 1969), 645–46.

PROLOGUE

Epigraph: Hortense Calisher, *Mysteries of Motion* (New York: Doubleday, 1983), 4.

1. George Fox, *The Journal,* 1651 (New York: E. P. Dutton, 1924), 39, 23.

2. The poem is "A Psalm of Life."

3. For Shiva as object of poetic adoration: A. K. Ramanujan, tr. and ed., *Speaking of Siva* (Baltimore: Penguin, 1973). For representations of Shiva in categories like "Androgyny and Unity" and "God of Dread and Terror" as well as lover, dancer, destroyer, etc., see Stella Kramrisch, *Manifestations of Shiva,* Philadelphia Museum of Art catalogue, 1981. The bisexual form of Shiva shows the left side of the body as female, the right side, male. His / her name then is Ardhanarisvara, the "metaphysical unity" implied by the marriage bond. Stella Kramrisch, *Presence of Siva* (Princeton: Princeton University Press, 1981), 350. For a subjective Siva "in your own face . . . ": ibid., 75. The passage is from the Svetasvatara Upanishad, 4, 3–4, slightly adapted. But that author warns, "Siva transcends all categories. He is existence, with all its paradoxes," xiv. Both spellings are accepted and Kramrisch uses both.

4. Diana Eck, "Kasi, City and Symbol," *Purana,* Vol. XX, No. 2, July 1978, 169–92. The article was enlarged into the book *Banaras: City of Light* (New York: Alfred A. Knopf, 1982).

5. *Bible of the World,* ed. Robert O. Ballou (New York: Viking, 1939), 5. *Rg Veda:* X, 90.

6. Kramrisch, *Presence of Siva,* op. cit., 81: "It is as a darkly attired uncanny stranger from the north that Rudra appeared . . . there is much darkness in Rudra."

7. It was the Hindu "Forest Scriptures" or Upanishads. These exist in many translations. A particularly artful one is *The Ten Principal Upanishads,* tr. Swami Shree Purohit and W. B. Yeats (New York: Macmillan, 1937).

POLESTAR SIGHTED

Epigraph: Herman Melville, *Clarel: A Poem and Pilgrimage in the Holy Land,* 1876. *The Portable Melville* (New York: Viking), 619.

1. The principle applies to the sun observed from north of the Tropic of Cancer; south of the Tropic of Capricorn, it moves E to N to W; between, its course fluctuates. At Benares, it always takes the southerly course, as it does in those regions of Europe, Africa, the Middle East, Asia, and the Americas where the sky-oriented religions began.

2. Lizelle Reymond, *My Life with a Brahmin Family* (Rider and Co. / Penguin Books, 1958 / 1972), 146.

3. Over one hundred cities pour raw sewage into the river, already choked with industrial effluents, pesticide and fertilizer runoff, and remains of cremated bodies. In Benares alone some four hundred are cremated daily, and the ashes— and often incompletely burned bodies—go into the river along with the waste of monkeys and sacred cattle. Yet the belief is that Ganges water is not only safe but healing.

4. There is a term for this sound: *Nadam,* cosmic vibration, perhaps comparable to Kepler's Music of the Spheres. Indeed Nadam-Brahma, Sound-as-god, is a prayer, along with Annam-Brahma and Shabdam-Brahma (Food-as-god and Word-as-god).

5. See Surinder Mohan Bhardwaj, *Hindu Places of Pilgrimage* (Berkeley: University of California Press, 1973). Though all India is holy (see below), and Benares auspicious for all ceremonies, there are other foci where cremation brings special benefit: for a dead male, the ancient town of Gaya; for a female, especially a mother who has died by violence, Siddhpur on the Saraswati River. See also Mrs. Sinclair Stevenson, *The Rites of the Twice Born* (London: Oxford University Press, 1920), 363.

6. Eck, op. cit. Also Betty Heimann, *Facets of Indian Thought* (London: George Allen and Unwin, 1964), especially "India's Biology." The process of redistribution of sacred places goes on. Only a sixth of official cult sites are now given to the Goddess though the universality of her appeal is recognized. Agehananda Bharati, "Pilgrimage in the Indian Tradition," *History of Religions,* Vol. 3, No. 1, 1963, 90.

7. Sudhir Kakar, conversation with author.

8. Her origin lies in pre-Hindu Indus Valley prototypes. Mircea Eliade, *Yoga: Immortality and Freedom* (Princeton: Princeton University Press, 1958), 354.

9. Kailas, the mythic Mount Meru, center of the Cosmos, is in Tibet, near the source of the Brahmaputra River. Hindus call it the Linga of Being rising from the Earth-vulva. For Buddhists, it marks the dividing point between matter and nothingness. To succeed in climbing it (a physical impossibility) would be to attain the unification of all contradiction. Marco Pallis, *The Way and the Mountain* (London: Peter Owen, 1960): "[A pilgrim] approaches from the golden plains of the south, from the noon of life. . . . He enters the red valley . . . in the light of the sinking sun, he goes through the portals of death between the dark northern and the multi-colored eastern valleys . . . and descends, as a new-born being, into the green valley on the east. . . . " 214.

10. This last teaching represents the most abstruse school of Hinduism, the Vedanta, heavily influenced by Buddhism. Romila Thapar, *A History of India,* Vol. 1

(New York: Penguin Books, 1966), 130. Also René Guênon, *Man and his Becoming, According to the Vedanta* (New York: Noonday Press, 1958); Christmas Humphreys, *Karma and Rebirth* (London: John Murray, 1943), 54–55.

11. The site is Amarnath Cave in Kashmir, where, at the August full moon, some 25,000 pilgrims may gather after a month or more on the road.

12. Bharati, "Pilgrimage in the Indian Tradition," op. cit., 139.

13. See Ananda Coomaraswamy, *The Dance of Siva* (New York: The Sunwise Turn, 1924), 64–66.

14. This is an ongoing question relevant to a discussion of pilgrimage rites and myths. The Victorians considered myths and the rites they generate to be the result of a defect in the reality-grasping mechanism of "primitive" peoples, a "disease of language" (Müller), representative of "pre-logical mentality" (Levy-Bruhl) or magical-thinking (Malinowski). Modern depth psychology revealed logical structures in myth, ritual, and art and so inspired the view of the human mind as a self-motivating system laboring to organize the world in its own terms. Idealist philosophers, symbolic logicians, and some linguists (Cassirer, Langer, Chomsky, etc.) went further and argued that no correlation can be drawn between these mental structures and the natural world. "All mental processes fail to grasp reality itself" (Cassirer, *Language and Myth*, 7, 11). By contrast, strictly naturalistic theories of myth include "euhemerism" (its origin in historic heroes like Alexander) and "geomythology" (its origin in earthquakes, floods, volcanic eruptions, etc.: see Dorothy B. Vitaliano, *Legends of the Earth* (Bloomington: Indiana University Press, 1976). More interesting to me, however, are hermeneutic philosophers, scientists, and historians of science and art who break the Kantian deadlock, proceeding on the assumption that the mind takes in data about the natural world, then processes it according to internal mechanisms. In other words, there are both variety in the world and also universally shared imaginative structures by which people comprehend that world. There are various local styles of pilgrimage but universal laws by which it is enacted: the thesis of this book.

15. Rudolf Arnheim, *Toward a Psychology of Art* (Berkeley, Los Angeles: University of California Press, 1966), 42.

16. Mircea Eliade, *Patterns in Comparative Religion* (Sheed & Ward/New American Library, 1974), 413.

17. See D. L. Snellgrove, *Buddhist Himalaya* (New York: Philosophical Library, 1957), 281: "[Buddhists of Tibet and Nepal] still believe the world to be flat and arranged like a mandala, with Mt. Meru at the center and four continents at the four directions."

18. Giorgio de Santillana and Hertha von Dechend, *Hamlet's Mill* (Boston: Gambit, 1969), 123: "This world conception with its three 'domains' . . . with the 'world pillar' running through the center . . . crowned by the 'world nail' . . . goes further back than Indian and Iranian culture, namely to the most ancient Near East, whence India and Iran derived their idea of a 'cosmos'—in itself by no means an obvious assumption." Also Peter G. Roe, *The Cosmic Zy-*

gote: Cosmology in the Amazon Basin (New Brunswick: Rutgers University Press, 1983).

19. The name Copernicus gave his treatise, *De revolutionibus orbium coelestium,* preserves the image of the Cosmos as a system of interlocked, revolving orbs. The paradigm-shift had to await those who "reshaped our cosmological self-image 65 years ago by shunting the solar system from the center to the distant outskirts of our galaxy." *Research Highlights,* Smithsonian Institution, Winter 1986.

20. "Ascetics worship the fire . . . [they] pass after death into light, from light into the sun, from the sun into lightning. The Spirit finds them there, and leads them to heaven. In that Kingdom of Heaven, they live, never returning to earth . . ." *Bhagavad-Gita,* 8.5–8.

21. *Astronomy of the Ancients,* ed. Kenneth Brecher and Michael Feirtag (Boston: MIT Press, 1981), 166. The Greek *okeanos* embraced earth and sky as their placenta. See also Diana Eck, "India's Tirthas: Crossings in Sacred Geography," unpublished ms., Harvard University, 1979; and Phyllis Ackerman, *Forgotten Religions* (1950), 6 (cited in de Santillana and von Dechend, op. cit., 260). Other places that may have appeared to be in line of contact with the sky were lightning-blasted trees and rocks, and places where rainwater collected.

22. *Ethnoastronomy: First Annual Conference on,* Smithsonian Institution program and abstracts, 1983. There is no fixed date for Eliade's "illud tempus," though it is known that "prehistoric hunters carrying torches entered the deepest cave recesses and [there] performed religious acts" as early as 30,000 before the historic era. (Frank E. Poirier, *In Search of Ourselves: An Introduction to Physical Anthropology* [Minneapolis: Burgess, 1977], 297). Lunar and solar notations on bones found in caves show that "careful astronomical observation, observation of seasonal periodicities in nature and complex problem-solving strategies for imaging and sequencing the periodicities of time" took place from the Upper Paleolithic period (28,000–20,000). (*Ethnoastronomy: First Annual Conference on,* 17)

23. In accord with modern historical usage, I use BCE to denote "Before the Common (or present) Era" and CE for "Common Era."

24. Thorkild Jacobsen, *Before Philosophy,* Henri Frankfort, ed. (Chicago: University of Chicago Press, 1946), 140.

25. Richard Hinckley Allen, *Star Names: Their Lore and Meaning.* (New York: Dover, 1963; ed. of G. E. Stechert, *Star Names,* 1899), 215. Eridanus has been associated with Homer's Ocean Stream that circumflows the earth, with the Po, Ebro, Rhine, and Vistula, with the Nile and Euphrates.

26. Mircea Eliade, *The Myth of the Eternal Return* or *Cosmos and History* (New York: Bollingen, 1954), 6, and de Santillana and von Dechend, op. cit., 205.

27. Surinder Mohan Bhardwaj, *Hindu Places of Pilgrimage in India: A Study in Cultural Geography* (Berkeley, Los Angeles: University of California Press, 1983), 29 et passim. The pilgrimage of these ancestral heroes was around a course of "tirthas" or sacred cross-points that defined the territory undergoing settlement. See also Stella Kramrisch, "Tirtha and Temple," *The Hindu*

Temple, (Calcutta: University of Calcutta, 1946), Vol. 1, and Eck, "India's Tirthas," op. cit., 14.

28. Cited in Ananda Coomaraswamy, *The Transformation of Nature in Art* (Cambridge: Harvard University Press, 1934), 155. Quoting Rao, *Elements of Hindu Iconography,* II.28. Compare: "Geometry serves Indian metaphysics through its notion of comprehensive space . . . like horns on the head of an animal or like the peak of a mountain, *Brahman* (the inner, Platonic essence . . .) protrudes and pierces through the limits and the contours of given empirical shapes." Heimann, op. cit., 123. Also: Blake's "the Gods of Greece and Egypt were mathematical diagrams."

29. De Santillana and von Dechend, op. cit., 177. Also Jerome Y. Lettvin, "The Gorgon's Eye" in *Astronomy of the Ancients,* op. cit., 135. Compare: Peter Brown, *The Making of Late Antiquity* (Cambridge: Cambridge University Press, 1978), 76: The pseudoscience of celestial motions "brought down into men's views of their lives . . . the complexities and conflicts which they saw in the planets as they moved like backgammon counters across the fixity of the heavens."

30. See W. R. Lethaby, *Architecture, Mysticism and Myth,* London, 1891 (reissued London: Architectural Press, 1974). The building of certain monuments, says the author, was a rite by which man identified himself with the source of order at the cosmic center, the *omphalos* or navel of the world. Eliade added that the monument represents not only its center but the dynamic event of its creation. See "Sacred Places: Temple, Palace, 'Centre of the World' " in Eliade, *Patterns in Comparative Religion,* op. cit., 367–85.

31. The major work on the subject is Stella Kramrisch's *The Hindu Temple,* op. cit. Her theme is the temple as embodied "impulse towards manifestation," human consciousness seeking embodiment under the control of "cosmic intelligence ordering the process of manifestation." 46.

32. Kramrisch, *Hindu Temple,* "Purification, Insemination and Levelling of the Site," 14–17.

33. J. McKim Malville, "Astronomical Discovery and the Evolution of Symbols in Hindu Mythology," *First International Conference on Ethnoastronomy,* op. cit., 17. This "astro-geophysicist" refers to "some 25 temples of Tamil Nadu state" in which "during a few days of the year for brief moments, sunlight enters the darkness of the sacred center to illuminate the symbol of the god." This takes place "near the time of vernal equinox." The event is "surya puja," or sun-worship.

34. Eliade, *Patterns in Comparative Religion,* op. cit., Chapter II, "The Sky and Sky Gods," especially 97–99 and the extensive bibliography 112–23. See also Harald A. T. Reiche, "The Language of Archaic Astronomy," in *Astronomy of the Ancients,* op. cit., 159.

35. See also Kramrisch, *Presence of Siva,* op. cit., 42–43.

36. As to whether this subtle movement in the heavens was perceptible to the naked eye in antiquity, many astronomers agree it was. "The effect is not really small. For instance, if the sun passes a given star at midwinter in a

man's youth, when he is 90 it will pass that same star one day after midwinter. The effect cannot be missed. And it would certainly be regarded by primitive astronomers as interesting and fundamental." NASA astronomer John O'Keeffe to author, 1983.

37. See *Astronomy of the Ancients*, op. cit., 160–61: "Parts of two major creation stories, those of the incestuous father . . . and the churning of the cosmic ocean, may be immediate responses to discoveries of the precession . . ." For example, Stella Kramrisch and others fix the time of generation of the Hindu myth of the incestuous father (see page 42) to the time when spring equinoctial sunrise would have been observed moving away from Canis Major (home of the star Sirius, which marks the tip of the father's arrow) toward Orion (the antelope, representing his daughter) around 4000–3000 BCE. Kramrisch, *Presence of Siva*, op. cit., 47, footnote 36.

38. Harald A. T. Reiche in *Astronomy of the Ancients,* op. cit., 184: These myths contain "a pseudohistorical description of one aspect of a continuous process that became critical about every two thousand years."

39. *Bible of the World*, op. cit., 5.

40. The ancient grinding mill or quern was a stationary, slightly convex stone on the ground and a rope-turned stone above, slightly concave. By medieval times in Europe, the mill had become an hourglass-shaped instrument, and so it is represented in carvings in Romanesque churches (see page 181). As to the persistence of the mill as an image for the delimited Cosmos, consider: "The shape of the universe may thus be compared to that of a grindstone or lens, the sun being situated about midway between the two surfaces." *Encyclopedia Britannica*, 13th ed., 1926, Vol. 25, 792.

41. Actually, two conjunctions herald the event: the entry of Jupiter into Aquarius and the sun into Aries. Now loosely coinciding also with the winter solstice, it heralds the sun's shift into its northward or "auspicious" track. The correlative events fall in February / March (in Hardwar), July / August (in Nasik), October / November (in Ujjain). See Ikbal Kaul, "Kumbh Mela," *The Illustrated Weekly of India*, February 20, 1977, 20–25. The Mahabharata calls Prayag the "King of pilgrimage-sites," and exhorts suicide there.

42. Richard Burghart, "Wandering Ascetics of the Ramanandi Sect," *History of Religions*, Vol. 22, No. 4, May 1983, 361–80.

43. Lama Anagarika Govinda, *The Way of the White Clouds* (New Delhi: B. I. Publications, 1960), 21. There is a contradiction here: the conventional "sunwise" pilgrimage is clockwise; "planetary" pilgrimage, as observed from the north pole, would be counterclockwise. But the Lama was not an astronomer. Some such contradiction may account for the doubled, counterbalanced directions of zodiacal layouts around some Christian medieval church portals.

44. Wallace Stevens, "Anecdote of the Jar," *The Palm at the End of the Mind: Selected Poems* (New York: Alfred A. Knopf, 1971), 46.

45. Georg Roppen and Richard Sommer, *Strangers and Pilgrims: An Essay on the Metaphor of Journey* (Oslo: Norwegian University Press), 12.

46. Out of this symbolism came the goat as sign for Polestar's son on earth: Christ. See Mary Sayre Haverstock, *An American Bestiary* (New York: Harry N. Abrams, 1979), 9. See page 141.

47. Some archaeologists believe these cities antedate even the earliest Mesopotamian settlements, dating from 6000 BCE or before.

48. Poirier, *In Search of Ourselves*, op. cit., 295. Compare Kramrisch, *Presence of Siva*, op. cit., 10–14.

49. See Hertha von Dechend, *World Ages*, unpublished ms. in author's possession, 60. The quotation is assembled from the *Bhagavata Purana* 4-8-10;5.23; and *Vishnu Purana* 1.12. See also *Hamlet's Mill*, op. cit., 138.

50. Eliade, *Yoga: Immortality and Freedom*, op. cit., 353–58: "If we are right in connecting the origins of Yogic asceticism with the proto-historical religion of the Indus, we may justifiably conclude that in it we have . . . a living fossil, a modality of archaic spirituality." He describes the Yogi's "petrified immobility of body . . . fixation of the psychological flux, immobility of thought, the 'arrest' and even the 'return' of semen." 361–62.

51. Cited in Ananda K. Coomaraswamy, "An Indian Temple," *Parabola*, Vol. III, Issue 1, 1978, 4–10. The author compares the Hindu Temple to the "Islamic doctrine of . . . the Perfect Man on which all things turn" and to Jacob's ladder.

52. See F.D.K. Bosch, *The Golden Germ* (The Hague: Mouton & Co., 1960), 210. The relationship between the axis of the sun's helical movement and Polestar is signified by the one-legged billy goat Aja ekapad, a creature "unborn, without parents," the "cosmic pillar," etc., ibid., 207–9. He is the "apex of the Cosmos" at the other end of the pole from the serpent of the deeps. Margaret E. Noble (Sister Nivedita) and Ananda Coomaraswamy, *Myths of the Hindus and Buddhists* (New York: Farrar and Rinehart), 388. A related figure of myth is Pusan, the sun-in-motion: "Aja ekapad is an image of the vertical axis of Pusan's cyclical path. . . . Aja ekapad is the axis of the cosmos." *Exploring India's Sacred Art: Selected Writings of Stella Kramrisch*, Barbara Stoller Miller, ed. (Philadelphia: University of Pennsylvania Press, 1983), 330, footnote 16; 332, footnote 47; 333, footnote 53. In early Orissan Shiva-temples, Aja ekapad was conventionally shown on the *north* of the sanctuary. But later, his images were placed on the *south* where they came under the influence of the death-god. Thus, the Shiva shrine itself stands midway on the cosmic axis—as does the star Sirius (see below, page 62). Thomas Donaldson, "Ekapada Siva Images in Orissan Art," *Ars Orientalis*, XIII, 153–67.

   Polestar generated corresponding offspring in the West: the goat-footed Phrygian Pan, the lame-footed Greek blacksmith Hephaistos, the one-eyed giant Cyclops. The Australian aboriginal polestar-god Turunblun has one eye and one foot. Noble and Coomaraswamy, op. cit., 387–88. See also Jane Harrison, *Themis: A Study of the Social Origins of Greek Religion* (Cleveland: World Publishing Co., 1912), 406–12.

53. See Diana L. Eck, *Darsan: Seeing the Divine Image in India* (Chambersburg, Pa.: Anima Books, 1981). "Darshan" is the term for open-eyed adoration of

a holy person or image, signifying the passage of a stream of energy between worshiper and object. Corresponding concepts in Hindu cosmology are "Karma"—a forward flow of causal effect through living substance—and "Dharma"—a flow of causal effect through material substance according to laws of momentum, attraction, repulsion, etc. See Edward Rice, *Eastern Definitions* (New York: Anchor Press, 1980), 118.

54. Kramrisch, *Hindu Temple,* Vol. 1, Part 1, 7.

55. In an abstract sense, an Asian mantra—OM MANI PADME HUM, NAMAH SHIVAYA, even OM / HE / SRA / HA / KSHA / MA / LA / VA / RA / YAM, emitted as an ongoing groan—functions as a hinge between earth and sky, for its vibrations fill the Cosmos. The same function is served by the perpetual praying of a Christian mystic (*The Way of a Pilgrim,* tr. from Russian by R. M. French, New York: Seabury Press / Ballantine, 1974 ed.). Works of art and literature may also function as hinges: "The past is hidden in some material object (in the sensation which that material object will give us) which we do not suspect." Here the tangible hinge is the *madeleine,* which joins two abstractions, past and present time. Ultimately, the mind itself is the hinge through which "human beings can be said to occupy a place . . . extending boundlessly . . . reaching far back into the years . . ." Marcel Proust, *The Past Recaptured* (New York: Modern Library, 1959), 402. On the other hand, among visualized hinge-images the strangest may be pre-Columbian divinities like the Mexican Quetzalcoatl, garbed in snakeskins and feathers, who sets himself afire and ascends as the morning star. For conceptual support: see Art Brenner, "The Structuralism of Claude Lévi-Strauss and the Visual Arts," *Leonardo,* Vol. 10, 303–6.

56. Allen, *Star Names,* op. cit., 64–72. Since there is no bright star at the actual southern pole, this one—some 40 degrees away—has served navigation and myth. It was named, says legend, by Menelaus for the pilot of his fleet, who, returning from Troy, landed in Egypt and died there. On Canopus's grave, Menelaus set up a stone pillar and gave the antipodal star its name. The pilot Canopus was not the only survivor of Troy to die on the sea route home; so did Aeneas's pilot, Palinurus, in the Bay of Naples. According to archaeoastronomical interpretation, drowning was a metaphor used by the ancients for the disappearance of a constellation or star into the abyss, as a result of the precessional shift. By this reading, drownings and other deaths of ships' pilots refer to the ending of the old World Age, with the fall of Troy. See Harald A. T. Reiche, "The Language of Archaic Astronomy," *Astronomy of the Ancients,* op. cit., 169 ff.

57. De Santillana and von Dechend, op. cit., 269. Canopus, sighted low in the southern sky along the southern border of the Caspian Sea, remains so to the upper bend of the Indus, thereafter rising degree by degree as one descends the subcontinent. Therefore, this theory if correct could help account for the descent of the star-following Aryans into the Gangetic plain.

58. Mystery-associations in myth and folklore with the north-south axis are manifold. To take only a couple: among the American Ojibway Indians, the house for rites for the dead, the "Ghost midewiwin," is oriented north / south,

while the "Life midewiwin" is oriented east / west. John A. Grim, *The Shaman: Patterns of Siberian and Ojibway Healing* (Norman: University of Oklahoma Press, 1983), 70. On Chartres cathedral, while the West Portal is the Virgin's and Christ reigns within at the East, the North Portal provides a theater of sculptures on the subject of Creation itself, enacted by the Father-creator or Polestar, who brings sky and earth into existence as well as sun, moon, and Adam. Compare: W. B. Yeats, "A Dialogue of Self and Soul": "Set all your mind upon the steep ascent . . . / Upon the star that marks the hidden pole . . . / That quarter where all thought is done: / Who can distinguish darkness from the soul?"

59. "Give me my robe and scepter," says Shakespeare's Cleopatra. "I have immortal longings."

60. For Sirius's qualities and related myths and rites: Allen, *Star Names,* op. cit., 120–29.

61. In support of this proposition: von Dechend, *World Ages,* op. cit., 90–100. She describes "the heliacal rising of Sirius, [that] fell on the same day of the Julian calendar every year" as it had for two millennia before. "This remarkable phenomenon, that Sirius by itself 'fabricates' the Julian year, has long been known. The famous Jesuit astronomer, Dionysius Petavius Aurelianus, began his dissertation of 1775 with the words, 'Admirabiliter contigit . . .'— 'Wondrously it happened that . . .', namely, the heliacal rising of Sirius in Heliopolis in [the second century CE] fell on the 20th of July by the Julian calendar, as it had" in millennia past. Thus, Frazer could state with assurance that "Sirius . . . on July mornings, [rose] from the eastern Mediterranean . . ." *The Golden Bough* (New York: Macmillan, 1922), 384. Previously, i.e., during the early Egyptian period, the star rose heliacally in June, signaling the floods. Now it does so in August. I witnessed this phenomenon myself thanks to modern technology and the aid of astronomer Dr. K. L. Franklin at the Hayden Planetarium, New York. "Can you turn the sky back?" I asked. "Back to where and when?" he inquired. I specified 3500 BCE, 35th parallel, late June, shortly before sunrise. He touched some dials, and lo, Sirius rose in the southeastern sky. Then I specified the year One, late July, the same time before sunrise. He turned switches, and lo, the star rose again, just where it should. Dr. William Gutsch also demonstrated this to me at the Planetarium.

For the relevance of this arcane material to pilgrimage rites and traditions, see pages 142 and 184.

62. The connection between Sirius and rites of circumcision is made in many ways and places. It is the "circumcision star" for the Mande people of the Sudan (see *Hamlet's Mill,* 430) and of the Dogon in Mali (see Maurice Griaule, *Conversations with Ogotemmeli,* Oxford University Press, 1965). For the connection between Sirius and the traditional overseer of circumcision for the Jews, Elijah, see below, page 101.

63. Richard Krautheimer, "Introduction to an 'Iconography' of Medieval Architecture," *Journal of the Warburg and Courtauld Institute,* Vol. 5, 1942, 1–33.

64. Kramrisch, *Presence of Siva*, op. cit., 44. "Rudra in the sky is Sirius, star of stars, most exalted among them . . ." The correspondence between Rudra and Shiva is that between Sirius and the sun. "Siva has the sun for his metaphor. Among stars, it is Sirius who represents Rudra." The compound myth of Rudra / Shiva enfolds both star and sun. Ibid., 136. As, I propose, will the compound myth of the Magdalene / Christ. See page 142.

65. Kramrisch, ibid., 164. "Even the circular luminous spot which the sun casts on a mirror" is a Shiva-linga.

66. Kramrisch, ibid., 164, and *Manifestations of Shiva*, op. cit., xxiii. "The myth of Rudra/Siva is the myth of God as consciousness . . ." A pilgrim of Shiva may wear a small linga around his neck; the "linga represents the wearer's soul, which is not different from the divinity. . . ."

POLESTAR GONE

Epigraph: William Shakespeare, *The Tempest*, Act V, Scene 1.

1. Johann Wolfgang von Goethe, *Theory of Colors*, tr. Charles Lock Eastlake (London: John Murray, 1840), Introduction. The actual line is "colors are the deeds of light, its deeds and sufferings."

2. Nirad C. Chaudhuri, *The Continent of Circe* (Bombay: Jaico Publishing House, 1965), 167. Also *Autobiography of an Unknown Indian* (Bombay: Jaico, 1951), 514. The author's thesis is that the Aryan Hindu is genetically European, consigned by "terrible destiny" to the Gangetic plain, always longing for the mountains and steppes of the northwest, a historic paradise.

3. Unclassified quotation in author's possession. Compare: " 'Women are the snakes,' a merchant said to me, 'they want our virility and they will not let us reach the supreme.' " Swami Agehananda Bharati, *The Ochre Robe* (Seattle: University of Washington Press, 1962), 261.

4. Though some dispute the prevalence of "dowry murders" in modern India, Reuters in March 1983 carried a report from New Delhi that "more than 1000 Indian women have died in 'dowry deaths' over the past three years. . . . The custom is still widely practiced, especially among Hindu families in the north." Source was the Minister of State for Home Affairs. The same month, Reuters/Kyodo reported 50,000 people gathered at a cremation ground in Rajasthan "and eagerly waited for flames to consume a 45 year old widow . . . the widow's five sons and three daughters backed their mother's plan to immolate herself."

5. Sadhir Kakar, *The Inner World: A Psychoanalytic Study of Childhood and Society in India* (Oxford, New Delhi: Oxford University Press, 1981), 187. The author relates early conditioning to later metaphysical thinking. He describes the "maternal cosmos of infancy" in a Hindu household. "Till a boy is eight years old, he is like one newly-born," 206. Later stages of "individuation" are marked by rites that symbolically immerse then deliver the child from Ganges-water. Lifelong, "the 'ultimate' reality of the maternal

cosmos of infancy is held superior to the 'worldly' reality of post-maternal childhood."

6. There are as many sources for Buddha legends and sayings, both canonical and apocryphal, as for Western myths and folktales. I have used, among many others: Joan Lebold Cohen, *Buddha* (New York: Delacorte, 1969); *The Bible of the World*, op. cit.; *The Dhammapada*, tr. Irving Babbitt (New York: Oxford University Press/New Directions, 1965); etc.

7. The "cult" is thus an enactment of the universal human inclination to organize the visual field according to vertical and horizontal axes. See Arnheim, op. cit. Compare the "Turning Ceremony" of the Omaha Indians, wherein a child of age two or three is turned to the "four hills of life," the four corners of the Cosmos. A grotesque example: Buchenwald camp was laid out around the stump of an oak to which Goethe legendarily made pilgrimage. By joyous contrast, here is a modern writer's "cosmos": "[The book *Ulysses*] turns like the huge earthball . . . round and round, spinning. Its four cardinal points being the female breasts, arse, womb and . . ." James Joyce, Letter 170, in William York Tindall, *A Reader's Guide to James Joyce* (New York: Noonday, 1959), 232.

8. Many elaborations on this Ur-event survive, for example: the Buddha as a child sat under an apple tree and looking up through the leaves envisioned himself seated years hence under another tree, making some as yet unknown leap of mind. Then "nostalgia for the return and deepening of this experience, as much as disillusionment with the rewards of worldly life, led to his [search for] a new mode of experience." Huston Smith, *The Religions of Man* (New York: Harper and Row, 1958), 123. The search *back* to that motivating event then becomes the "pilgrimage." See Eleanor Munro, *Originals: American Women Artists* (New York: Simon & Schuster, 1979).

9. For this and other scriptural passages, I have used, among other sources: *The Dhammapada*, tr. Babbitt, op. cit.; Edward Conze, *Buddhist Thought in India* (Ann Arbor: University of Michigan Press, 1967); Christmas Humphreys, *Buddhism* (New York: Penguin Books, 1951); D. L. Snellgrove, *Buddhist Himalaya* (New York: Philosophical Library, 1957).

10. Conze, op. cit., 136: "This our worldly life is an activity of nothingness, of Nirvana itself. There is not the slightest distinction between them."

11. Two Chinese pilgrims, Fa-Hsien and Hsuan-Tsang, visited this town in the fifth and seventh centuries and left reports of a populated sanctuary with a famous statue of the Buddha "turning the wheels of the law" (now in the local museum), a commemorative pillar topped with lions, and a 300-foot-high stupa, still one of the wonders of this quiet place. It was abandoned in the ninth century in the course of resurgent Hinduism, and what structures remained were toppled during a Moslem campaign against nearby Benares.

12. This ancient humanistic ethos bore fruit in 1956 when 250,000 Hindu untouchables converted en masse to Buddhism.

13. There were no supernatural bonds implied in original Buddhism, only with the Teacher, his moral principles and the community of like-minded people. Nor was there talk of heaven or hell. He denied the existence of cosmological

entities, like the ebbing and waxing Vedic universes. He spoke out against primitive instruments of social control predicated on cosmic metaphysics, like caste and the Brahmin hierarchy. At most, the Buddha referred to causal responsibility over a cycle of rebirths, suggesting that, in some unseen way, life-experience shaped further existence. The Hindu-Buddhistic notion of reincarnation survived as undercurrent in Christian thought until it was pronounced anathema at the Council of Constantinople in 551.

14. This sculptural type was invented in what is now Pakistan as an outgrowth of decadent Greco-Roman style. Thus all Buddhist sculpture looks back to Hellenism, and one can say that "the art of the Barabadur [sic] is a distant relation of the altar-reliefs and reliquaries of our medieval cathedrals." Claire Holt, *Art in Indonesia* (Ithaca: Cornell University Press, 1967), 47. Only a few other figure-types emerged in Buddhist iconography: by the second century CE, there were at Anuradhapura in Sri Lanka (then Ceylon) big stone figures of the Buddha standing in hieratic, frozen frontality or lying on one side, asleep or dead. As Mahayana Buddhism spread, it generated other figure-classes, guardians, saints, etc., to represent various human emotions. But where the axial or Ur-Buddha appears he is invariably static and inward.

15. Lama Anagarika Govinda, *Psycho-cosmic Symbolism of the Buddhist Stupa* (Emeryville, Calif.: Dharma Publishing Co., 1976), among other sources. The ancient Aryan hut with its central shaft-chimney may have been a further inspiration for the structure. The symbolism of the closed circle was widespread and its use in Buddhist iconography reinforced by Chinese ritual use of the jade PI to signify the sky. Thus hut and heaven are joined by the stupa-shrine. Eventually the stupa was set on a square base oriented to the cardinal points, signifying the plane of the earth and so theoretically extending its power. Kramrisch, *Hindu Temple*, op. cit., 14. Further geometric features include the tripartite vertical structure of base, body, and spire, referring to the Buddhist trinity: community on earth, connective law or Dharma, nothingness or Nirvana.

16. Paul Mus, *Barabudur* (Hanoi, 1935).

17. A British art historian argues the so-called Ashokan pillars were actually remnants of chthonic-cosmogonic pillar-cults, taken over by Buddhist promulgators, as Christians would build churches over pagan shrines. John Irwin, "The Lat Bhairo at Benares," *Proceedings of the Fifth Conference of South Asian Archaeology* (Berlin: Reimer, 1981), 313 ff. Ashoka legendarily undertook other measures to spread Buddhism, wedding a daughter into Nepalese nobility and dispatching a son, Mahindra, to Ceylon with a sprig of the original Bo tree. Also he installed a major cult site, Sanchi, in the center of the Indian subcontinent, on a north/south axis at the juncture of two rivers, perhaps "in the middle of the world," so it might outdraw the Hindu circuit around the continental perimeter or at least mark its axis.

18. The transmission of Indian Buddhist ideas and styles to China began in the first century CE, and by the fourth century the famous chain of Buddhist oasis-shrines had been installed across the northeastern desert wastes. Midrashes attended this flow of influence: the young Buddha dreamed he lay on

the whole earth as if it were a bed, with his head on the Himalayas, his hands in the oceans, and his feet in the southern seas. Then when the first Buddhist icons arrived in China, they shone like the sun for four days, then burst into flame.

19. By the second century CE, the new Mahayana cult had become popular enough to create schism at a council in Kashmir and soon was generating subcults and a cosmology with hierarchies of saints burgeoning through time toward the Maitreya or Savior of the future. But the best-known Mahayana elaboration on the original teaching was its provision that people need not accept their mortal end *now* but might, or better *should,* delay that fate until all sentient beings were ready to go together. Meanwhile they might enjoy, or suffer, reincarnation. As the forms of Mahayana spread, the Buddha as a character also invaded syncretic Christianity and Hinduism. *The Golden Legend* (Jacobus de Voragine, [New York: Longmans, Green, 1941 ed.]), for example, includes the Buddha story in terms of the Christian tale of Saints Barlaam and Josaphat. The Hindu Vishnu cycle of myths embraced the Buddha whole as one of the avatars of the god, appearing on earth after Krishna and before Christ. The tooth of this incarnate Buddha is probably the empowering mystery-"substance" in the wood icon worshiped by millions in the Indian town of Puri today. Unless that tooth is, as others claim, in Sri Lanka, or nowhere.

20. Diana L. Eck, "The Church in Bali: Mountainwards and Seawards," *The Harvard Divinity Bulletin,* April–May 1982, 8–11.

21. All aspects of the shadow play reflect its sacred character. The puppets are made by craftsmen ritually purified and dressed in white. The figures, of animal hide, preferably a water buffalo never whipped, should be made in one day, though if more are needed, no more than twice seven. As to the plays' themes, one concerns Prince Rama, an aspect of the sun-god, pursuing his wife into the shadow kingdom of Ceylon: a mythic response to the annual solar descent. The other dominant theme is the battle between good and evil: the Pandavas (puppets on the shadow master's pure right hand) against the Kauravas (on his polluted left).

22. Bosch, *Golden Germ,* op. cit., 184. See page 48.

23. The deciphering of the Borobodur is a tale unto itself. A conceptual unity to what looked like a random collection of sculpture was not detected until 1835, when the linguist Karl Wilhelm von Humboldt, brother of the universal scientist-philosopher Alexander, applied to the puzzle his theory that any coherent human endeavor must be structured around a unifying internal law. Eventually, he discovered in Mahayana texts the source and theme of the Borobodur's plan and sculpture. See Mus, *Barabudur,* op. cit. Also Jan Fontein, *The Pilgrimage of Sudhana* (The Hague / Paris: Mouton, 1967).

24. For descriptions of Nalanda: Sacheverell Sitwell, *Touching the Orient* (London: Duckworth, 1934), and Major Raven-Hart, *Where the Buddha Trod: A Buddhist Pilgrimage* (Colombo, Sri Lanka: Lake House, 1956). Buddhist cosmology was elaborated there on the basis of astronomical observation. A pyramidal structure was perhaps used for the purpose. Raven-Hart says it

resembled "something Aztec or Babylonian," more suited to "star worship than Buddhism" (89).

25. Giuseppe Tucci, *The Theory and Practice of the Mandala* (London: Rider, 1961). The Buddhist mandala, like the Hindu, is a map of the Cosmos, with an entryway at the east and a central axis connecting earth to the North Star. The interior space is divided into twelve segments. The cardinal directions and turning-points of a trek through it are guarded by gods or demons. A practitioner undertakes a mental pilgrimage through its passages until the trip's end, when theoretically he renounces the whole experience. There are also sculptural mandalas on altars, with guardian figures bilaterally flanking a Buddha. Beyond these microcosmic diagrams, geographical ones have been laid over much of Asia. Nepal's Kathmandu Valley is a mandala pinned at its four corners by mountain shrines. The Buddhist who travels it thereby circumambulates the Cosmos. In Burma, Pagan is a mandala, with gates and palaces replicating structures in the sky. Thailand is overlaid by a mandala whose circuit-road leads through twelve sacred cities. Both Hindu Angkor Wat and Buddhist Angkor Thom in Cambodia are mandalas.

The mandala of Chinese geo-cosmology had a north-south axis bifurcating the imperial city and, at its center, the emperor's palace. Where the emperor sat was the foot of the North Star, and the Buddha was that star itself (Allan G. Grapard, "Flying Mountains and Walkers of Emptiness: Toward a Definition of Sacred Space in Japanese Religion," *History of Religions,* Vol. 21, No. 3, February 1983, 195–221: "The Polestar is Sakayamuni"). When he had to reset the Cosmos at the winter solstice, the emperor went into the Temple of Heaven, faced north, and bowed to a diagram of the sky. Then, impersonating that star, he turned to face south to receive the people's kowtows. The temple *was* the sky: to build it, the geomancer laid down one stone in a field, then nine in a circle, then more in each ring till 360 were reached. Chinese still make pilgrimage to four peaks of Buddhist fame. At the center of the mandala is the one that penetrates heaven.

But modern Japan best preserves the ancient Indo-Chinese geo-cosmological ideas. The Shingon Buddhist sect regards the whole island nation overlaid by Womb and Diamond mandalas, intersecting at Omine mountain in Kii peninsula. That cult was remotely fathered by an eighth-century Sinhalese Buddhist who traveled to Indonesia, thence China, where he became the teacher of the founder of Shingon. The relevance of this chain of influence: "Although no specific historical evidence remains, it is probable that the Buddhists responsible for designing the Borobodur knew something of the thought" of that original teacher from Ceylon. Hiram W. Woodward, Jr., "Borobodur and the Mirrorlike Mind," *Archaeology,* Vol. 34, No. 6, November / December 1981, 40–47.

26. Grapard, op. cit., 220.

27. A debarking place for Buddhist refugees was Mahaballipuram, where the first free-standing Hindu temples were then being built. Master builders may have sailed along with geomancers and priests in the train of the patrons of the

Borobodur, the Calliendra princes, once patrons of Nalanda. In Java, they ruled 778–864.

28. The ascending "worlds" of the Borobodur are Kamadhatu (Matter), Rupadhatu (Form), Dharmadhatu (Law), and Arupadhatu (No-form). This four-rung ladder is the vertical correlative to the horizontal quarters. At the cross-point of vertical and horizontal stands the stupa-temple.

29. *The Silk Route and the Diamond Path*, ed. Deborah E. Klimburg-Salter, exhibition catalogue, UCLA Art Council, Frederick S. Wight Gallery, University of California (Los Angeles, 1982). Each Directional Buddha has attributes: colors, costume, mudras, associated saints and consorts, etc., by which he is also recognizable in Tibetan, Nepalese, and Chinese art. Compare the Aztec system: four directional gods, red for east, blue for south, white for west, black for north, aligned on the square base of the cosmic pyramid. Atop, in the center, the Lord of Fire and Time, Omoteotl. But examples of geo-cosmological systems are many. See Hiram W. Woodward, Jr., op. cit.

30. For a Chinese meditation on this ultimate immortality-providing Buddha: "The Dharmakaya has no image; it is eternal and formless. [But though] the ultimate Principle is nothingness, it yet responds . . . in the dead of night, the darkness is split open. For the humblest there is eternal life, without years, without aging." Shen Yo (?–513 CE), Kuang Hung Ming Chi, xvi, quoted in Lawrence Soper, *Literary Evidence*, 72.

31. Ernest Becker, *The Denial of Death* (New York: The Free Press, div. Macmillan, 1973).

POLESTAR THE PILGRIM

Epigraph: Claude Lévi-Strauss, "The Structural Study of Myth," in *Myth: A Symposium*, ed. Thomas A. Sebeok (Bloomington: Indiana University Press, 1958), 65.

1. *Bible of the World*, op. cit., 12.

2. De Santillana and von Dechend, op. cit., 216.

3. An ongoing argument among historians is whether the Great Pyramid at Giza—and by extension other pyramids and temples—contained built-in pipes focused on Alpha Draconis (Thuban), Gamma Draconis, or others. Recently (*Sky and Telescope*, 1985) Richard L. Walker of the U.S. Naval Observatory, on the basis of calculations of stars' positions at the time the Pyramid was built, lent his name to the nay-sayers. But the question remains.

4. Diane Wolkstein and Samuel Noah Kramer, *Inanna: Queen of Heaven and Earth* (New York: Harper & Row, 1983), 99.

5. Plate 19, Savina J. Teubal, *Sarah the Priestess* (Athens, Ohio: Swallow Press, 1984), 117.

6. De Santillana and von Dechend, op. cit., 430.

7. For Alpha Draconis and its related myths: Allen, op. cit., 206–7.

8. For Gamma Draconis, ibid., 208–9: "It was nearer the pole than any other bright star about 4000 years ago."

9. Allen, op. cit., 454: citing John de Mandeville, fourteenth-century English traveler.

10. See above, note 58, "Polestar Sighted."

11. The point at issue is whether ancient Near Eastern peoples designed their theo-cosmological systems on the basis of observed facts. An early-twentieth-century school of scholars known as the Pan-Babylonists—led by astronomer Hugo Winckler—argued they did and that cosmic myths date from the First Babylonian Period, around 1800 BCE. The idea was that this pseudoscience spread through the ancient world. A divergent group of Revisionist Babylonists date the myths to the Second Babylonian Period, around 700 BCE. In general, these scholars read events in Homer and the Old Testament as solar and sidereal myths and saw the Patriarchs as personifications of the sun and moon. Unfortunately for Winckler, when the clay tablets on which he based his theories were deciphered, they turned out not to support his ideas. Still, some scientists have returned to the idea, finding evidence now not in clay tablets but in orally transmitted myth. Contrary "historicist" opinion called (and calls) this an "absurd doctrine" and holds there was no knowledge of celestial systems including the precession until the time of Hipparchus, 161–126 BCE. See Franz Cumont, *Astrology and Religion Among the Greeks and Romans* (New York: Putnam's Sons / Dover, 1912 / 1960), 4–6. Also Richard M. Dobson, "The Eclipse of Solar Mythology," in *Myth: a Symposium*, op. cit., 15–38.

12. David Biale, "The God with Breasts: El Shaddai in the Bible," *History of Religions*, Vol. 21, No. 3, February 1982, 240–56.

13. This and succeeding scriptural passages from *The New English Bible* (New York: Oxford University Press, 1976). Compare Exodus 4.23–27 and footnotes 24–26, that "obscure passage," as the NEB puts it, that suggests the mystery-relationship between circumcision and the rescue of fathers and sons from sacrificial death.

14. Barbara Kirschenblatt-Gimblett, "The Cut That Binds: The Western Ashkenazic Torah Binder as Nexus between Circumcision and Torah," in *Celebration: Studies in Festivity and Ritual*, ed. Victor Turner (Washington, D.C.: Smithsonian Institution Press, 1982), 136. "For a male, initiation into [the Torah] is made by a cut that binds." The author shows the clear symbolism of the Torah as a female person. The circumcision is, symbolically, a cutting-free of the male from an enclosing symbiotic female. The author further relates the covenant itself to a length of unbleached linen on which the eight-day-old infant is laid for the circumcision and which is later torn into strips and resewn into a binder for the Torah scroll.

15. Gershom Scholem, *Major Trends in Jewish Mysticism* (New York: Schocken Books, 1954), 37.

16. NEB footnote: "Twelve stones and twelve jars of water, and the complex of altar (land) and trench (water) probably symbolize the cosmic order."

17. Jezebel, who paints her eyes, dresses her hair, and looks down from a high window (2 Kings 9.30), must be yet another typological overlay on the Star-queen. Thus we have not merely a *war* in the skies but a *civil war*, Elijah

against Jezebel, the male Sirius against its female figuration. In effect the conflict must be a gloss on the symbolism of circumcision.

18. Wolkstein and Kramer, op. cit., 190, footnote 60.

19. In these approaches, the personified Polestar is one of those constructs of forced thought whose ontology contradicts logic, like the Hindu Shiva or the Buddhist Diamond Point.

20. Exodus 35.7 and 36.19: The tent was to be of rams' skins and porpoise hides, signifying the cosmic realms of land and sea.

21. For the Messiah as perpetual wanderer: Luke 9.58 and Northrop Frye, *The Great Code: The Bible and Literature* (New York: Harcourt Brace Jovanovich, 1982), 159. For the endurance of the idea of "the Church as a pilgrim on Earth . . .": "The Mystery of the Church," *Final Report of the Synod of Bishops in Rome,* 1985, Section 1.3.

22. Frank Moore Cross, *Canaanite Myth and Hebrew Epic* (Cambridge: Harvard University Press, 1973). Also *Israel Pocket Library: History Until 1880* (henceforth *IPL*) (Jerusalem: Keter Publishing House), 22–23.

23. Allen, op. cit., 452. Citing the Surya Siddhanta, Chapter 12, Verse 34.

24. H. V. Morton, *In the Steps of the Master* (London: Methuen & Co., 1947 ed.), 72.

25. Scholem, op. cit., 7.

26. Adin Steinsaltz, *The 13-Petalled Rose* (New York: Basic Books 1980).

27. NEB footnote: "The army of Gog is composed of elements from the four corners of the author's world: Gomer, north; Ethiopia, south; Tarshish, west; Dedan, east. It is called out from the far recesses of the north, the mythological dwelling of good and evil." In this cosmogram, Jerusalem is "the very center of the world." As now, a conflict involving Jerusalem involves whole opposed Worlds.

28. Scholem, op. cit., 280.

29. R. J. Werblowsky, Zwi, "The Meaning of Jerusalem to Jews, Christians and Muslims," The Chas. Strong Memorial Lecture, Israel University, 1972, reprint *Jaarbericht Ex Orient Lux* 23 / 1973–74: "The identification of Jerusalem with the widowed, sorrowful and mourning mother . . . is one of the main motifs of traditional Jewish imagery."

30. The Roman Julian calendar, initiated in 64 BCE, was solar-based as was the calendar of the Essenes, who abandoned the moon orientation of the Jewish year for what they considered a more stable, eternal order, fixed by the "laws of the Great Light of Heaven." G. Vermes, *The Dead Sea Scrolls in English* (New York: Penguin ed., 1981). Passover and Easter are now set by both solar equinox and moon.

31. Cited in Joan Comay, *The Temple of Jerusalem* (London: Weidenfeld & Nicolson, 1975), 49.

32. Pilgrims climbed to the Temple chanting Psalms, especially 120–134, known as Songs of Ascent: "Open unto me the gates that I may enter and give thanks . . . / Our feet shall stand within thy gates, O Jerusalem . . . / Now we stand in your gates, O Jerusalem" (Psalm 122).

33. Leviticus 16.29 and NEB footnote.

34. *IPL*, op. cit., 128–29.

35. *IPL*, op. cit., 146–201, mentions "grave terrorist acts."

36. See Louis Finkelstein, *Akiba: Scholar, Saint and Martyr* (New York: Atheneum, 1985), 349, footnote 44.

37. Ibid., 260–77.

38. Allen, op. cit., 454.

39. Perhaps the image influenced Russian-born Abstract Expressionist Mark Rothko.

40. Cited in Teddy Kollek and Moshe Pearlman, *Pilgrims to the Holy Land* (London / Jerusalem: Weidenfeld & Nicolson, 1970), 38. This intrepid pilgrim, traveling through Constantine's imperial network, covered, as he wrote, some 3,200 miles and changed horses 360 times, traversing Italy, Syria, and Palestine.

41. Cited in Laurie Magnus, *The Jews in the Christian Era* (New York: E. P. Dutton, 1929).

42. Yehuda Halevi, born Spain 1086, died Jerusalem 1142. Cited in Zev Vilnay, *The Guide to Israel,* 21st Edition (Jerusalem: Ahiever, 1979), 570.

43. J. Abelson, *The Immanence of God* (Hermon Press edition, London 1912, New York 1969), 163.

44. Cited ibid., 353.

45. Kirschenblatt-Gimblett, op. cit., 136: "Like a human, the scroll is 'dressed' in its finery. . . . Like a queen, the scroll wears a regal mantle and bears a precious crown. . . . The 'naked' scroll is not to be touched with bare hands."

INTERREGNUM

Epigraph: Wallace Stevens, "The Pastoral Nun," *The Palm at the End of the Mind* (New York: Alfred A. Knopf, 1971), 293.

1. Allen, op. cit., 454.

2. See Frye, *Great Code,* op. cit., 96. Many writers speculated on the correlation between customs and the precessing skies. When the constellation into which the vernal sun rose was Taurus, bull-worship and -sacrifice was the dominant rite in the Near East. As the vernal sunrise passed into Aries, lamb-slaughter became the dominant rite; the Christ-sacrifice was made when the equinox coincided with Pisces.

3. Wendell Clausen, "Virgil's Messianic Eclogue," paper delivered at a symposium "On Poetry and Prophecy," sponsored by Harvard University Center for Literary Studies, 1986. His thesis, widely shared, is that the prophecy concerned the return of Hesiod's Golden Age.

4. Philippe Borgeaud, "The Death of the Great Pan: The Problem of Interpretation," *History of Religions,* February / March 1983, 254–83.

5. Jane Ellen Harrison, *Themis: A Study of the Social Origins of Greek Religion* (Cleveland: World Publishing, 1912), 468.

6. See Eliade, *Patterns in Comparative Religion,* op. cit., Chapter X: "Sacred Places: Temple, Palace, 'Centre of the World.' "

7. Joseph Fontenrose, *The Delphic Oracle* (Berkeley and Los Angeles: University of California Press, 1978), 402. See also his *Python: a Study of the Delphic Myth and Its Origins* (Berkeley and Los Angeles: University of California Press, 1959).

8. Fontenrose, *Delphic Oracle*, 206.

9. Sir James George Frazer, *The Golden Bough*, (New York: Macmillan, 1931). 384.

10. Marie-Louise von Franz, *Time* (New York: Thames & Hudson, 1978), 6.

11. George E. Mylonas, *Eleusis and the Eleusinian Mysteries* (Princeton: Princeton University Press, 1961), 205. Also C. G. Jung and C. Kerenyi, *Essays on a Science of Mythology* (New York: Bollingen, 1949), 190.

12. Cited in Coomaraswamy, *Dance of Siva*, op. cit., 56.

13. Gerardus Van der Leeuw, *Sacred and Profane Beauty* (New York: Holt Rinehart & Winston, 1963). The author speculates the first enclosed shelters may have been circular "dance houses." See also Mircea Eliade, *A History of Religious Ideas*, Vol. 1. (Chicago: University of Chicago Press, 1978), 25: "As for the 'circular dance' . . . this ritual choreography was well known to the Paleolithics." See also Martha Stone, *At the Sign of Midnight: The Concheros Dance Cult of Mexico* (Tucson: University of Arizona Press, 1975) and William Simpson, *The Buddhist Praying-Wheel: Circular Movements in Custom and Religious Ritual* (New York: University Books, 1970).

14. Fontenrose, *Python*, op. cit., 382, footnote 25. The author cites Herodotus, Virgil, Pindar, Pliny, etc., on "Apollo's visits to the Hyperboreans" in the North or among "the gold-guarding griffons on the borders of India."

15. Pindar, Fragment 102; Sophocles, Fragment 710. Both cited in Jung and Kerenyi, op. cit., 199–200; Mylonas, op. cit., 299.

16. Peter Brown, *The Cult of the Saints* (Chicago: University of Chicago Press, 1981), 80. Citing Aelius Aristides.

17. See Victor Turner, *Dramas, Fields and Metaphors* (Ithaca: Cornell University Press, 1974), Chapter 6: "Passages, Margins, and Poverty: Religious Symbols of Communitas." The author credits Arnold van Gennep with first use of the term "liminality" to describe the mid-phase in transition rituals, the period of "real or symbolic threshold" characterized often by mysterious darkness, fluidity, ambiguity of time and place, etc.

18. See above, note 52, "Polestar Sighted."

19. Cited in Edgar Heurnecke, "The Apocryphal Gospel of John" in *New Testament Apocrypha*, Vol. II., Westminster, 228–32. Also see note 13 above and compare the circular dance, "Mandala," performed by the Hindu god Krishna, standing in a circle of milkmaids. He plays the flute while simultaneously multiplying himself so each maid thinks he dances with her only (see letter by Peg de Lanater in *The Art Bulletin*, March 1986, 154). Both Krishna and Christ are, in Vishnu mythology, avatars of the one Sun-god, as is Buddha, and as will be the messiah, Kalkin.

20. Compare: Frye, *Great Code*, op. cit., 98: "The coming of Jesus into the world . . . seems to have taken place historically at one of those dialectical confrontations in which history suddenly expands to myth . . ."

21. *The Golden Legend,* op. cit., 355–64. Her name is here derived from *amarum mare*—"bitter sea, or light-giver, or enlightened"—and from *manes rea*—"remaining in guilt, or . . . unconquered or magnificent." She is a creature of sea and starlight, guilt and glory. Her contradictory, protean character marks her as a mythological being outside the confinements of Church dogma.
22. Renaissance sculptor Donatello may have understood the traditional import of the Magdalene's hair when he carved her entirely robed in wavy tresses. The sign also connects her with John the Baptist, famous for his hair coat and diet of winged locusts and honey.
23. Theodor H. Gaster, *The Dead Sea Scrolls* (New York: Doubleday, 1976), 8, 59. This biblical historian suggests that influence from "remote Indian antiquity" may have reached Palestine via pilgrims and missionaries traveling through Persia. He mentions such specifics as the theory of cyclical time, the virtue of meditation on abstract universals, and the use of the left hand for "unclean" bodily functions.
24. The standard of the twins, Gemini, lashed to Saul / Paul's ship's mast, generated a further transparency, the legend of Erasmus, martyred in the fourth century by this atrocious means: his intestines were wound out of his body onto a windlass. His alternate name is St. Elmo, applied to the glow sometimes seen atop ships' masts that sailors believed was the visible sign of their protector: Stella Maris.
25. Franz Cumont, *Astrology and Religion Among the Greeks and Romans* (New York: Putnam's / Dover, 1912 / 1960 ed.), 61.
26. *Confessions,* Book XI, Section XIII, 16–17.
27. Magnus, op. cit., 46.
28. Cited Fontenrose, *Delphic Oracle,* op. cit., 349.
29. G. W. Bowersock, *Julian the Apostate* (Cambridge: Harvard University Press, 1978), 84, 16.
30. Book XIII, Section XXV, 50–51; Section XXVI.

SON OF STAR

Epigraph: Thomas Kuhn, *The Structure of Scientific Revolutions,* 2nd ed. (Chicago: University of Chicago Press, 1970), 22.

1. The curiosity of this effort is added to by the Christian bias against designated sacred spaces. As N. Frye says: "For Christianity . . . a central sacred place could no longer exist. The Messiah himself was a wanderer and Christianity was not centered symbolically on Jerusalem as Judaism was. . . ." *Great Code,* op. cit., 159. All the more does the labor prove what power sacred geometry had on those who constructed the Christian Cosmos.
2. Peter Brown, *Cult of the Saints* (Chicago: University of Chicago Press, 1982), 93–105.
3. This famous typology goes back to Leviticus 29.1–46 and the rule that remnants of sacrificed animals be deposited "outside the gates."
4. Frye, *Great Code,* op. cit., 174.

5. Steven Runciman, *Byzantine Civilization* (New York: St. Martin's Press /
Meridian, 1933 / 1956), 23.

6. John Wilkinson, *Jerusalem Pilgrims Before the Crusades* (Jerusalem: Ariel,
1977), 149–78.

7. Ibid., 177 traces the flight of inference from 1 Corinthians 15.22, to Origen,
to the "bloodstains" that are still pointed out to pilgrims today.

8. El Hakim reigned 996 to 1021 and "progressed through religious enthusiasm
to fanaticism and, eventually, madness, acting throughout with unusual cru-
elty." Ibid., 13–14.

9. This is the so-called Madaba Map. Ibid., 31 and endpapers. It provides unique
information about the city layout in its Byzantine development, around the
year 660.

10. Rosemary Jeanes, "Labyrinths," *Parabola* 4.2. 12–14.

11. De Santillana and von Dechend, op. cit., 342.

12. Wilkinson, op. cit., 101.

13. *The Golden Legend*, op. cit., 269–76.

14. John Wilkinson, *Egeria's Travels to the Holy Land* (Jerusalem: Ariel).

15. Cited in Wilkinson, *Jerusalem Pilgrims*, op. cit., 144.

16. Wilkinson, *Egeria's Travels*, op. cit., 83–88.

17. Since the rupture between Latin West and Orthodox East, the rites have celebrated separate Easters. Both make it the first Sunday after the full moon
after the equinox, but for the Orthodox, the day must also follow Jewish
Passover, hence in some years it comes a week later. Since tradition has Jesus
sharing a seder with his disciples before his death, the Latins can be said
sometimes to place his Resurrection before his Crucifixion. But common logic
is not the rule in myth.

18. Cited in Marina Warner, *Alone of All Her Sex* (New York: Random House,
1976), 209.

19. Helen Huss Parkhurst, *Cathedral: A Gothic Pilgrimage* (London: Lovat
Dickson, 1936), 194.

20. The long chain of mythological associations that bind the buried pine tree,
that was the dead Attis, to the resurrected wood of the cross also engages
other ancient symbols for the generation of new life out of inert matter,
including the Hindu linga and the Buddhist stupa. Orthodox Easter liturgy
still includes the hiding of a wooden flower-decked cross and its "discovery"
on Easter morning.

21. See *Pelerins de Rome: Visages de Rome* II (Paris: Les editions du cerf, 1976).

22. Matthew 16.14–17. The compound Man had of course been presented before
in art and myth. In the third millennium BCE, the Sumerian King Gudea
recorded a dream: he saw a living man "equal to the heavens" and also "equal
to the earth," who therefore could tell him how to measure and lay out the
sky-houses on earth that were ziggurats and temples (André Parrot, *Babylon
and the Old Testament* [New York: Philosophical Library, 1958]). So did
Ezekiel's Bronze Man come to him in a dream (40.3): a man of alloy, both
copper and tin, who showed him how to build the heavenly Temple in Jerusalem, that lay in the midst of the cosmic river. But the doubled-figure as

hinge between earth and sky goes back to the twin beacons of the Golden Age, Castor and Pollux (see page 48). The Essenes, like the Hindu Shiva-priesthood, seem to have understood the principle. They said the Messianic Age would be announced by *two sons of God,* one an anointed priest, the other a layman. Elsewhere, it was prophesied that at Passover of the messianic year, "Moses shall come out of the wilderness, and the King-Messiah out of Rome." G. Vermes, *The Dead Sea Scrolls in English* (New York: Penguin ed., 1981), 51.

23. The Holy Ghost was, shall we say, a mystery-blend of Shekinah and Wisdom, an immanence that would give rise to the heresies of Antinomianism and Transcendentalism. Jewish tradition also gives embodied form to a free-floating, mystical "Divine Presence": a white dove (female) that sits atop the Wailing Wall on the eve of Tishah be-Av. Vilnay, op. cit., 138.

24. During the intervening centuries, that entryway whether standing or only remembered acquired other names. For a while it was known as the Beautiful, later the Golden, Gate, and as the latter it passed into Western literature.

25. Zoé Oldenbourg, *The Crusades* (New York: Random House, 1966), 484 et passim. The author emphasizes that it was during these twelfth-century battles that the tone of Moslem chronicles "gradually changes from war in general to the idea of a holy war. Not that the theme of the jihad was unknown" to earlier historians, but from the time of Saladin "Moslem warriors could no longer be killed without becoming martyrs . . . soldiers of God." However, Saladin agreed to spare Jerusalem's population and to allow pilgrimage to the Holy Sepulchre on payment of a body tax.

26. Ibid., 549.

27. Unclassified newspaper clipping in author's possession.

28. L. G. A. Cust, *The Status Quo in the Holy Places* (Jerusalem: 1919; facsimile edition, Jerusalem: Ariel, 1980).

29. Ibid., 26. I saw it there, at the foot of a nun selling candles, who tossed her change into it.

30. Poirier, op. cit., 297: "Fire obsession may be of ancient origin; fire may be a stimulant as potent as drugs in arousing visions."

31. Wilkinson, *Egeria,* op. cit., 133–39. Egeria describes the bishop in Jerusalem entering the Tomb and bringing out paschal fire to light the people's candles. Five centuries later, the Breton pilgrim Bernard the Wise put it that "an angel comes and lights the lamps . . . the patriarch gives this fire to the bishops and to the rest of the people . . ." (Wilkinson, *Jerusalem Pilgrims,* op. cit., 142). After the Crusaders enclosed the Tomb within the Holy Sepulchre Church, the event became vastly more charged with energy and also peril. In a panic in 1837, over four hundred people were crushed and suffocated there. The British therefore controlled every step of the event, from the opening of the church doors "by the Armenians" and the taping shut of the Tomb "by the Moslem Guardian in the presence of one Archimandrite of the Orthodox and one of the Armenian rites" to the holding of the tapes by "two bishops, behind them two dragomans, behind these two sextons (always Orthodox and Armenian)." (Cust, op. cit., Appendix C).

FOLLOWING STAR

Epigraph: De Santillana and von Dechend, op. cit., 65.

1. A. Kingsley Porter, *Romanesque Sculpture of the Pilgrimage Roads* (Boston: Marshall Jones, 1923), 171.

2. A. Kingsley Porter and other authors offer variants of this figure of speech, as does Walter Starkie, *The Road to Santiago: Pilgrims of St. James* (New York: Dutton, 1957), 81–82.

3. Dante, *Vita Nuova*, 4.

4. Jonathan Sumption, *Pilgrimage: An Image of Medieval Religion* (Totowa, N.J.: Rowman and Littlefield, 1975).

5. *Pilgrims' Guide to Santiago de Compostela*, eds and trans. Paula L. Gerson, Annie Shaver-Crandall, M. Alison Stones. (Forthcoming from London: Harvey-Miller / Oxford University Press), typescript p. 51. In popular texts of the late nineteenth and twentieth centuries, the author is given as Aymery Picaud, a French priest. Study now reveals Picaud played little part in its preparation. Among the documents (see page 198) is a false Bull of Pope Innocent in which is written, "This manuscript is being carried to Compostela by Aymery Picaud [and friends]. . . . Whoever touches a hair on their heads shall suffer excommunication." This is his only mention save as a signer of a piece of liturgical music.

6. Brown, *Cult of the Saints*, op. cit., 73.

7. Rev. James S. Stone, *The Cult of Santiago: Traditions, Myths and Pilgrims* (London: Longmans, Green, 1927), 121.

8. The Library of Congress Information Bulletin publishes 23 pages of bibliography on the astronomical background of the Nativity. Sightings most often mentioned are Sirius, Halley's comet of 12 / 11 BCE, a conjunction of Jupiter and Saturn in Pisces in midwinter 6 BCE or with Mars the next year, or a supernova in Capricorn the year after that. The mention in Matthew 2.9 (dated ca. 80 CE) is of course antitype of star mentions in Numbers, 2 Samuel, the Psalms, Isaiah, and Micah. For a recent view, see Dorrit Hoffleit, "The Christmas Star, Novae and Pulsars," *Journal of the American Association of Variable Star Observers*, Vol. 12, No. 1, 15–20.

9. Sumption, op. cit., Chapter 11.

10. *Pilgrims' Guide*, op. cit., 28.

11. Stone, op. cit., 24, and other recent writers agree on this point.

12. The biblical name is Boanerges. See (James) Rendel Harris, *Boanerges* (Cambridge: Cambridge University Press, 1913).

13. De Santillana and von Dechend, op. cit., 226.

14. *The Homeric Hymns*, tr. Apostolos N. Athanassakis (Baltimore: Johns Hopkins University Press, 1976), 69.

15. Luke 9.52–56 and NEB footnote *d*. Also *The Golden Legend*, op. cit., 369.

16. *The Golden Legend*, 363.

17. See above, note 61, "Polestar Sighted."

18. *Encyclopedia Britannica*, 13th ed., Vol. 9 / 10, 274. Elijah's feast day is so celebrated in both Latin and Orthodox Christianity.

19. *The Golden Legend*, 368–77. But many English narratives by missionaries and clergy of the nineteenth century also include these mixed-up snatches of myth and folktale. Among this type seems to be that of Stone, op. cit. He lists his own sources, pp. 11–26. More recent: Starkie, op. cit., 1–59.

20. Compare: Edward Gibbon, *Decline and Fall of the Roman Empire:* "A stupendous metamorphosis was performed in the 9th century, when from a peaceful fisherman of the lake of Gennesareth, the Apostle James was transformed into a valorous knight . . . the sword of a military order, assisted by the terrors of the Inquisition, was sufficient to remove every object of profane criticism."

21. Starkie, op. cit., 25, footnote 1, cites a Spanish source for discovery of the bones before 860. However, even standard sources disagree on details of these chaotic centuries when Visigothic remnants in Galicia were engaging in guerrilla warfare with the Saracens. The House of Asturias itself begins in clouds. "Pelayo [is] well nigh legendary . . ." *Encyclopedia Britannica*, 13th ed., Vol. 25, 541. Of Spanish Christendom of the time, the *Shorter Cambridge Medieval History* says, "Visigothic Spain presents the first, though unsuccessful, blending of a battered classic and a nomad barbaric inheritance." (Cambridge: Cambridge University Press, 1952), 150. Against this background, the tale of Santiago enlarged from myth-grounded folktale to propagandistic epic. See also Otto von Simson, *The Gothic Cathedral* (Princeton: Princeton University Press / Bollingen, 1962), 84.

22. Starkie suggests "ancient chroniclers attributed to the Battle of Clavijo events that took place a hundred years later" at the Battle of Simancas, when King Ramiro II did butcher a considerable number of foe.

23. Santiago was not alone in so doing. In 1124, some English pilgrims saw, "on midsomer night, the Lord . . . in the Firmament in crucified forme and bloudy" (Stone, op. cit., 175). Joan of Arc also made morale-boosting appearances, as did, over World War I trenches, St. George. And lest one think the fever has ended: "Suddenly we saw the Holy Spirit in the sky. We followed his hands as he guided us to the center of the battlefield and gave us zeal and energy to fight." A fourteen-year-old Iranian in *Newsweek*, March 21, 1983, 51.

24. Porter, op. cit., 176.

25. Cited in Donald Attwater, *The Penguin Dictionary of Saints* (Middlesex: Penguin, 1965), 62.

26. Joseph Gantner and Marcel Pobe, *The Glory of Romanesque Art* (New York: Vanguard Press, 1956), 43.

27. *Pelerins de Rome*, op. cit.

28. Gantner and Pobe, op. cit., 11.

29. Von Simson, op. cit., 80.

30. Brown, op. cit., Chapters 3, 4. Note that all relics were not beneficent. Pontius Pilate's corpse became charged with taint and by some accounts was thrown into the Tiber where it spawned demons. Or else the body was thrown into the Rhone from Vienne or walled up in an Alpine gorge outside Lausanne. How to rid the earth of pollution is not a new problem.

31. Sumption, op. cit., 210.

32. See above, note 5.

33. Griaule, *Conversations with Ogotemmeli*, op. cit. See above, note 14, "Polestar the Pilgrim."

34. Warner, op. cit.

35. Carol de Veguar, "From Great Mother to Mother of God: Problems of Iconographic Continuity," unpublished ms., 5.

36. Wilkinson, *Jerusalem Pilgrims*, op. cit., 117 footnote 4. See also Warner, op. cit., and Evelyn Underhill, *The Miracles of Our Lady Saint Mary* (London: William Heinemann 1905).

37. Attributed to Cyril of Jerusalem. Warner, op. cit., 345.

38. Mrs. Anna Jameson, *Sacred and Legendary Art* (London, 1864), Vol. I, 347.

39. Victor Turner, *Image and Pilgrimage in Christian Culture* (New York: Columbia University Press, 1978), 143.

40. Warner, op. cit., 274–75.

41. See above, note 13.

42. Warner, op. cit., 275.

43. Warner, op. cit., 305–90; also Frye, *Great Code*, op. cit., 70–71: "the Virgin Mary took on some of the attributes of a Queen of Heaven [and] . . . some developments in Judaism assigned something parallel to a female Schekinah [but] neither was ever regarded as in any sense a supreme God, who remained thought of as symbolically male in all Biblical religions." Yet, elsewhere Frye writes: "Apocalyptic mother figures include the Virgin Mary and the mysterious woman crowned with stars who appears at the beginning of Revelation 12 and who is presented also as the mother of the Messiah. . . . (also) the symbolic Jerusalem of Revelation 21 who descends to earth . . . and is finally identified with the Christian Church." Ibid., 140. That cosmic person appears in the last of the Glorious Mysteries of the Rosary, an aid-to-meditation on the pilgrimage of the Virgin toward Assumption to the uppermost Cosmos.

   As I understand it, *pace* Frye, in such postures and acts the female is the unifier of the Three Worlds and so must be equivalent to the cosmic axis itself and so a "supreme God." Compare: "Placing the Mother of the Three Worlds upon a golden throne studded with precious gems, [Siva] dances on the heights." Coomaraswamy, *Dance of Siva*, op. cit., 57. Compare also the Latin American cult of the Virgin of Guadalupe, who stands on the moon in an aureole of fire. And Robert Graves writes in *The White Goddess* (New York: Farrar, Straus and Giroux, 1966 ed), 492: "None greater in the universe than the Triple Goddess!" Many local festivals grant this towering figure dominance over a neighborhood or city. See Kay Turner, "The Virgin of Sorrows Procession: A Brooklyn Inversion," Folklore Papers, University Folklore Association, University of Texas (Austin, 1980), No. 9, 1–25.; also Robert Anthony Orsi, *The Madonna of 115th St.: Faith and Community in Italian Harlem* (New Haven: Yale University Press, 1986). The event in such cases is the processional search of the transcendent Mother for her lost Son. Their eventual reunion, not Christ's appearance alone, serves to save and preserve the human community.

44. Von Simson, op. cit., 89; "armed pilgrimages . . . ," ibid., 79. Sources in addition to those cited below include Georges Duby, *The Age of the Cathedrals* (Chicago: University of Chicago Press, 1981); Emile Mâle, *The Gothic Image* (New York: Harper Torchbook, 1958); Erwin Panofsky, *Studies in Iconology* (Oxford: Oxford University Press, 1939); and other standard texts.

45. "Adam Lay Ybounden," *The Cassell Book of English Poetry*, ed. James Reeves (New York: Harper, 1965), No. 9.

46. From its location atop these burial grounds, some have said, came the name Compostela with its root *compost*. Others trace it to "Giacomo Postola," the road's original name (Stone, op. cit., 158). But popular faith always held the name means "field of stars."

47. Von Simson, op. cit., 140.

48. *The Golden Legend*, op. cit., 771.

49. See the inspired description of Gothic illumination in Parkhurst, op. cit., 72–76.

50. Motto of the Carthusian Order of monks.

51. Von Simson, op. cit., 36, footnote 38.

52. Ibid., 221: "The great Gothic builders thought of themselves above all as geometricians."

53. Parkhurst, op. cit., 189.

54. See Henry Adams, *Mont-Saint-Michel and Chartres* (Princeton: Princeton University Press, 1905 / 1935), Chapter XIV, "Abelard," 285–319.

55. Gantner and Pobe, op. cit., 40.

56. Adams, op. cit., 383: "The equilibrium is visibly delicate beyond the line of safety; danger lurks in every stone. The peril of the heavy tower, of the restless vault, of the vagrant buttress; the uncertainty of logic, the inequalities of the syllogism . . . ," etc.

57. Gantner and Pobe, op. cit., 12.

58. See Roppen and Sommer, op. cit., 12 et passim.

59. Stone, op. cit., 343.

60. *Encyclopedia of World History*, ed. William L. Langer (Boston: Houghton Mifflin, 1948), 390.

61. *Dark Night of the Soul*, Book II, Ch. 9.5: "The spirit must be straitened and inured to hardships . . . and brought by means of this purgative contemplation into great anguish and affliction . . . and have an intimate sense and feeling that it is making a pilgrimage . . ."

62. *Pilgrim's Progress* (London: Everyman's Library ed., 1954), 160–61.

63. George Borrow, *The Bible in Spain* (London: J. M. Dent & Sons, 1906 / 61), 244–53.

64. Nigel Pennick, *The Subterranean Kingdom* (Wellingborough, England: Turnstone Press, 1981), 66.

65. *Pilgrims' Guide*, op. cit.

THE END

Epigraph: Calisher, op. cit.

1. Starkie, op. cit., 15.
2. Mircea Eliade, *No Souvenirs* (New York: Harper and Row, 1977), xii: "The correct analyses of myths and of mythical thought, of symbols and primordial images, are, in my opinion, the only way to open the Western mind and to introduce a new planetary humanism."
3. Sociologist Daniel Bell has described the present state of culture as "a breaking down of a rational cosmology." And Fouad Ajami, of Johns Hopkins School of Advanced International Studies, wrote in *The New York Times* (April 17, 1986): "A terrible wind was blowing throughout the realm of Islam. . . . The middle ground in much of the Moslem world was caving in."
4. Tyler Dennett, *The Democratic Movement in Asia* (New York: YMCA Association Press, 1918), 6. "All the nations and races of Asia are standing on end like a circle of dominoes. If any one of them is knocked over or disturbed, the resulting commotion is immediately communicated to all the others." China missionary Dennett was undoubtedly read by John Foster Dulles from whom the image entered post–World War II political vernacular.
5. "Shiva" is the name given the world's biggest laser, used for nuclear fission research at California's Lawrence Livermore National Laboratory.
6. Compare Czeslaw Milosz, *Native Realm, A Search for Self-Definition*, 2–3: "There is a new organ which we may call the telescopic eye, which perceives simultaneously not only different parts of the globe, but also different moments in time. . . ."
7. Calisher, op. cit., 1.
8. Joan Colebrook, "Twilight of the Ananda," *Geo*, May 1979, 102–30. The Ananda inhabit an incomparably savage wasteland. Then the horrific procedures to which they ritually submit their bodies—circumcision, subincision, drawing out of fingernails, bloodletting, burning, striking at the skull until blood flows—could be called technics for the correction of the Cosmos, employed against the human axis to stave off wider catastrophe.
9. Such a tunnel, dated ca. 1000, was recently discovered in Chaco Canyon northwest of Albuquerque in which solstice and equinoctial suns appear to cast daggers of light onto a spiral on the far wall, locking sky and earth together.
10. The "first generation" of Earth-works, by Robert Smithson, Robert Morris, Michael Heizer, etc., afforded such experience to solitary travelers far off the beaten track. But the "second generation" of Earth-works are conceived with social purpose, to engage people in beneficently orienting rituals. For example, the Vietnam Monument in Washington, D.C., at first shocking to people used to pompous verticality in monuments to dead heroes, proved its revolutionary power by drawing multitudes into its arms in communal pity for lives lost to old myths of power. Related works are being erected nationwide by artists like Nancy Holt, Patricia Johanson, Charles Ross, James Turrell, etc.
11. Compare the invented term "Tellurianism" by E. T. Stringer—from the Greek *tellus*, the living earth—to denote the notion that each human is one of the

earth's brain cells. A related theory is called, by British scientist James Love-lace, the "Gaia principle."

12. The "anthropic principle," a new astrophysical concept, provides that only the universe as it exists could have supported the rise of intelligent life. Thus, teleology returns in purportedly respectable guise: the study of design, purpose, or final cause in natural evolution.

13. See Mylonas, op. cit., 222, 242: "panspermia," in Greece, denoted cereal seeds—sage, poppy, wheat, barley, peas, vetches, okra, lentil, beans, rice, oats: "the produce of the earth"—offered Demeter at Eleusis.

14. Georgio de Santillana, *The Crime of Galileo* (Chicago: University of Chicago Press, 1955 / 76). The author portrays a Galileo who "never felt himself . . . a rebel," who spoke "in the name of the community of the faithful which joins the ancient dead to the yet unborn" (xi), but who was politically destroyed for "Reasons of State . . . a constellation of accidents and personal motives." What the world fears today.

AFTERWORD

Epigraph: Louise Bogan, "Poem in Prose," from *The Blue Estuaries: Poems 1923–1968* (New York: Farrar, Straus & Giroux, 1968). Reprinted in *Journey Around My Room: The Autobiography of Louise Bogan. A Mosaic by Ruth Limmer.* (New York: Viking Press, 1980), 98.

1. The poem was, again, Longfellow: "The Arrow and the Song."

SELECTED
BIBLIOGRAPHY

Abelson, J. *The Immanence of God*. New York: Hermon Press, 1969 ed. of London, 1912.

Albright, William Foxwell. *From the Stone Age to Christianity: Monotheism and the Historical Process*. New York: Doubleday / Anchor ed., 1957.

Allen, Richard Hinckley. *Star Names: Their Lore and Meaning*. New York: Dover, 1963 ed. of G. E. Stechert, *Star Names and their Meanings*, 1899.

Archaeoastronomy: Journal of the Center for Archaeoastronomy. College Park, Md.: Vols I–IX, 1978–present.

Arnheim, Rudolf. *Toward a Psychology of Art*. Berkeley / Los Angeles: University of California Press, 1966.

―――. *Art and Visual Perception:* Berkeley / Los Angeles: University of California Press, 1954 / 1974.

Astronomy of the Ancients. ed. Kenneth Brecher, Michael Feirtag. Cambridge, MIT Press, 1981.

Attwater, Donald, *The Penguin Dictionary of Saints*. New York: Penguin, 1965.

Auerbach, Erich. *Mimesis: The Representation of Reality in Western Literature*. Princeton: Princeton University Press, 1953.

Babbitt, Irving, tr. *The Dhammapada*. New York: New Directions.

Bachelard, Gaston. *The Poetics of Space*. tr. Maria Jolas. Boston: Beacon Press, 1969.

Barfield, Owen. *Poetic Diction: A Study in Meaning*. Middletown, Conn.: Wesleyan University Press.

Beardsley, John. *Probing the Earth: Contemporary Land Projects*. Washington, D.C.: Smithsonian Institution Press, 1977.

Benedict, St. *The Rule*. tr. Anthony C. Meisel and M. L. del Mastro. New York: Image Books, 1975.

Bernbaum, Edwin. *The Way to Shambhala*. New York: Doubleday / Anchor, 1980.

Bharati, Swami Agehananda. *The Ochre Robe*. Seattle: University of Washington Press, 1962.

———. "Pilgrimage Sites and Indian Civilization," in *Chapters in Indian Civilization*, ed. J. W. Elder, Vol 1. Dubuque: Kendall Hunt Publishing Co., 1970.

Bhardwaj, Surinder Mohan. *Hindu Places of Pilgrimage in India: A Study in Cultural Geography*. Berkeley / Los Angeles: University of California Press, 1983.

The New English Bible. Oxford: Oxford University Press, 1976.

The Bible of the World. ed. Robert O. Ballou. New York: Viking Press, 1939.

Black Elk. *The Sacred Pipe*. University of Oklahoma Press / Penguin, 1953 / 1971.

Bliss, Frederick Jones. *The Development of Palestine Exploration*. London: Hadden & Stoughton, 1906.

Bosch, F. D. K. *The Golden Germ: An Introduction to Indian Symbolism*. Gravenhage, the Hague: Mouton & Co., 1960.

Bowersock, G. W. *Julian the Apostate*. Cambridge: Harvard University Press, 1978.

Brown, Peter. *The Cult of the Saints*. Chicago: University of Chicago Press, 1982.

Buber, Martin. *The Way of Man*. Secaucus, N.J.: Citadel Press, 1966.

Burl, Aubrey. *Prehistoric Avebury*. New Haven: Yale University Press, 1979.

Campbell, Joseph. *The Masks of God. Creative Mythology*. New York: Penguin, 1970.

Canetti, Elias. *Crowds and Power*. New York: The Seabury Press, 1978.

Carpenter, Edward. *Pagan and Christian Creeds*. New York: Harcourt Brace & Howe, 1920.

Cassirer, Ernst. *Language and Myth*. tr. Susan K. Langer. New York: Harper, 1946.

Chaudhuri, Nirad C. *Autobiography of an Unknown Indian*. Bombay: Jaico Press, 1951.

———. *The Continent of Circe*. Bombay: Jaico Press, 1965.

Clark, Sir Kenneth. *Landscape into Art*. New York: Harper & Row, 1976.

Clarke, Arthur C. *The Promise of Space*. New York: Harper & Row, 1968.

Comay, Joan. *The Temple of Jerusalem*. London: Weidenfeld & Nicolson, 1975.

Conze, Edward. *Buddhist Thought in India*. Ann Arbor: University of Michigan Press, 1967 ed.

Coomaraswamy, Ananda K. *The Dance of Siva*. New York: The Sunwise Turn, 1924.

————. *Myths of the Hindus and Buddhists,* with Sister Nivedita (Margaret E. Noble). New York: Farrar & Rinehart.

————. *The Transformation of Nature in Art.* Cambridge: Harvard University Press, 1934.

Cowan, Paul. *An Orphan in History: Retrieving a Jewish Legacy.* New York: Doubleday, 1982.

Cross, Frank Moore. *Canaanite Myth and Hebrew Epic.* Cambridge: Harvard University Press, 1973.

Cumont, Franz. *Astrology and Religion Among the Greeks and Romans.* New York: Dover / Putnam's, 1960 / 1912.

Curzon, Robert. *Visits to Monasteries in the Levant.* London: Murray, 1881.

Cust, L. G. A. *The Status Quo in the Holy Places.* Jerusalem: Ariel, 1980 facsimile.

Daumal, René. *Mount Analogue.* Baltimore: Penguin ed., 1974.

Day, Dorothy. *On Pilgrimage.* New York: Curtis Books, 1972.

Dechend, Hertha von. *World Ages.* Unpublished ms. in MIT library, courtesy Harald A. T. Reiche.

Dempsey, Rev. T. *The Delphic Oracle.* New York: Oxford University Press, 1918.

Doughty, Charles M. *Travels in Arabia Deserta.* New York: Doubleday / Anchor, 1955.

Duby, Georges. *The Age of the Cathedrals.* Chicago: University of Chicago Press, 1981.

Dumézil, Georges. *Gods of the Ancient Northmen.* Berkeley: University of California Press, 1973.

Eck, Diana. *Banaras: City of Light.* New York: Alfred A. Knopf, 1982.

————. "The Church in Bali: Mountainwards and Seawards," *Harvard Divinity Bulletin,* April / May 1982.

————. *Shiva & Shakti in the Land of India.* Kenyon College pamphlet, 1982.

Eisler, Robert. *Orpheus the Fisher: Comparative Studies in Orphic and Early Christian Cult Symbolism.* London: J. M. Watkins, 1921.

Ekholm, Gordon F. "Transpacific Contacts" in *Prehistoric Man in the New World.* Chicago: University of Chicago Press, 1964.

Eliade, Mircea. *From Primitives to Zen.* New York: Harper, 1967.

————. *History of Religious Ideas.* Chicago: University of Chicago Press. 1978.

————. *The Myth of the Eternal Return, or Cosmos and History.* Princeton: Princeton University Press, 1954.

————. *No Souvenirs.* New York: Harper & Row, 1977.

————. *The Quest: History and Meaning in Religion.* Chicago: University of Chicago Press, 1969.

————. *Sacred and Profane.* New York: Harcourt Brace Jovanovich, 1959.

————. *Yoga: Immortality and Freedom.* Princeton: Princeton University Press, 1958.

Encyclopedia Britannica. 13th ed.

Encyclopedia Judaica.

Epstein, Perle. *Pilgrimage: Adventures of a Wandering Jew.* Boston: Houghton Mifflin, 1979.

Ethnoastronomy: First Annual Conference on: Indigenous Astronomical and Cosmological Traditions of the World. Smithsonian Institution Program and Abstracts, 1983.

Field, Henry M. *Among the Holy Hills.* New York: Scribners, 1884.

Flusser, David. "Jewish-Christian Schism." Unpublished ms. Jerusalem: 1985.

Fontein, Jan. *The Pilgrims of Sudhana.* The Hague: Mouton & Co., 1967.

Fontenrose, Joseph. *The Delphic Oracle.* Los Angeles: University of California Press, 1978.

————. *Python.* Los Angeles: University of California Press, 1959.

Fox, George. *The Journal.* New York: Dutton, 1924 ed.

Franco, Juan José Cebrian. *Santuarios de Galicia.* Santiago: Arzobispado de Santiago de Compostela, 1982.

Frankfort, Henri. *Before Philosophy.* New York: Penguin, 1954 ed.

————. *The Birth of Civilization in the Near East.* Bloomington: Indiana University Press, 1951.

Franz, Marie Louise von. *Time.* New York: Thames & Hudson, 1978.

Frazer, Sir James George. *The Golden Bough.* New York: Criterion, 1959.

Frye, Northrop. *The Great Code.* New York: Harcourt Brace Jovanovich, 1982.

Gantner, Joseph, and Marcel Pobe. *The Glory of Romanesque Art.* New York: Vanguard Press, 1956.

Gaster, Theodor H. *The Dead Sea Scrolls.* New York: Doubleday / Anchor, 1976.

Geertz, Clifford. *The Interpretation of Cultures.* New York: Basic Books, 1973.

Gibbon, Edward. *The Decline and Fall of the Roman Empire.* New York: Modern Library, 1932.

Glueck, Nelson. *The River Jordan.* London: Lutterworth Press, 1946.

The Golden Legend. Jacobus de Voragine. tr. and adapted by Granger Ryan and Helmut Ripperger. London: Longmans, Green, 1941.

Goodfield, June. *An Imagined World: The Story of Scientific Discovery.* New York: Harper & Row, 1981.

Govinda, Lama Anagarika. *Psycho-cosmic Symbolism of the Buddhist Stupa.* Emeryville, Calif.: Dharma Publishing Co., 1976.

————. *The Way of the White Clouds.* Bombay: B. I. Publications, 1960.

Graham, Stephan. *With the Russian Pilgrims to Jerusalem*. London: Macmillan, 1914.

Graves, Robert. *The White Goddess*. New York: Farrar, Straus & Giroux, 1948, 1979.

Griaule, Maurice. *Conversations with Ogotemmeli: An Introduction to Dogon Religious Ideas*. Oxford: Oxford University Press, 1965.

Guénon, René. *Man and His Becoming, According to the Vedanta*. New York: Noonday Press, 1958.

Guthrie, W. K. C. *A History of Greek Philosophy*. Cambridge: Cambridge University Press, 1962.

Hamilton, Edith. *The Greek Way to Western Civilization*. New York: Mentor, 1948.

———. *Mythology*. New York: New American Library, 1942.

Harris, (James) Rendel. *Boanerges*. Cambridge: Cambridge University Press, 1913.

Harrison, Jane. *Themis: A Study of the Social Origins of Greek Religion*. Cambridge: Cambridge University Press, 1912.

Hawkins, Gerald S., and John B. White. *Stonehenge Decoded*. New York: Dell, 1965.

Hazleton, Lesley. *Where Mountains Roar*. New York: Holt Rinehart, 1980.

Heimann, Betty. *Facets of Indian Thought*. New York: Schocken Books, 1964.

Heurnecke, Edgar. *New Testament Apocrypha*. Philadelphia: Westminster, 1965.

Highwater, Jamake. *The Primal Mind*. New York: Harper, 1981.

Hogben, Lancelot. *Astronomer, Priest and Ancient Mariner*. New York: St. Martin's Press, 1973.

Holt, Claire. *Art in Indonesia.* Ithaca: Cornell University Press, 1967.

Hudson, G. F. *Europe and China*. London: E. Arnold, 1931.

Humphreys, Christmas. *Karma and Rebirth*. London: John Murray, 1943.

Israel Pocket Library, Vol. 1: *History to 1880*. Jerusalem: Keter, 1973.

James, William. *Varieties of Religious Experience*. London: Longmans, Green, 1902.

Jameson, Anna. *Sacred and Legendary Art*, Vol. 3: *Legends of the Madonna*. London, 1864.

Jung, C. G. *Memories, Dreams, Reflections*. London: Collins, 1969.

———. *Modern Man in Search of a Soul*. London: Routledge & Kegan Paul, 1933.

———. *Symbols of Transformation*. New York: Bollingen, 1956.

Jung, C. G., and C. Kerenyi. *Essays on a Science of Mythology: The Myth of the Divine Child and the Mysteries of Eleusis*. New York: Bollingen, 1949.

Kakar, Sudhir. *The Inner World: A Psychoanalytic Study of Childhood and Society in India*. Delhi / New York: Oxford University Press, 1981.

Kendall, Alan. *Medieval Pilgrims*. New York: Putnam's, 1970.

Kenton, Edna. *The Book of Earths*. New York: Morrow, 1928.

Klagsbrun, Francine. *Voices of Wisdom*. New York: Pantheon, 1980.

Kollek, Teddy, and Moshe Pearlman. *Pilgrims to the Holy Land*. London / Jerusalem: Weidenfeld & Nicolson, 1970.

Kramrisch, Stella. *The Art of India*. London: Phaidon, 1955.

———. *Exploring India's Sacred Arts: Selected Writings of Stella Kramrisch*. ed. Barbara Stoller Miller. Philadelphia: University of Pennsylvania Press, 1983.

———. *The Hindu Temple*. 2 vols. Calcutta: University of Calcutta, 1946.

———. *Manifestations of Shiva*. Philadelphia: Philadelphia Museum of Art, 1981.

———. *Presence of Siva*. Princeton: Princeton University Press, 1981.

Krauss, Rosalind E. *Passages in Modern Sculpture*. New York: Viking, 1977.

Krom, N. J. *Barabudur: Archaeological Description*. The Hague: Martinus Nijhoff, 1927.

Larousse *Encyclopedia of Mythology*. tr. Richard Aldington and Delano Ames. London: Batchworth Press, 1959.

Laski, Margharita. *Ecstasy*. Bloomington: Indiana University Press, 1962.

Leeus, Gerardus van der. *Sacred and Profane Beauty*. New York: Holt, Rinehart, 1963.

Lethaby, W. R. *Architecture, Mysticism and Myth*. New York: Braziller, 1975.

Lévi-Strauss, Claude. *Myth and Meaning*. New York: Schocken Books, 1979.

———. "The Structural Study of Myth," in *Myth: A Symposium*. ed. Thomas A. Sebeok, for The American Folklore Society. Bloomington: Indiana University Press, 1958.

Lewis, C. S. *The Discarded Image*. Cambridge: Cambridge University Press, 1964.

———. *Surprised by Joy*. New York: Harcourt Brace Jovanovich, 1955.

Lifton, Robert Jay. *Boundaries: Psychological Man in Revolution*. New York: Simon and Schuster / Touchstone, 1967.

Lippard, Lucy R. *Overlay: Contemporary Art and the Art of Prehistory*. New York: Pantheon, 1983.

Lloyd, Seton. *The Art of the Ancient Near East*. New York: Praeger, 1961.

Macrobius. *Commentary on the Dream of Scipio*. tr. and with introduction and notes by William Harris Stahl. New York: Columbia University Press, 1952.

Magnus, Laurie. *The Jews in the Christian Era*. New York: Dutton.

Mâle, Emile. *Religious Art*. New York: Noonday, 1949.

Marnham, Patrick. *Lourdes: A Modern Pilgrimage.* New York: Coward McCann and Gohegan, 1981.

Matthews, John. *The Grail.* New York: Thames & Hudson, 1981.

Mehta, Ved. *Portrait of India.* New York: Farrar, Straus & Giroux, 1970.

———. *The New India.* New York: Viking Press, 1978.

Merleau-Ponty, Jacques, and Bruno Morando. *The Rebirth of Cosmology.* Athens: Ohio University Press, 1982.

Miller, Perry. *Errand into the Wilderness.* Cambridge: Harvard University Press, 1975.

Morrison, Diana. *A Glossary of Sanskrit: From the Spiritual Tradition of India.* Petaluma, Calif.: Nilgiri Press, 1970.

Muller, Herbert J. *Freedom in the Ancient World.* New York: Harper & Row, 1961.

Munro, Eleanor. *Originals: American Women Artists.* New York: Simon & Schuster, 1979.

Munro, Thomas. *The Arts and Their Interrelations.* New York: Liberal Arts Press, 1951.

Mus, Paul. *Barabudur.* Hanoi, 1935.

Narayan, R. K. *Gods, Demons and Others.* New York: Viking, 1964.

Neumann, Eric. *Art and the Creative Unconscious.* New York: Bollingen Foundation, 1959.

———. *The Great Mother.* Princeton: Princeton University Press, 1972.

———. *The Origins and History of Consciousness.* New York: Bollingen Foundation, 1954.

Novak, Barbara. *Nature and Culture.* New York: Oxford University Press, 1980.

O'Flaherty, Wendy Doniger. *Siva.* New York: Oxford University Press, 1973.

Oldenbourg, Zoé. *The Crusades.* New York: Random House, 1966.

Oliver, Paul. *Shelter, Sign and Symbol.* New York: Overlook Press, 1977.

Otto, Rudolph. *Mysticism East and West.* New York: Macmillan, 1952.

Pallis, Marco. *The Way and the Mountain.* London: Peter Owen, 1960.

Panofsky, Edwin. *Gothic Architecture and Scholasticism.* Meridian, 1957.

———. *Studies in Iconology.* Oxford: Oxford University Press, 1939.

Parke, H. W., and D. E. W. Wormell. *The Delphic Oracle.* Oxford: Blackwell, 1950.

Parke, H. W. *Greek Oracles.* Hillary House, 1967.

Parkes, James. *Judaism and Christianity.* Chicago: University of Chicago Press, 1948.

Parkhurst, Helen Huss. *Cathedral: A Gothic Pilgrimage.* London: Lovat Dickson, 1936.

Parrot, André. *Babylon and the Old Testament.* New York: Philosophical Library, 1958.

Pennick, Nigel. *The Subterranean Kingdom.* Wellingborough, England: Turnstone Press, 1981.

Percy, Walker. *The Message in the Bottle.* New York: Farrar, Straus & Giroux, 1975.

Pfeiffer, John E. *The Creative Explosion.* New York: Harper & Row, 1982.

Plato. *The Collected Dialogues.* ed. Edith Hamilton and Huntington Cairns. New York: Bollingen / Pantheon, 1961.

Poirier, Frank. *In Search of Ourselves: An Introduction to Physical Anthropology.* Minneapolis: Burgess, 1977.

Porter, A. Kingsley. *Romanesque Sculpture of the Pilgrimage Roads.* Boston: Marshall James, 1923.

Rambach, Pierre. *The Secret Message of Tantric Buddhism.* New York: Rizzoli, 1979.

Rank, Otto. *Art and Artist.* New York: Agathon, 1968.

Raven-Hart, Major R. *Where the Buddha Trod: A Buddhist Pilgrimage.* Colombo, Sri Lanka: Lake House, 1956.

Rawson, Philip. *Tantra: The Indian Cult of Ecstasy.* London: Thames & Hudson, 1973.

Reflections of Minds: Western Psychology Meets Tibetan Buddhism. ed. Tarthang Tulku. Emeryville, Calif.: Dharma Publishing Co., 1975.

Reymond, Lizelle. *My Life with a Brahmin Family.* London: Rider / Penguin, 1958 / 1972.

Rice, Edward. *Eastern Definitions.* New York: Doubleday / Anchor, 1980.

Rizzuto, Ana-Maria, M.D. *The Birth of the Living God: A Psychoanalytic Study.* Chicago: University of Chicago Press, 1979.

Roiphe, Ann. *Generation Without Memory.* Boston: Beacon, 1981.

Roppen, Georg, and Richard Sommer. *Strangers and Pilgrims: An Essay on the Metaphor of Journey.* Oslo: Norwegian University Press.

Runciman, Steven. *Byzantine Civilization.* New York: St. Martin's, 1933.

Sagan, Carl. *Dragons of Eden.* New York: Random House, 1977.

Santillana, Giorgio de, and Hertha von Dechend. *Hamlet's Mill: An Essay on Myth and the Frame of Time.* Boston: Gambit, 1969.

Schauss, Hayyim. *The Jewish Festivals.* New York: Schocken, 1962.

Scholem, Gershom G. *Major Trends in Jewish Mysticism.* New York: Schocken, 1941.

Schroedinger, E. *What Is Life?* Cambridge: Cambridge University Press, 1967.

Scully, Vincent. *The Earth, the Temple and the Gods.* New Haven: Yale University Press, 1962.

———. *Pueblo: Mountain, Village, Dance.* New York: Viking, 1975.

Seiss, Joseph A. *The Gospel in the Stars, or Primeval Astronomy.* Philadelphia: Lippincott, 1885.

Serrano, Miguel. *The Serpent of Paradise: The Story of an Indian Pilgrimage.* tr. Frank MacShane. London: Routledge & Kegan Paul, 1963.

Shawn, Ted. *Gods Who Dance.* New York: Dutton, 1929.

Simson, Otto von. *The Gothic Cathedral.* Princeton: Princeton University Press / Bollingen, 1962.

Sitwell, Sacheverell. *Touching the Orient.* London: Duckworth, 1934.

Smith, Rev. George Adam. *The Historical Geography of the Holy Land.* London: Collins, 1894 / 1974.

Smith, Huston. *The Religions of Man.* New York: Harper & Row, 1958.

Snellgrove, D. L. *Buddhist Himalaya.* New York: Philosophical Library, 1957.

Starkie, Walter. *The Road to Santiago.* Pilgrims of St. James. New York: Dutton, 1957.

Steinsaltz, Adin. *The Thirteen-Petalled Rose.* New York: Basic Books, 1980.

Stevenson, Mrs. Sinclair. *The Rites of the Twice-Born.* London: Oxford University Press, 1920.

Stokstad, Marilyn. *Santiago de Compostela.* Norman: University of Oklahoma Press, 1978.

Stone, Rev. James S. *The Cult of Santiago: Traditions, Myths and Pilgrims.* London: Longmans, Green, 1927.

Stone, Martha. *At the Sign of Midnight: The Concheros Dance Cult of Mexico.* Tucson: University of Arizona Press, 1975.

Stutterheim, W. F. S. *Studies in Indonesian Archaeology.* The Hague: 1956.

Sumption, Jonathan. *Pilgrimage: An Image of Medieval Religion.* Totowa, N.J.: Rowman & Littlefield, 1975.

Teubal, Savina J. *Sarah the Priestess: The First Matriarch of Genesis.* Athens, Ohio: Swallow Press, 1984.

Thapar, Romila. *A History of India.* New York: Penguin, 1966.

Thompson, William Erwin. *Passages About Earth: An Exploration of the New Planetary Culture.* New York: Harper, 1974.

Tillich, Paul. *The Courage to Be.* New Haven: Yale University Press, 1952.

Tucci, Giuseppe. *The Theory and Practice of the Mandala.* London: Rider, 1961.

Turner, Victor. *Dramas, Fields and Metaphors.* Ithaca: Cornell University Press, 1974.

———. *Image and Pilgrimage in Christian Culture.* with Edith Turner. New York: Columbia University Press, 1978.

Underhill, Evelyn. *Mysticism.* New York: Dutton / Noonday, 1955.

Urton, Gary. *At the Crossroads of the Earth and the Sky.* Austin: University of Texas Press, 1981.

Vermes, G. *The Dead Sea Scrolls in English*. New York: Penguin, 1981.

Visages de Rome. Vols. 1–4. Paris / Rome: Centre Saint Louis de France, 1979–82.

Vitaliano, Dorothy B. *Legends of the Earth: Their Geologic Origin*. Bloomington: Indiana University Press, 1973.

Waley, Arthur. *Three Ways of Thought in Ancient China*. New York: Doubleday / Anchor, 1956.

Wetering, Janwillem van de. *The Empty Mirror: Experiences in a Japanese Zen Monastery*. New York: Houghton Mifflin, 1975.

Wilkinson, John. *Egeria's Travels to the Holy Land*. Jerusalem: Ariel.

———. *Jerusalem Pilgrims*. Jerusalem: Ariel, 1977.

Williamson, G. A. *The World of Josephus*. Boston: Little, Brown, 1964.

Wind, Edgar. *Pagan Mysteries in the Renaissance*. New Haven: Yale University Press 1958.

Wolkstein, Diane, and Samuel Noah Kramer. *Inanna: Queen of Heaven and Earth*. New York: Harper & Row, 1983.

Yates, Francis A. *The Art of Memory*. Chicago: University of Chicago Press, 1966.

Young, Jean, and Michael Lang. *Woodstock Festival Remembered*. New York: Ballantine Books, 1979.

Selected Periodicals

Babb, Lawrence A. "The Physiology of Redemption." *History of Religions* Vol. 22, No. 4, May 1983. 293–312.

Berger, Peter. "The Third World as Religion." *Partisan Review* No. 2, 1983.

Bharati, Agehananda. "Pilgrimage in the Indian Tradition." *History of Religions* Vol. 3, No. 1, 1963. 135–67.

Biale, David. "The God with Breasts: El Shaddai in the Bible." *History of Religions* Vol. 21, No. 3, February 1982. 240–56.

Borgeaud, Philippe. "The Death of the Great Pan: The Problem of Interpretation." *History of Religions* Vol. 22, No. 3, February 1983. 254–83.

Bronowsky, J. "Copernicus the Humanist." *Smithsonian,* April / May 1973.

Burghart, Richard. "Wandering Ascetics of the Ramanandi Sect." *History of Religions* Vol. 22, No. 4, May 1983.

Colebrook, Joan. "Twilight of the Ananda." *Geo,* May 1979. 102–30.

Eck, Diana L. "Kasi, City and Symbol." *Purana* XX, no. 2, 1978.

Fairservis, Walter A., Jr. "The Script of the Indus Valley Civilization." *Scientific American*, March 1983. 58–66.

Fleming, James. "The Undiscovered Gate Beneath Jerusalem's Golden Gate." *Biblical Archaeology Review*, January / February 1983. 24.

Fleury, Helene. "Cosmos in Stone." *Parabola* Vol. III, No. 1.

Grapard, Allan G. "Flying Mountains and Walkers of Emptiness: Toward a Definition of Sacred Space in Japanese Religions." *History of Religions* Vol. 21, No. 3, February 1982. 195–221.

Green, Peter. "Answering Service." Review of Joseph Fontenrose, *The Delphic Oracle. New York Review of Books*, April 5, 1979.

Heisenberg, Werner. "The Representation of Nature in Contemporary Physics." *Daedalus*, Summer 1958. 95–109.

Hori, Ichiro. "Mountains and Their Importance for the Idea of the Other World in Japanese Folk Religion." *History of Religions* Vol. 6, 1966. 1–23.

Huxley, G. L. "Cosmogonical Connections." Review of M. L. West, *The Orphic Poems. Times Literary Supplement*, May 25, 1984. 597.

Jeanes, Rosemary. "Labyrinths." *Parabola* Vol. 4, No. 2, 12–15.

Kane, P. V. "Tirthayatra." *Dharmasastra* Vol. 4. Gvmt. Oriental Series (Poona, Bhandarkar Oriental Research Institution, 1930–62. 2nd ed. 1973–74).

Kaufman, A. "Where the Ancient Temple of Jerusalem Stood." *Biblical Archaeology Review*, March / April 1983. 40–59.

Komar and Melamid. "In Search of Religion." *Artforum*, June 1980. 30.

Krautheimer, Richard. "Introduction to an 'Iconography of Medieval Architecture.' " *Journal of the Warburg and Courtauld Institute*. Vol. 5, 1942. 1–33.

Lawlor, Robert. "Geometry at the Service of Prayer: Cistercian Mystic Architecture." *Parabola* Vol. 3, No. 1. 12–20.

Lenz, Mary Jane. "Star Gods of the Northwest Coast." *Bulletin of the American Museum of Natural History*, February 1983. 5.

Maccoby, Hyam. "The Greatness of Gershom Scholem." *Commentary*, September 1983. 37–46.

Parsons, Talcott. "Religious Organization." *Daedalus*, Summer 1958. 65–85.

Peterson, Indira Viswanathan. "Lives of the Wandering Saints: Pilgrimage and Poetry in Tamil Saivite Hagiography." *History of Religions* Vol. 22, No. 4, May 1983. 338–60.

Reiche, Harald A. T. Review of de Santillana and von Dechend, *Hamlet's Mill. Classical Journal* Vol. 69, No. 1, October / November 1973. 81–83.

Renfrew, Colin. "The Social Archaeology of Megalithic Monuments." *Scientific American,* November 1983. 152–63.

Rensberger, Boyce. "Roots of Writing Traced Back More Than 10,000 Years." *The New York Times,* July 9, 1977. 19–20.

Rosenberg, Harold. "The Mythic Act." *The New Yorker,* May 6, 1967.

Schein, Bruce E. "The Second Wall of Jerusalem." *Biblical Archaeologist,* Winter 1981. 21–26.

Speck, Frank G., and Jesse Moses. "The Celestial Bear Comes Down to Earth: The Bear Sacrifice Ceremony of the Munsee-Mohicans." Reading Public Museum and Art Gallery. Reading, Pa. 1945.

Steinsaltz, Rabbi Adin. "Repentance: The Upward Spiral." *Parabola* Vol. 8, No. 1. 34–39.

Turner, Kay F. "The Virgin of Sorrows Procession: A Brooklyn Inversion." *Folklore Papers.* University Folklore Association Center for Intercultural Studies in Folklore and Ethnomusicology. University of Texas. No. 9, 1980. 1–26.

Turner, Victor. "The Center Out There: Pilgrim's Goal." *History of Religions* Vol. 12, No. 3, 1973.

Veguar, Carol de. "From Great Mother to Mother of God: Problems in Iconographic Continuity." Unpublished ms.

Werblowsky, R. J., Zwi. "The Meaning of Jerusalem to Jews, Christians and Muslims." Israel University Study Group for Middle Eastern Affairs, repr. *Jaarbericht Ex Orient Lux.* Vol. 23. 1973 / 4.

Whitehead, Alfred N. "Uses of Symbolism." *Daedalus,* Summer 1958. 109–23.

Woodward, Hiram W., Jr. "Borobodur and the Mirrorlike Mind." *Archaeology* Vol. 34, No. 6, November / December 1981. 40–47.

Yu, Anthony C. "Two Literary Examples of Religious Pilgrimage: The Commedia and the Journey to the West." *History of Religions* Vol. 22, No. 3, February 1983. 202–30.

ACKNOWLEDGMENTS

One travels in a long project and draws from many sources on the way. Gratefully, I acknowledge the help of kind friends, among them: Suresh Vasant, who guided me through India, and Walter and Nesta Spink, who sent me to Suresh; also in respect to my Asian pilgrimages, Jerome Alan and Joan Lebold Cohen, Jill Cowan, Diana Eck, Eleanor Gadon, John Irwin, Ruth Jhabvala, O. K. and Helena Joshee, Ved Mehta, Muriel Peters, David Shainberg, Laurence Shainberg, Robert Shaplen, Daphne Hellman Shih, Clare Brett Smith, Dwight W. and Nancy Webb, Hiram W. and Ann Woodward. In Delhi: Sudhir Kakar, Michael T. Kaufman, Herbert and Cornelia Levin, Rear Adm. Gautam and Umi Singh. In Jaipur: Krishna and V. K. Thanvi. In Benares: Anand Krishna and Sushila Koirala. In Bombay: Ansuya Dutt, Gopal Ratnam, Mr. and Mrs. Armarsey, and Mulk Raj Anand. The late former prime minister of Nepal, B. P. Koirala, gave me guidance about Nepal, as did Todd Lewis.

Bruce and Naomi Bliven sent me to Father Edmund Bliven and Judith Elizur in Jerusalem. Once there, I was kindly helped also by Ruth Cheshin of The Jerusalem Foundation; David and Annette Crohn; David Flusser; Mr. and Mrs. Avrain Lewensohn; Colette and Arie Muscat; Edgar E. Siskin of the Jerusalem Center for Anthropological Studies; Naomi Teasdale, head of pilgrimage for the Municipality of Jerusalem; and Zev Vilnay. Archimandrite Nickiphoros A. Baltatzis, Greek Orthodox Patriarchate, and parish priests Elias Yaghnam and Jabra D. Baddour of that community helped me find standing room at the Holy Fire Ceremony.

Apropos of Compostela, the following were companions or help-givers: Jane Aiken, Harry Bober, Lynn Boillot, Paula Gerson, Hannah Green, Miguel and Ellen Junger, Mervin Jules, and Annie Shaver-Crandall.

In the field of archaeoastronomy, I am grateful to John B. Carlson of The Center for Archaeoastronomy, K. L. Franklin and William Gutsch of the Hayden Planetarium, Harald A. T. Reiche of MIT; and an astronomer from NASA who prefers to remain anonymous who read the manuscript for errors of scientific fact and emphasis.

The following also read the typescript in part or whole. In temporal sequence: John Cox, E. J. Kahn, Jr., Walter Spink, Annie Dillard, Phyllis Rose, Francine Klagsbrun, Katharine Kuh, Stella Kramrisch, Lynn Boillot, Donald J. Munro, David T. M. Frankfurter, Alexander M. Frankfurter, David and Catherine Shainberg, Edith Turner.

I thank Swami Durgananda, the former Sally Kempton, at the Siddha Yoga Dam Ashram in the U.S., and Mina Kempton and Lenore Tawney who guided me at its several campgrounds. Thanks too to the Mishkenot Sha'ananim in Jerusalem and its director Ruth Bach, and to Yaddo and Curtis Harnack. Such utopian communities, religious or secular, work on the heart as well as the mind and afford a glimpse of a better world.

And for general advice and help, I thank John Appleton, Cynthia Beeker, Gary Clevidence, Joan Colebrook, Margaret Croyden, Hertha von Dechend, Wilton Dillon, Perle Epstein, Margit van Leight Frank, Capt. and Mrs. Charles Glaze, the supportive Kahn family—Joan, Olivia, E. J. III, Joseph, Hamilton—, Betty Jean and Robert Jay Lifton, Roger Lipsey, Ted Morgan, Jacob Needleman, Ann Norton, Necee Regis, Jean Sulzberger, and Abby Zito.

The late Roland Gelatt of Thames & Hudson, London, opened the door for this project, Stanley Baron held it open, and New York editor Peter Warner, perhaps because he is also a novelist, let me run my course and then encouraged me to shape the tale. Thanks too to Susan Dwyer. Georges Borchardt, my agent, was kindly still there when I came home at last, and Amy Robbins in his office provided cheer and help. John Anderson was a perfect model of a copy editor.

Special thanks, finally, to sculptor-printmaker Mary Frank and to the Zabriskie Gallery for the use of the distinguished monoprint on the cover. I also acknowledge my debt to her and other artists whose work involves ideas contiguous to my own, among them Patricia Johanson, Nancy Holt, Lowrey Burgess, Charles Ross, Elisabeth Munro Smith, and James Turrell. Indeed, the end reward of a project is not the product so much as the continuum to which one has contributed and of which one thereby feels a part. My respectful gratitude, then, to Dr. Kramrisch, who appeared to find my approach to this subject worthy, and, in the other generational direction, to the pilgrim of Tinker Creek.

INDEX